T0319173

"Vinod embarks on an excellent treatise on the convergence between the physical and digital worlds. Alongside, he at once recognizes that fundamental economic principles are no longer sacrosanct; be they the concepts of scarcity and choice, or the dictates of diminishing returns to scale. What we know from textbooks are no longer textbook! *Global Meets Digital* challenges business leaders to think differently about strategic implications of the global-digital world."

Dr. Janamitra Devan,
Head of Executive Office/Chief Strategy Officer,
NEOM, Saudi Arabia; former Vice President, The World Bank Group;
former Director, Global Strategy Practice, McKinsey & Co.

"This 'must-read' book for students and executives is a deeply reasoned and authoritative review of how digitalization speeds the international expansion of service providers like Netflix or Spotify, but it also covers examples of companies that provide physical products to global markets, such as Nestlé, Bosch, Starbucks, and Peloton. For the latter category of firms selling tangible products, digitalization has not only speeded up innovation, but for several it has entailed a fundamental organizational restructuring of their global operations and strategy decisions such as the choice between internal development and production *versus* strategic alliances *versus* acquiring foreign companies."

"The book is a 'deep dive' into one of the fundamental changes occurring in business today—as evidenced by as many as 264 useful references on the subject. Yet, at the same time, it is written in language accessible to students and executives, with lessons for strategy clearly delineated. This book should be essential reading."

Dr. Farok J. Contractor,
Distinguished Professor in Management & Global Business,
Rutgers Business School, New Brunswick & Newark, New Jersey

"It is rare to find a book on business strategy that combines the scope and depth of Vinod's understanding of strategy with the rigor of academic research that is as accessible in clear prose to the multinational executive who needs to formulate a strategy that is executable. He provides a terrific framework at the intersection of economics, strategy, and technology for understanding the dynamic dialectical process of the global (thesis) meeting digital (antithesis) that enables one to see opportunities and exigencies in the resulting synthesis in ways far superior to vain efforts to predict the future."

R. Lemuel Lasher,
Chairman, Leading Edge Only, Ltd., Managing Director,
Boehme Eckhart LLC; former Vice President-Strategic Projects and Chief Innovation Officer,
Computer Sciences Corporation

"In this excellent book, Jain provides a roadmap for how global firms should leverage digitalization to enhance their global competitiveness. Whether your firm is big or small, young or old, a B2C or a B2B company, Jain shows you how to craft a digital strategy and stay ahead of competitors. Peppered with hundreds of examples from diverse industries and countries, Jain's book is a treasure trove of practical insights for managers, academics, and students alike."

Dr. Ravi Ramamurti,
University Distinguished Professor of International Business & Strategy, and Director,
Center for Emerging Markets, Northeastern University

"The book is far more than a study of the intersection of two megatrends—globalization and technology. It recognizes that while the axes are nominally orthogonal, they interact powerfully as the two phenomena evolve in the business world—along with the consequential impacts on our personal and professional lives. In fact, the author makes clear that this deepening intersection creates a new need for business capabilities demanding new models and new strategies to succeed in the global-digital world. The text is clear, well organized and meticulously punctuated with relevant case studies, and the scholarly works of those attempting to understand the why's and broader implications of these phenomena. Finally, it offers a framework for leaders to examine their corporate strategies and evaluate them for future relevance in a methodical way."

Dr. Alpheus Bingham,
author of The Open Innovation Marketplace *and*
One Smart Crowd, *and founder of InnoCentive*

"Professor Vinod Jain's latest book *Global Meets Digital: Global Strategy for Digital Businesses-Digital Strategy for Global Businesses* is very timely. It used to be no firms had digital strategy; then some firms had a digital strategy; and today all firms should have a digital strategy, but many do not. This book will help you learn how to develop a successful one. Professor Jain has written a very accessible book that clearly explains complex issues about digital strategy and includes many interesting case studies which help readers to better understand the issues discussed and learn about international best practice in the area. *Global Meets Digital* is unique in that it covers strategies for physical, digital, and smart products like the Internet of Things. The book also covers many important current themes like digital disruption, the paradox of globalization, exponential technologies, industry 4.0, disruptive business models, competition in digital markets, and winner-take-all market dynamics. This book is a must-read for any student or executive concerned about digital strategy."

Dr. Carl Fey,
Professor of Strategy, BI Norwegian Business School,
Oslo, Norway; former Dean, Nottingham University Business School China

"At last, a book that addresses the inescapable reality of the fusion between the physical and digital worlds. What impacted me most about this world-class book is the practical and pertinent applications of its content. Vinod Jain managed to combine his research, knowledge, and industry experience with relevant case studies delivering a superb book. I'm glad Vinod Jain has so well and so fully shed light on these two vital and here-to-stay forces."

Humberto "HAP" Patorniti,
Partner at Tenacity Inc. and Adjunct Professor,
Rutgers State University; former CEO and President, SODEXO, Mexico, North America

"Globalization has been going on since humans started to consume something that was built somewhere else. It started with the Silk Road and then to ships to railways to trucks to airways and finally the Internet. All of these modes of knowledge and service transport have helped increase the speed at which the services can move across the globe, and it is just continuing to pick up speed. "Global Meets Digital" gives you the whole perspective on what is happening and what is yet to come, and how one by one each industry is getting transformed. If you are in any position in a business and are thinking about what Digital means for your business, then this is the book for you!"

Lokesh Kumar,
Chief Technology Officer, sheeva.ai and Co-founder
and Chief Architect, urgent.ly

"I highly recommend Dr. Vinod Jain's new book, 'Global Meets Digital', for several reasons. It is a book for our time in business that will enable us to also prepare for the future environment of the melting of 'older business axioms' into new, adaptable business strategies to take any business enterprise into the near and far-reaching future. Jain critically examines not only how we got here, but more importantly, how we should think about next steps in navigating the ever dynamic and changing world of business where 'giants have fallen' and new entries can generate a meteoric rise in shareholder value. Essentially, the rules have changed and ALL business must recognize and plan for the future. I enjoyed the mixture of real-world business case studies with the lessons learned to prepare one's own business. In my opinion, this is a 'must read' for any organization or person contemplating how to grow in a digital business environment."

H.E. The Hon., Dr. Thomas A. Cellucci,
former First Chief Commercialization Officer of the United States of America,
Author of 30 books, and Serial Entrepreneur

"Vinod writes an extremely timely book for today's executives. It captures two pressing, inter-connected issues of our time—globalization and digitalization, and offers numerous insights about how we can address them—in an integrated manner. I highly recommend the book, particularly to executives aiming to expand their global footprint through a digital strategy."

Dr. Tony Tong,
Senior Associate Dean for Faculty & Research and Professor of Strategy & Entrepreneurship,
Leeds School of Business, University of Colorado Boulder

"Dr. Jain has long shared his expertise regarding the relationship between global and digital business. His latest book, *Global Meets Digital*, provides a look at the historical evolution of this relationship. Further, given the unprecedented rate of change today, driven by the twin forces of globalization and technology, he points to the business revolution that is unfolding real time. Dr. Jain provides an insightful strategic context to the growing interconnectedness between the two and offers numerous case examples that allows the reader to peer into the future. *Global Meets Digital* explores the opportunities and challenges and is a must read for business leaders who are struggling to reimagine today's new normal."

Keith Darcy,
President, Darcy Partners Inc.; former Independent Senior Advisor,
Deloitte & Touche LLP, and former Chairman, Better Business Bureau Foundation

"Vinod has a unique style of explaining even complex concepts in a simple manner, which makes this book enjoyable to read. He addresses the challenges of global expansion for new-age digital businesses and the need for digital transformation of traditional global enterprises in a lucid fashion with authentic case studies across the spectrum. I recommend this book as compulsory reading for business leaders looking for practical guidance on several topics not covered in other management books."

Sridharan Rangarajan,
Vice President, Platforms, Viessmann, Germany;
former Director, Hybrid Cloud Strategy, Bosch, Germany; and former Program Director,
Bluemix Practice, IBM Software Group

"Dr. Jain captures the importance of growth strategies for Global and Digital businesses through his impressive research, extensive case studies, academic excellence, and many years of engagement with the world's leading corporations. This is a brilliant book for executives facing a highly charged market dynamic in the global-digital world. While most books on strategy tend to focus on B2C businesses, what I, with over 30 years of senior-level experience in B2B businesses worldwide, really appreciated is that *Global Meets Digital* has a whole chapter devoted to competing in B2B businesses."

Steven R Zirkel,
President & CEO of Blue Everest LLC;
former Managing Director, Owens Corning Asia Pacific

"As an active practitioner in international business for over 30 years I really appreciated reading *Global Meets Digital* by Vinod Jain. I strongly recommend reading this book as it is timely and it discusses the real issues companies are facing right now. The important concepts are clearly explained and supported by practical cases so that the reader is able to relate to real situations. The ideal content to bring ourselves up to date on critical issues that impact global strategy, Vinod Jain's new book is, in my view, a must read."

Jean-Paul DAVID,
CEO of Mercadex Europe & Director of Institut MX, Paris, France

"The title of this book—Global Meets Digital—captures starkly the new reality. In the new era, global enterprises will thrive only if they embrace the new opportunities and sidestep the challenges created by the exploding digitization of the global economy. Digitization affects every aspect of your global strategy—what markets to target, how to win in these markets, and how to design and manage the global value chain. This book covers these and related topics."

Dr. Anil K. Gupta,
Michael Dingman Chair in Strategy and Globalization, The University of Maryland,
College Park; Author, The Quest for Global Dominance *and* Getting China and India Right

"In modern times, it's not enough to have strategy, you need to have a flexible and resilient execution feedback loops to maximize outcomes. Vinod combines an approach that does both and explains in his book how businesses can benefit from taking advantage of the natural contradictions that exist between the physical and digital, the local and the global, and between theory and practice."

PV Boccasam,
Chairman of Jôrn Capital

Global Meets Digital

The world today is at the intersection of two megatrends—Globalization and Digitalization—a business revolution unfolding in real time. *Global Meets Digital* captures the many nuances of this revolution succinctly, including its impact on our lives and business. An immediate implication of this revolution is that the economic principles that underpinned business and strategy for hundreds of years, such as diminishing returns to scale and resource scarcity, are no longer valid for a large and growing number of products and services. The book will challenge you to think differently not just about digital products, but also about physical products.

In the global-digital world, products are of three kinds—physical, digital, and smart machines (products that are both physical and digital, and connected to the internet)—a distinction missed by most books on strategy and global business. The economics of each kind of products is distinct from that of the others, which has strategic implications for all kinds of businesses—implications such as how to compete and how to create and capture value.

With several mini case studies and over 300 company examples, the book covers themes and cutting-edge issues like the paradox of globalization, digital disruption, disruptive business models, exponential technologies, Internet of Things, competition in digital markets, winner-take-all market dynamics, Industry 4.0, how to innovate, strategizing for the New Normal, and value creation and value capture in both B2C and B2B contexts. The book derives its underpinnings from the practice of global and digital business, while theory remains in the background.

Intended specifically for an executive/professional audience, *Global Meets Digital* should also be of value to business students and professors learning to dip their toes into a digital world.

Vinod K. Jain is an expert in global and digital strategy, award-winning professor, Fulbright Scholar, and author of an MBA textbook, *Global Strategy*. He taught at the Rutgers Business School, Newark and New Brunswick, and the Robert H. Smith School of Business, University of Maryland, College Park. At Maryland, he was also the Founding Director of the federally funded Center for International Business Education and Research and Academic Director of Smith School's Executive MBA program in China. Since leaving Maryland, he has taught in China, Denmark, Finland, Poland, and India as a visiting or term professor. His opinion pieces have appeared in *The Washington Post*, *The Baltimore Sun*, *Mensa Bulletin*, and *Economic Times* and *Mint* (India's #1 and #2 business dailies), among other media. In the past, he worked as a middle- and senior-level executive with American and British multinationals. Vinod has a PhD in Strategy and International Business from the University of Maryland, College Park, MS in Management from UCLA, and MS and BS (Hons) in Statistics from the Indian Statistical Institute, Calcutta.

Global Meets Digital

Global Strategy for Digital Businesses -
Digital Strategy for Global Businesses

Vinod K. Jain, Ph.D.

Routledge
Taylor & Francis Group

A PRODUCTIVITY PRESS BOOK

First published 2023
by Routledge
605 Third Avenue, New York, NY 10158

and by Routledge
4 Park Square, Milton Park, Abingdon, Oxon, OX14 4RN

Routledge is an imprint of the Taylor & Francis Group, an informa business

© 2023 Vinod K. Jain

The right of Vinod K. Jain to be identified as author of this work has been asserted by him in accordance with sections 77 and 78 of the Copyright, Designs and Patents Act 1988.

ISBN: 978-0-367-47968-8 (hbk)
ISBN: 978-0-367-47907-7 (pbk)
ISBN: 978-1-003-03744-6 (ebk)

DOI: 10.4324/9781003037446

Typeset in Adobe Garamond Pro
by codeMantra

For

Kamal, Sumita, and Anupama

Contents

Preface...xi
Acknowledgments xiii
Author xv

SECTION 1   THE CONTEXT

1   Global Meets Digital 3
The Global–Digital Economy 4
Old Is New Again!.. 5
Business in the 2020s
    Globalization: From Divergence to Interdependence to Convergence to… 8
    Technology—On Steroids...13
        What's behind the growth of IT?...14
    Competition—A Changing Paradigm..15
Notes 17

2   Paradox of Globalization...19
Global Business in 1914
When Did Globalization Begin?.. 20
What Is Behind the Growth of Globalization in Recent Periods? 23
    Multilateral Institutions 24
    Governments... 24
    Multinational Enterprises...25
    Information and Communication Technologies...25
Globalization Today 25
    Reversal of Attitudes toward Globalization 25
    Reverse Innovation 27
    Reverse FDI 28
    Reverse Outsourcing/Offshoring... 30
Globalization Today versus in Earlier Eras...31
The Paradox 32
Notes 32

3   Digital Business: Technology at Warp Speed...35
Crossing the Chasm
Economics of Digital Products 36
Technologies 38

Artificial Intelligence...38
Robotics...41
3D Printing..43
Cloud...44
Blockchain...45
5G...46
Exponential Characteristics of Information Technologies.............................46
Digital Disruption 46
Value Creation and Capture with Technology 50
Notes 53

SECTION 2 STRATEGY

4   Entering Foreign Markets **57**
Netflix Goes Abroad
Foreign Market Selection 59
The PRISM Framework 59
P: Political Economy 61
Political Systems 61
Economic Systems 62
R: Resources..63
I: Institutions and Infrastructure 63
S: Society and Culture..64
M: Market Potential...65
Industry Structure...67
A Systematic Approach...68
Learning about Foreign Markets...69
Entering Foreign Markets 69
Exporting/Importing 69
Licensing..70
Franchising..70
Foreign Direct Investment...72
Strategic Alliances 73
Notes 73

5   Global Strategy for Digital Businesses **75**
Digitization-Digitalization-Digital Transformation
Spotify..77
How Spotify Creates Value 78
How Spotify Captures Value..80
Spotify's Global Strategy 81
Peloton...82
How Peloton Creates Value 85
How Peloton Captures Value...86
Peloton's Global Strategy 86
The Globalization–Localization Dilemma 87
Global Strategy for Digital Businesses 88
Network Effects 88

Technology and Innovation 88
First Movers, Fast Seconds, and Imitators 89
Localization 90
Licensing and Partnering 92
IP Protection 93
Notes 94

6 Digital Business Models 97
Direct Selling 98
Subscription 99
Freemium 101
Outcome Based 102
Razor and Blade 103
Data Monetization 104
Platform 105
Ecosystem 108
Business Models for Professional Services Firms 111
How Law Firms Bill Their Clients 111
Productization of Services 112
Notes 113

7 Digital Strategy for Global B2C Businesses 115
Three Kinds of Businesses
What Is a Global Business? 115
What Is Digital Strategy? 117
Economics of Digital Markets 117
Value Creation and Value Capture 118
How Value Is Created 120
How Value Is Captured 122
Competition and Competitive Advantage in Digital Markets ... 123
Establishing Competitive Advantage in Digital Markets ... 124
Digital Strategy for Global B2C Businesses 126
Nestlé 127
Digital Transformation at Nestlé 127
Nestlé's Digital Strategy 128
Notes 129

8 Digital Strategy for Global B2B Businesses 131
The Four Industrial Revolutions 131
Industry 4.0 132
How IoT (IIoT) Changes Manufacturing 133
Some Specific Advantages of the IIoT 133
How XCMG Benefits from the IIoT 134
Value Creation-Value-Capture Framework for IoT (IIoT) Businesses ... 135
Value-Creation Layer 1: Physical Thing 137
Value-Creation Layer 2: Sensors and Actuators 137
Value-Creation Layer 3: Connectivity 138
Value-Creation Layer 4: Analytics 138

Value-Creation Layer 5: Digital Service 138
Bosch 139
Digital Transformation at Bosch 140
Bosch Group's Digital Strategy...141
Notes 143

9 Reinventing Innovation...**145**
InnoCentive Reinvents Innovation
How Innovation Happens...147
Serendipity 148
Invisible Hand of Market 149
Visible Hand of Management 149
How to Innovate 153
The Build|Buy|Ally Framework 153
Build: Innovation through Internal Development 153
Buy: Acquiring Innovation through M&A...155
Ally: Acquiring Innovation through Alliances 157
Open Innovation 160
Notes 161

10 Reimagining Business **163**
The Five Megatrends...164
Globalization...164
Digitalization 165
Competition..165
The Fourth Industrial Revolution 166
The New Normal 166
Strategizing for the New Normal...167
It's a Global–Digital World 168
Reach and Richness...169
Improved Performance 170
Value Creation and Value Capture...171
1. Globality 172
How to Leverage Globality 172
2. Competition's New Logic and Logistics 173
Some Features of Digital Markets...174
How to Establish and Sustain Competitive Advantage in Digital Markets 175
3. Innovation's New Logistics...175
4. Disrupt/Cannibalize Yourself...175
5. The Fourth Industrial Revolution 176
6. Disruptive Business Models..177
7. Exponential 178
Notes 179

Index **181**

Preface

The confluence of the physical and digital worlds is well underway. It has meant, among other things, that digital players are moving into physical spaces, and physical incumbent businesses are fast pursuing digitalization—blurring boundaries between global and digital. That is the context of *Global Meets Digital*, with value creation and value capture as the central theme that pervades throughout the book.

Intended specifically for an executive/professional audience, *Global Meets Digital* derives its underpinnings from the practice of global and digital business, while theory remains in the background. It is imperative for multinational enterprises (MNEs) to learn from the experiences of other MNEs about how they do business and how they succeeded (or failed) in international and digital markets.

Well, MNEs have existed for a very long time. So, why now? The context of business in the last decade, especially in the last 5–6 years, has undergone major changes: (1) growing interconnectedness between the physical and digital worlds; (2) accelerating growth of technologies, such as artificial intelligence and cloud computing, used not only by IT firms but also increasingly by firms in practically all industries; (3) growing role of cross-border data flows as international trade in physical goods is not growing as in the past; (4) health, social, and economic crises brought forth by COVID-19; (5) a changed political, economic, and social environment in many parts of the world, including the US, Europe, Asia, and Latin America—with strategic implications for business.

All these factors pose great challenges (and great opportunities!) for businesses to create and capture value. That's because the economics and strategy of physical products are different from the economics and strategy of digital products, which, in turn, are different from the economics and strategy of smart machines (products that are both physical and digital and connected to the internet).

With several minicase studies and over 100 company examples, the book covers themes and cutting-edge issues like the paradox of globalization, digital disruption, disruptive business models, exponential technologies, Internet of Things, competition in digital markets, winner-take-all market dynamics, Industry 4.0, how to innovate, strategizing for the New Normal, and value creation and value capture in both B2C and B2B contexts.

During my academic career spanning some 30 years, I have taught strategy, global business, and global strategy at business schools in the US, Europe, China, and India. Prior to that, I worked with American and British multinationals for many years. As a result, I have been an observer and a participant in the changing context of business—from legacy to digital. As the cliché goes, digital changes everything!

Acknowledgments

Over the years, I have learned a great deal during my digital learning journey from many people, many authors, and many companies, too numerous to mention individually; I am deeply grateful to all of them. Some, who read and commented on parts of the manuscript, deserve very special thanks. They are Dr. Alph Bingham, President, Cascade Consulting LLC and former President and CEO of InnoCentive; Lokesh Kumar, CTO of Sheeva.ai and co-founder of urgent.ly; Humberto "HAP" Patorniti, faculty member at Rutgers Business School and former President and CEO of SODEXO Mexico City; and Sridharan Rangarajan, Vice President, Platforms at The Viessmann Group, Germany.

I am grateful to Kristine Mednansky, senior editor, Taylor & Francis Group, for her patience and advice during the manuscript's slow progress over almost 3 years. Also to Rebecca Lyles of the TextCPR editorial service for continuing help with editing. I would be remiss if I did not express thanks to my friends at TiE-DC, the Washington DC chapter of TiE.org, a global association of entrepreneurs and CEOs, most of whom run technology businesses, for helpful conversations with them, as well as to participants in my seminars and webinars for their questions and thoughtful comments.

Last, but not least, very special thanks to my wife, Kamlesh (Kamal), a good human being and a profound thinker, and to our daughters, Sumita and Anupama, for their unflagging support, love, and pleasant company during our life journeys.

Author

Vinod Jain is an expert in global and digital strategy, Fulbright Scholar, award-winning professor, and author of an MBA textbook, *Global Strategy*, published by Routledge (New York and London, 2016). Vinod taught at the Rutgers Business School, Newark and New Brunswick, Nottingham University Business School China, and the Robert H. Smith School of Business, University of Maryland, College Park. At Maryland, he was also the Founding Director of the Center for International Business Education and Research (CIBER) and Academic Director of Smith School's Executive MBA program in China. He has been a visiting/term professor at Aalto University, Finland; Copenhagen Business School, Denmark; Hult International Business School Shanghai, China; Indian Institute of Management Bangalore, India; and Polish American Management Center at University of Lodz, Poland.

In the past, Vinod worked with British and American multinationals for many years, including Macmillan Publishers (Vice President), Molins (Manager Coordination), and Coca-Cola (Marketing Research Executive). He has conducted over a hundred executive and academic seminars in Bahrain, Brazil, Canada, China, Europe, India, and the US, and has been active on many boards and professional and trade associations.

Not a techie, Vinod is fascinated by and has flirted with digital strategy and digital business ever since the dotcom days. (He registered his first internet domain in 1998.) For instance, in April–May 2000, he conducted a six-Saturday, executive seminar on e-Business Strategy. The same year, he designed and chaired an All-Academy Symposium on "Business Models in the New Economy" at Academy of Management's annual, international conference in Toronto, Canada. The symposium attracted over 200 participants and had presenters from several universities, including Alabama, INSEAD, Oregon, Rutgers, Wharton, and a think tank in Canada. Since then, he has presented talks and seminars on global and digital strategy and even once ran a digital business for a few years. In March and May 2022, he was invited by the Academy of Management to offer a webinar on digital strategy for its members.

Vinod's articles and opinion pieces have appeared in *The Washington Post*, *The Baltimore Sun*, *Mensa Bulletin*, *Economic Times* and *Mint* (India's #1 and #2 business dailies), and other media. He has been honored by the Governors of both Ohio and Maryland for his services to international and internationalizing businesses in their states.

Vinod has a PhD in Strategy and International Business from the University of Maryland, College Park, MS in Management from UCLA, and MS and BS (Hons.) in Statistics from the Indian Statistical Institute, Calcutta. www.vinodjain.com.

THE CONTEXT

1

Chapter 1

Global Meets Digital

It's all so simple, Anjin-san. Just change your concept of the world.

James Clavell, Shōgun, 1975

The world has practically always had global business.

Arab traders had been traveling to spice-producing lands since 4,000–5,000 years ago, along what have come to be known as the Spice Routes, bringing spices and herbs with them to the Middle East. During the earliest evolution of trade, spices such as cardamom, ginger, pepper, and turmeric were important items of trade, some even as valuable as gold today. The Arabs kept the source of spices (the East Indies) secret for a long time to avoid competition. Over time, the Romans and other Europeans took control of the spice trade. The Silk Road, a network of trade and cultural land routes connecting China, India, Persia, the Arabian Peninsula, East Africa, and Southern Europe, existed around the same time and intermittently brought together traders, merchants, monks, pilgrims, thieves, and soldiers from different countries. The Silk Road is said to have begun around 3,200 BCE and lasted several millennia. In addition to silk and other goods and cultural influences, Buddhism, Islam, Christianity, and even disease and technologies of the time traveled along the road. The Spice Routes and the Silk Road met and extended each other at some places—furthering global business.

Digital business, however, is of recent origin. It involves business models that use digital technologies for products ranging from physical products (such as plant and machinery) to purely digital (software) to smart machines[1] (products that are both physical and digital and connected to the internet, such as the electric vehicle and drone). Lately, more and more traditional (physical) businesses in the automotive, consumer goods, and other industrial sectors have been moving into the digital world—creating a new class of products (smart machines).

The confluence of global business and digital business, a shift long in the making, is now well underway. Of the important factors that account for this confluence, two, in particular, stand out. Continuing advances in technology and innovation, now growing at an exponential pace, and the growing interconnectedness between the physical and digital worlds mean that the boundaries between global business and digital business are getting increasingly blurred—creating a global–digital world (Figure 1.1).

The confluence of the physical and digital worlds means, among other things, that digital players are moving into physical spaces (e.g., Amazon's move into physical retailing with the acquisition

DOI: 10.4324/9781003037446-2

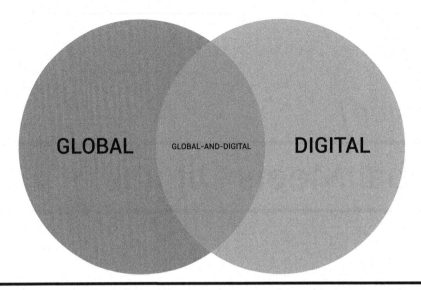

Figure 1.1 A global-digital world.

of Whole Foods in 2017 and into healthcare with the acquisition of primary care provider One Medical in 2022), and physical incumbent businesses are fast pursuing digitalization and digital business models. For example, John Deere, the agricultural, forestry, and construction machinery company, which used to manufacture separate engines for a wide range of users, each requiring a different level of horsepower, can now modify the horsepower of a standard engine using just software. John Deere is meeting global customer needs for varying designs through software, rather than hardware. Though it is not just software, other elements of digital technology, such as artificial intelligence (AI), 3D printing, Internet of Things (IoT), and robotics, are helping to blur the distinctions between physical business and digital business.

In addition to blurring the distinctions between physical business and digital business, *global meets digital* is happening across multiple geographies in multiple contexts. One such context is the blurring of boundaries between the *old economy* and the *new economy* to create what we might call a *connected economy*. Another somewhat related context involves repurposing of the old, abandoned industrial sites into new uses—old becomes new again.

The Global–Digital Economy

New economies emerge following major technological innovations, which typically redefine the rules of the game and how people live and work. The term *new economy* has been in use as a metaphor for transformational change in societies for a long time. The world has seen many new economies since the first Industrial Revolution of the late eighteenth century, which ushered in disruptive change in most industries of the time and led to rising prosperity in England. These changes then spread to the rest of Europe, North America, and eventually to the rest of the world. The end point of a new economy typically merges with the beginning of another new economy, though both continue to co-exist and co-evolve. And so it was with the dawn of the second Industrial Revolution in the early twentieth century with Henry Ford's moving assembly line that launched the era of mass production and continuing rise of prosperity in America. This transformational change in manufacturing technologies and processes indeed changed how people lived and worked in the decades that followed—all hallmarks of the arrival of a new economy in America.

The term *new economy* acquired almost a new meaning in the dot-com era of the late 1990s and early 2000s when the *digital economy* was the new economy. This new economy, like the earlier ones, was born out of technological innovations (e.g., the internet), had its own players (the dot-coms), playing fields (the World Wide Web), rules of the game (*information rules*), and business models (e.g., clicks-and-bricks).

Today the world has both the old economy and the digital economy, as well as a *new* economy that has emerged in the last decade or so. This *new* economy has been called by various names, such as the second Machine Age[2], the third industrial revolution[3], and the age of smart machines[4]. For sake of simplicity, we will refer to today's economy as the *global-digital economy*. This term comprises the old economy, the digital economy, and the age of the smart machines.[5]

The global–digital economy consists of consumers, firms, markets, nations, governments, and other actors that are more connected to each other than at any time in previous eras. As in the past, such connections are facilitated by the twin forces of globalization and technology, the latter now at an unprecedented and increasing speed of change.

Some key features of the global–digital economy are:

- Global—encompassing both developed and developing nations.
- Goods—range from physical goods, digital goods, and smart machines (goods with digital characteristics, e.g., hardware, software, and sensors, embedded into them and connected to the internet).
- Services—range from simple location-bound services to services that can be performed anywhere and everywhere, not necessarily close to customers.
- Processes—both physical and digital.
- Connectivity—provided by multilateral institutions, governments, multinational corporations, competition, digital technologies, and networks.
- Speed—business and economic phenomena operate in real time, 24/7, and at increasing speeds.

Old Is New Again![6]

Many of the manufacturing estates and cities in what was once known as the Rust Belt have experienced a transformational spit and polish in recent years—so much so that some of them positively shine with dynamism built around high-technology and creative industries. What I have found is that the old, abandoned industrial sites have been converted into new productive uses in hundreds of cities across the US and around the world. The story of converting former abandoned industrial sites into new powerhouses of creative and high-tech industries is a story of reinvention and renewal that is being witnessed worldwide. Cities and towns formerly known as major manufacturing hubs—the *old economy*—are increasingly transitioning to the *new economy*.

For instance, the old Studebaker automotive plant in South Bend, IN, that closed down in 1963 is now the Renaissance District, the Midwest's largest mixed-use technology campus, which houses a data center and educational, industrial, commercial, coworking, residential, and retail spaces. Ignition Park, located on 140 acres of Studebaker's famous Engineering Department, is one of the two state-certified technology parks in South Bend, the other being Innovation Park at the University of Notre Dame just north of downtown South Bend. Ignition Park's focus is on high-potential technologies and ventures such as nanotechnology and turbomachines; Notre Dame's Turbomachinery Laboratory is located within the Ignition Park. South Bend has perhaps the densest concentration of fiber optic cables in the country, ideal for data centers and telecom and cloud services companies.[7] It even has a commuter rail offering direct access to downtown Chicago. The University of Notre Dame provides the intellectual capital for the Ignition Park and the city's other businesses.

As President of the (then) Toledo Area International Trade Association and a member of the faculty of the business school at Bowling Green State University some 20 years ago, I had the opportunity to explore northwest Ohio, a part of the Rust Belt region, in some depth. Around that time, I also obtained a Business and International Education (BIE) federal grant with the theme "Northwest Ohio: From Rust Belt to Prosperity in a Global Economy," which gave me further insights into this industrial decay and its potential. The 2-year BIE grant was intended to help strengthen the international competitiveness of regional businesses through education, research, and outreach. Over time, I have become quite interested in how some of the old, shuttered manufacturing estates and cities resurrected themselves into something new, dynamic, and exciting.

Manchester, NH, reputed to be a global textile capital before World War I, is now home to knowledge businesses, research institutes, and fancy restaurants. The old, once-crumbling Riverside Mill District has been reincarnated into a complex of 30 technology firms, including Texas Instruments and Autodesk. Dyn, an internet performance company with more than 400 workers during its heyday, was headquartered in one of the repurposed industrial buildings. Its office space looked like that of a high-tech company in Silicon Valley, complete with indoor putting greens and playground slides (Oracle acquired Dyn in 2017 but permanently closed it in January 2020). Some of the nineteenth-century industrial buildings that previously served as tenement housing for textile mill workers are now stylish, eclectic residential condominiums, and retail stores.

The University of New Hampshire, which maintains an urban campus in Manchester, has been strengthening its STEM offerings and has a new biotechnology major. Many members of its large student body find for-credit internships in the immediate business community, often in STEM-oriented fields at high-tech companies. The Department of Defense is setting up an $80 million research institute, the Advanced Regenerative Manufacturing Institute, for the biofabrication of human tissue and organs.

The Crown Cork and Seal Company started operations in Baltimore in 1897 and was once the largest bottle cap factory in the world. After relocating its headquarters to Philadelphia in 1958, the company sold 30 of its industrial buildings to the City of Baltimore for $1.5 million, but manufacturing continued at its Highlandtown plant for another 30 years. (It closed its Baltimore operation in 1987.) The repurposed Crown Cork and Seal building now houses artists' studios and light manufacturing enterprises. One of the company's buildings, the Copycat Building (named after Copy Cat Printing, which operated in the building decades ago), is now the centerpiece of Baltimore's Station North Arts and Entertainment District. It offers studio and living space for more than 100 artists, musicians, and performers. Another building now houses the Emerging Technology Center, a nonprofit tech incubator that has worked with more than 100 tech startups at different stages of their evolution.

In the mid-2010s, James and Deb Fallows went on a 3-year journey across the US in their single-engine Cirrus SR22 airplane, exploring small- and medium-sized cities that had previously suffered economic, political, environmental, or some other hardship, but came out of the hardship successfully. They traveled to about four dozen cities, spending up to 10 days in some of them. The March 2016 issue of *The Atlantic* magazine has their detailed story, titled "How America Is Putting Itself Back Together."[8] Everywhere they went, they saw signs of reinvention and renewal. They found that despite the major talent destinations of the East and West Coasts, talent and ambition are widely distributed throughout the US. Duluth, MN, for example, is now a key aerospace center in the nation and also has new firms in medical equipment, environmental technology, and other high-tech fields. The space occupied by the former Bethlehem Steel plant in Bethlehem, PA, now has a performing arts center, a casino resort, and outdoor music venues. Pittsburgh has metamorphosed from a dying steel city into a major technology hub, aided by its key universities and local philanthropists (the Mellon, Heinz, Carnegie, and Frick families) committed to the city's development.

Such phenomenal changes are not limited to the US. Dozens of European cities have experienced similar evolution. Like Pittsburgh in the US, entire cities—not just old manufacturing plants—have been transformed into creative and high-tech spaces. For example, the city of Sheffield[9] in the UK was the birthplace of stainless steel manufacturing and a major player in the first Industrial Revolution. After four devastating rounds of deep recession and other natural disasters during the 1970s and 1980s, Sheffield's resurgence during the 1990s and especially during the early 2000s can be attributed to high levels of public investment, its strong university anchors, advanced engineering and technical skills, manufacturing heritage, preexisting infrastructure, and some 13,000 small- and medium-sized enterprises (SMEs) that account for more than 80% of all private sector jobs in the city. Its new economy companies are involved in hydrogen and other renewables, digital innovation, environmental technologies, and advanced manufacturing.

One of the reasons for the comeback of downtrodden communities and cities has been the availability of cheap land in once-abandoned manufacturing estates. But none of the industrial renaissances would have been possible without the backing of universities with preexisting specialized research and educational facilities, their manufacturing and industrial heritage, infrastructure, local philanthropies and economic development agencies, and public investment. These factors have led to the establishment of incubators and other resources that attract entrepreneurs, startups, artists, and others looking for affordable places to establish themselves.

In their 2016 book, *The Smartest Places on Earth: Why Rustbelts Are the Emerging Hotspots of Global Innovation*, Antoine van Agtmael and Fred Bakker explored why the rust belts of the rich world are developing into what they call brainbelts. With dozens of examples of rust belt and nonrust belt cities from the US and Europe, they told stories of how people from different cultures and backgrounds came together to find global solutions for global problems. They highlighted several factors that helped create the brainbelts, such as visionary thinkers, local universities, public initiatives, startups, and even big corporations. These emerging islands of creativity and innovation have transformed local economies through collaboration between business, academia, and regional governments working together with ingenuity, new technologies, and new materials.

The January 21, 2001 issue of the *Newsweek* magazine published a list of ten dying cities of America, based on the largest population declines in America's metro cities, that included South Bend, IN, and Pittsburg, PA.[10] Despite declining population, these and many other cities now present growth trends that span high-tech and creative industries, even growing population in some—hallmarks of economic resurgence. They offer lessons for erstwhile industrial cities to benefit from their preexisting industrial and infrastructural assets, universities, corporations, local philanthropists and visionary thinkers, and governments to work together for a new future.

Business in the 2020s is global and digital, almost by definition. Every company today is global—whether it does business abroad or competes with companies from abroad. With 7.98

BUSINESS IN THE 2020S

Predicting the future is hard. But preparing for its uncertainties, while you lie on the beach, can at least be entertaining. It can also broaden the mind and subtly change your understanding of the present... Speculating about the future, even if it is far-fetched, can help people and institutions cope with what comes next.

The Economist, July 6, 2019 (p. 12)

billion people in the world (as of July 2022), hundreds of millions of businesses, and over 13 billion devices connected to the internet, they are all now part of the digital economy... every business is a digital business.[11]

To explore the likely trajectory of business in the 2020s, it is helpful to study some of the major trends we observe in the fall of 2022 that could define the boundaries of business. Here is a list of three trends which we believe will have the most impact on multinationals' strategy in this decade and beyond, though unexpected risks can derail any strategy no matter how carefully it is designed. (Other trends, including climate change, the rise of international terrorism, and growing global risks, are not included here—not because they are not important—but because of the space needed to adequately cover them.)

- Globalization—from divergence to interdependence to convergence to...
- Technology—on steroids.
- Competition—a changing paradigm.

Globalization: From Divergence to Interdependence to Convergence to...

Globalization is today's big reality and a *defining issue* for the twenty-first century.[12] It is driven by technology, international trade and investment, knowledge and cross-border data flows, communication and transportation networks, the arrival of several developing countries onto the global stage, multinational enterprises from both developed and developing countries, the actions of governments and multilateral institutions such as the International Monetary Fund and the World Trade Organization, geopolitics, and even the actions of nongovernmental organizations. Most of these actors have been in business for decades, but their impact today is much greater than it used to be in the earlier eras. (Globalization is, of course, not new. There are many kinds of globalization, including ecological globalization, economic globalization, and globalization of terrorism, disease, and money laundering. We are concerned mainly with economic globalization in this book.)

The Industrial Revolutions created extraordinary economic growth, but also huge *divergence* in living standards between industrialized countries and the rest of the world. Over time, however, the world has been experiencing greater interactions between and among countries with the rise of cross-border trade, investment, people migration, technology and data flows, and through the efforts of multilateral institutions. *Interdependence* among nations has been the hallmark of growing globalization in recent decades.

While the Industrial Revolutions and the digital economy continue to bestow great benefits upon advanced countries, many developing countries that had previously been left out of the bounty have also lately been experiencing dramatic increase in growth and prosperity. Hence, the term *emerging markets* is used for such countries. In China, for example, hundreds of millions of people have been lifted out of poverty. Now, as industrialized countries are experiencing lower growth rates, and developing countries higher growth rates, there is growing *convergence* between developed and developing countries on several dimensions. According to Michael Spence, the winner of the 2001 Nobel Prize in Economic Sciences,

> The huge asymmetries between advanced and developing countries have not disappeared, but they are declining, and the pattern for the first time is convergence rather than divergence.[13]

Lately, however, there has been talk of slowing globalization, even of deglobalization, meaning decreasing interdependence and integration among nations. And there has been backlash against globalization and multilateral

THE RISE OF EMERGING MARKETS

In terms of size, speed, and directional flow, the global shift in relative wealth and economic power now under way – roughly from West to East – is without precedent in modern history.

Global Trends 2025: A Transformed World. Washington, DC: U.S. National Intelligence Council, November 2008

institutions for at least 20 years as well as, more recently, the rise of nationalism in many parts of the world (e.g., BREXIT in Britain and the election of far-right candidates in the US, Italy, and Brazil). In parts of Europe and some other countries, antiestablishment political parties have made significant electoral gains. Even in developing countries, rising living standards are making citizens demand more. Ian Bremmer, in his 2018 book, (*Us vs. Them: The Failure of Globalism*), argued that the worst is yet to come.

As the world's center of gravity shifts decisively in favor of emerging markets, competitive challenges and opportunities are being continually and dramatically transformed. Let us take just three examples of how some developing countries are beginning to have the characteristics of developed countries, even surpassing them on certain dimensions, such as GDP (gross domestic product), the number of Fortune Global 500 companies, and middle-class consumption.

Gross domestic product. Ranked number six in the list of the world's top 10 economies in 2010, China's GDP was only $1.193 trillion (at current prices) compared to $10.285 trillion for the US, less than 12% of the US GDP (Table 1.1). Few could have imagined that in 22 years, China's economy would be second only to that of the US in terms of GDP at current prices, and larger than that of the US in terms of GDP at purchasing power parity, or PPP—making China the largest economy in the world. India's GDP at PPP ranked number three in 2022, compared to number nine in 2000, surpassing all the G7[14] countries except the US. The list of top 10 economies (GDP at PPP) now includes Russia, Brazil, and Indonesia.

Fortune Global 500 companies. Table 1.2 shows the number of Fortune Global 500 (FG500) companies headquartered in the G7 and BRIC[15] countries for 2000, 2005, 2010, and 2019. Each of the G7 countries shown in the table experienced a decline in the number of FG500 companies headquartered there over the 19-year period, with the US, the UK, and Japan experiencing the largest decline. The 2019 list had more than 50 fewer US-headquartered FG500 companies than in 2000. (This does not indicate the decline of American business, but the rise of everyone else and the fact that there can be only 500 companies in the FG500 list.) The biggest increase was achieved by China, with an increase of 110 FG500 companies from 2000 to 2019; a large number of these companies are state-owned enterprises (SOEs). Among the top 10 FG500 companies are three Chinese SOEs, Sinopec Group (ranked #2), China National Petroleum (#4), and State Grid (#5). Several Chinese technology companies also significantly improved their rank in FG500, including Alibaba Group Holdings which climbed 182 places and Tencent Holdings which climbed 94 places compared to their ranks in 2018.

Table 1.1 World's Top 10 Economies Ranked by GDP at Current Prices and PPP, 2000 and 2022

Rank (2000 GDP at Current Prices)	Country	2000 GDP		Rank (2022 GDP at Current Prices)	Rank (2022 GDP at PPP)	Country	2022 GDP	
		At Current Prices ($ Trillion)	At PPP ($ Trillion)				At Current Prices ($ Trillion)	At PPP ($ Trillion)
1	US	10.285	10.285	1	2	US	25.347	25.347
2	Japan	4.731	3.237	2	1	China	19.912	30.178
3	Germany	1.892	2.341	3	4	Japan	4.912	6.110
4	UK	1.497	1.467	4	5	Germany	4.257	5.270
5	France	1.372	1.678	5	3	India	3.535	11.745
6	China	1.193	3.608	6	7	UK	3.376	3.372
7	Italy	1.107	1.565	7	9	France	2.937	3.678
8	Brazil	0.645	1.524	8	15	Canada	2.221	2.234
9	India	0.477	2.148	9	12	Italy	2.058	2.972
10	Russia	0.260	1.531	10	8	Brazil	1.833	3.681
					6	Russia	1.829	4.365
					10	Indonesia	1.289	3.395

Source: IMF World Economic Outlook Database (2000, 2022).

Note: PPP stands for purchasing power parity; it indicates the value of GDP after taking into account cost of living differences between countries (e.g., 1 dollar in China has a much larger purchasing power than 1 dollar in the US).

The BRIC nations now account for 165 of the FG500 companies (145 are in China), compared to just 14, 19 years ago. Clearly, the world's economic center of gravity is moving from the developed toward the developing world and generally from West to East.

Size of middle class. Research by Homi Kharas of the Brookings Institution shows that by 2030, about 65% of the world's total middle class will likely be living in Asia Pacific (Table 1.3).[16] When the middle-class populations in Central and South America, Sub-Saharan Africa, and Middle East and North Africa are added to this total, it comes to about 80% of the total worldwide middle-class population. In fact, by the end of 2018, over half the world's population was *middle class* or *rich*.[17]

The consumption by the middle-class population in Asia Pacific (including Japan) will likely be 57% of the total world consumption by 2030 (Table 1.4).

Further, as Table 1.5 shows, India and China are going to be the big spenders in the coming decades, their share in worldwide consumption eclipsing that of individual countries in the rest of the world by orders of magnitude. In 2015, the US had the largest middle-class market in the world ($4.7 trillion), but was overtaken by China in 2020 and will likely be overtaken by India

Table 1.2 Number of Fortune Global 500 Companies in the G7 and BRICs, 2000, 2005, 2010, and 2022

Category	Country	2000	2005	2010	2022
G7	US	175	175	141	124
	UK	39	33	29	18
	Germany	34	34	36	28
	France	43	40	40	25
	Japan	107	81	71	47
	Canada	12	14	11	12
	Italy	10	10	11	5
BRICs	Brazil	2	4	8	7
	Russia	2	3	6	4
	India	1	5	8	9
	China	9	18	47	145

Source: Fortune Magazine, various issues.

Table 1.3 Size of the Middle Class, 2015, 2020, and 2030 (Millions of People and Global Share)

Region	2015		2020		2030	
North America	335	11%	344	9%	354	7%
Europe	724	24%	736	20%	733	14%
Central and South America	285	9%	303	8%	335	6%
Asia Pacific	1,380	46%	2,023	54%	3,492	65%
Sub-Saharan Africa	114	4%	132	4%	212	4%
Middle East and North Africa	192	6%	228	6%	285	5%
World	3,030	100%	3,766	100%	5,412	100%

Source: Homi Kharas, "The Unprecedented Expansion of the Global Middle Class, An Update", February 2017 (Brookings Institution).

in 2030. According to estimates by Homi Kharas of the Brookings Institution, the middle-class market in advanced economies, having reached maturity, is growing at only 0.5–1% per year. The middle-class market in emerging economies, by contrast, will likely grow at 6% per year.

There is of course a lot more to globalization than discussed here, which we will explore in greater detail in Chapter 2.

Table 1.4   Global Middle-Class Consumption in Top 10 Countries, 2015, 2020, and 2030 (PPP, Constant 2011 Billion $ and Global Share)

Region	2015		2020		2030	
North America	6,174	18%	6,381	15%	6,681	10%
Europe	10,920	31%	11,613	27%	12,573	20%
Central and South America	2,931	8%	3,137	8%	3,630	6%
Asia Pacific	12,332	36%	18,174	43%	36,631	57%
Sub-Saharan Africa	915	3%	1,042	2%	1,661	3%
Middle East and North Africa	1,541	4%	1,933	5%	2,679	4%
World	34,614	100%	42,279	100%	63,854	100%

Source: Homi Kharas, "The Unprecedented Expansion of the Global Middle Class, An Update", February 2017 (Brookings Institution).

Table 1.5   Middle-Class Consumption, Top 10 Countries, 2015, 2020, and 2030 (PPP, Constant 2011 Trillion $ and Global Share)

2015			2020			2030		
Country	Tn$	Share (%)	Country	Tn$	Share (%)	Country	Tn$	Share (%)
US	4.7	13	China	6.8	16	China	14.3	22
China	4.2	12	US	4.7	11	India	10.7	17
Japan	2.1	6	India	3.7	9	US	4.7	7
India	1.9	5	Japan	2.1	5	Indonesia	2.4	2.4
Russia	1.5	4	Russia	1.6	4	Japan	2.1	2.1
Germany	1.5	4	Germany	1.5	4	Russia	1.6	1.6
Brazil	1.2	3	Indonesia	1.3	3	Germany	1.5	1.5
UK	1.1	3	Brazil	1.2	3	Mexico	1.3	1.3
France	1.1	3	UK	1.2	3	Brazil	1.3	1.3
Italy	0.9	3	France	1.1	3	UK	1.2	1.2

Source: Homi Kharas, "The Unprecedented Expansion of the Global Middle Class, An Update", February 2017 (Brookings Institution).

Technology—On Steroids

Technology is the second big reality in today's world, and, in fact, it provides the glue for the global–digital economy. Technology and globalization have gone hand in hand for centuries, each impacting and being impacted by the other. As noted earlier, technology has been behind the evolution of new economies ever since the first Industrial Revolution. Over the last several decades, technology has been advancing at an increasing rate of change in multiple fields, including information technology (IT), manufacturing and automation, life sciences, genetic engineering, renewable energy, materials, automotive, services, processes, and more—so much so it is now ubiquitous in our everyday lives.

Information technology has seen the greatest advances during the last two decades. There are many more advances yet to come, most of which cannot even be visualized at this time. (This book focuses largely on digital technologies.)

As Donald Rumsfeld, the former US Secretary of State for Defense, might say, there are "unknown unknowns." This is partly because information technologies are general-purpose technologies[18] that can be used in multiple industries in multiple ways. According to Erik Brynjolfsson's and Andrew McAfee's, today's IT is quantitatively and qualitatively different from its earlier heyday in that it is digital, exponential, and recombinant.[19] Digital technologies are behind most of the innovations we see today in practically all fields of human endeavor, and their progress has been exponential as suggested by Moore's law and Metcalfe's law of network effects. Moore's law states that, for a given price, computing power doubles every 18–24 months, and according to Metcalfe's law, the value of a network equals the square of the number of its users; hence, the exponential characteristic of the digital revolution. Finally, borrowing the term recombinant from genetics research, Brynjolfsson and McAfee observe that digital innovation is recombinant in the sense that each innovation "becomes a building block of future innovations."[20] Innovations from multiple sources get connected and enhanced through networks and open innovation to create entirely new products and services which may or may not bear any semblance to the products/services from which they evolved.

> There are known knowns. There are things we know that we know. There are known unknowns. That is to say, there are things that we now know we don't know. But there are also unknown unknowns. There are things we do not know we don't know.
>
> Donald Rumsfeld, US Secretary of State for Defense, 2002

Computers and IT form the backbone of new products and services that simply did not exist even 10 years ago. In manufacturing, the 3D printing technology has taken the world by storm. One can now literally print not only complex pieces of jewelry at home, but also a handgun using a 3D printer and design software downloaded from the internet. Several companies now construct (print) houses, even large buildings, using 3D printing technology. For instance, in 2019, Apis Cor of the US was hired by Dubai Municipality to print a two-story administrative building, the largest 3D printed building in the world at the time. The 6,998-square-foot building was completed in just 2 weeks.[21] Figure 1.2 shows a 3D printed house in Wallenhausen, Germany.

3D printing is, of course, only one of several disruptive technologies today. It was only a few years ago that social, mobile, analytics, and cloud (SMAC) were all the rage in technology innovation. Today, some of the maturing, disruptive technologies (in no particular order) are Artificial intelligence (AI), fifth-generation mobile cellular communications (5G), cloud computing, data analytics, Internet of Things (IoT), advanced robotics, virtual and augmented reality (VR and AR), 3D printing, and blockchain.

Figure 1.2 A house constructed with 3D printing.

Source: 3D-Druck-Haus Wallenhausen, September 19, 2021https://commons.wikimedia. org/wiki/File:3D-Druck-Haus_Wallenhausen_02.jpg.

Not just manufacturing and construction, these and other digital technologies are upending most other industries. Take, for instance, MoneyLion, a fintech company launched in 2013. It offers its members free checking accounts, debit cards usable at over 55,000 ATMs without a fee, managed investing in ETF portfolios, and, for a fee, cash advances and help with building credit. It targets people with less than $2,000 in savings on average and already has over 4 million members and $477.5 million in venture capital funding as of summer 2022. Or, in healthcare, consider TytoCare, a mobile-health platform that allows anyone to perform guided medical self-exam with a remote healthcare provider anytime, anywhere. With the Tyto exam kit handheld by a patient, the medical provider can remotely examine the patient's heart, throat, abdomen, skin, ears, and body temperature. The provider can then offer diagnosis, treatment plan, and even order a prescription, if needed. Founded in 2012, Tyto offers three telehealth products: TytoHome™ for consumers, TytoPro™ for professionals, and TytoClinic™ for remote point-of-care locations—all designed to replicate a face-to-face clinic visit.

What's behind the growth of IT?

In one word … digitization. At the very basic level, without digitization, computers, IT, and everything they enable would not have been possible.

Digitization involves the conversion of an analog source into a digital source, that is, converting it into a series of zeros and ones so it can be *read* by computers—a bridge between the analog and the digital worlds. The analog source can be a paper book converted into an e-book. It can be a musical score (a printed manuscript) or a phone conversation (physical sound) converted into a digital file. So, digitization simply involves converting an analog source into a digital source, without making any changes to the underlying process itself. That's the function of *digitalization*.

Digitalization is the process of moving to digital business; it cannot occur unless the different elements involved in a process have first been digitized. Digitalization thus involves transforming a business process using digital technologies. It makes processes easier to perform and more efficient. It is ubiquitous in our daily lives, so much so it is hard to visualize a world without digitalization. Digitization and digitalization are what used to be known as *computerization* in an earlier era.

All this growth and innovation are, however, not without challenges. A key challenge arising from the adoption and growth of digital technology revolves around digital disruption. Technologies like AI, data analytics, robotics, and others mentioned earlier (and new entrants into their industries) are fueling disruption for millions of companies, especially those in legacy industries wedded to older technologies and unwilling or unable to digitalize their processes, systems, and business models. A 2019 survey of decision makers conducted by market research firm Vanson Bourne, and sponsored by Teradata, found that 94% of the businesses surveyed experienced some form of disruption and were rethinking their business approaches. The survey also found that 61% of the respondents were unprepared to strategically address market-disruptive competitors. The top sources of disruption included keeping up with customer demands and market dynamics (87% of the respondents), workforce pressures such as skills shortages and employee retention (85%), and adapting to new business models (74%). Respondents in the survey, called "Adapt or Perish: The New Reality in a Hyper-digitized World," were from companies in the US, the UK, France, Germany, China, and Japan with 1,000 employees or more and annual revenue of at least $250 million—in financial services, IT, technology, and telecom industries.[22]

Refer to Chapter 3 for more on technology, its genesis, and its impact on the business world.

Competition—A Changing Paradigm

What pulls together the other forces in the global–digital economy is competition—competition for markets, technologies, investment, talent, and other resources. Economic competition typically refers to competition for markets, i.e., rivalry between two or more sellers for sales, market share, and profits. How firms go about trying to secure the business of prospective customers changes with the emergence of new economies and new technologies. There has also been a fundamental change in how firms compete and create and capture value in the global–digital economy, which is the crux of this book.

Talking of competition in an economic sense, Harvard Business School professor Michael Porter popularized the concepts of industry analysis, competitive strategy, and competitive advantage, among other core strategy ideas.[23] His theories developed at the height of the old economy (the 1970s and 1980s) are still relevant today, especially for old economy companies and industries, i.e., industries in the industrial economy that tend to be relatively stable and mature. Using Porter's five forces model for a digital economy industry would, however, be a stretch, though some of his other theories are still applicable for digital economy firms and industries.[24]

As economies become more services-oriented[25], more connected, and with digitized goods and services, competition is becoming ever more international in its reach. A company that operates in multiple markets has the opportunity to spread parts of its value chain among countries as it competes for customers, markets, and resources globally. In markets worldwide, it often meets the same global players and also has the opportunity to dovetail its competitive stance against specific competitors differently in different markets. At the same time, it must meet the assault on its home market by companies from throughout the world, and increasingly by companies from emerging markets.

With *new technologies* (e.g., AI and 3D printing), *new players* (digital startups), *new products* (IoT devices), *new playing fields* (digital and emerging markets), *new challenges* (digital disruption), *new rules of the game* (network effects), and *new market dynamics* (winner-take-all or winner-take-most), competition is now an entirely new ballgame.

New technologies. Competition in high-technology industries is generally very different from competition in old-economy industries. Platform-based business models, multisided markets, and network effects are especially important in considering the impacts of technology on competition. While new technologies can provide competitive advantage to a firm, for example, by creating entry barriers for competitors, technology markets also present some unique challenges for firms. Such challenges include digital disruption caused by newer technologies, startups, and other entrants into their industries (think Uber/Lyft in the taxi market) as well as by services such as price comparison websites (e.g., confused.com in the insurance and financial services industries in the UK). Besides, companies such as Uber/Lyft and Airbnb have not only disrupted the taxi and hospitality industries, respectively, they have also increased the market size of those industries and have often bred new startups.

New players. These are companies that have joined the ranks of global competitors from emerging markets, small and medium-sized enterprises (SMEs) new to international competition from both developed and emerging markets, as well as new digital players from everywhere. All of these have negative implications for incumbents in their industries.

New products. Digital technologies and innovation are giving rise to new products and services—both purely digital and IoT—whose economics and market behavior are very different from those of physical goods and services.

New playing fields. The fall of the Berlin Wall on November 9, 1989 opened up huge new markets—markets that had been behind the Iron Curtain for over 50 years—for companies from all over the world. The growth of developing economies since the 1990s and 2000s has created a much larger market for companies with international operations or aspirations. These new markets comprise some 4 billion consumers and millions of businesses—more than the world experienced at any other time in the past. Add online markets to these playing fields.

New challenges. Digital disruption is just one of the challenges brought on by digital. Businesses today face many other technology-related challenges such as fast-evolving technologies, budgetary constraints, and security concerns.

New rules of the game. In the global–digital economy, firms have many more competitive tools available to them than in any of the previous economies. This is partly because it consists of the old economy, the digital economy, and the age of smart machines—each with its own competitive tools. For old-economy firms, Michael Porter's generic strategies framework should work well, i.e., companies can compete through cost leadership, differentiation, and/or scope.

New market dynamics. Digital markets exhibit zero or near zero marginal cost and significant economies of scale. Such characteristics, along with network effects, whereby a product becomes more valuable the more users it has, can generate winner-take-all or winner-take-most market dynamics.[26]

Digital economy firms, for which economies of scale and scope tend to be very significant, are subject to Carl Shapiro's and Hal Varian's *information rules*.[27] Digital or information goods are goods that can be digitized, that is, converted into *bits* (the smallest possible piece of information, represented by a 1 or a 0) and *bytes* (groups of 8 bits each). As was observed earlier, the marginal cost of producing a digital good is zero or nearly zero. With zero or near zero marginal cost, and with significant economies of scale, "[T]he returns in such markets typically follow a distinct pattern—a power law, or Pareto curve, in which a small number of players reap a disproportionate share of the rewards. Network effects, whereby a product becomes more valuable the more users it has, can also generate these kinds of winner-take-all or winner-take-most markets."[28] Examples of such digital products (with one, two, or three winners in the market, the rest being niche players) are not hard to find. The Microsoft application software is but one.

Smart products (*connected things*), on the other hand, are both physical and digital and connected to other smart products through the internet. Because they are physical, they do not have zero marginal cost. Because they have software and sensors embedded into them, the cost of producing them is generally greater than for their purely physical equivalents. However, they are able to command premium prices. The rules of the game for the age of the smart machines are still evolving and would likely include technology leadership, increasing returns to scale, and first mover advantages, among others.

Truly, competition in the 2020s is an entirely new ball game! In this new global–digital world, everyone, including individuals and businesses, will need a new gameplan. That's where this book comes in.

Notes

1 This term was first used by The Economist, "The age of smart machines," on May 25, 2013, and popularized by Erik Brynjolfsson and Andrew McAfee in their January 2014 book, *The Second Machine Age* (W.W. Norton & Company). Michael E. Porter and James E. Heppelmann referred to such products as "smart, connected products" in their *Harvard Business Review* articles in November 2014 and October 2015.

2 Erik Brynjolfsson and Andrew McAfee, *The Second Machine Age: Work, Progress, and Prosperity in a Time of Brilliant Technologies* (New York: W.W. Norton & Co., 2014).

3 The Economist, "Manufacturing: The Third Industrial Revolution," *The Economist*, April 21, 2012.

4 The Economist, "The Age of Smart Machines," *The Economist*, May 24, 2013.

5 For more discussion, see Vinod K. Jain, *Global Strategy: Competing in the Connected Economy* (New York and London: Routledge, 2016).

6 An earlier version of this section appeared in the July 2020 issue of the *Mensa Bulletin*, Vinod K. Jain, "Old is new again: A dazzling new sheen on the rust belt." https://www.us.mensa.org/read/bulletin/features/old-is-new-again/.

7 Paul Tullis, "Pete Buttigieg revived South Bend with tech. Up next: America," *Wired*, April 11, 2019. https://www.wired.com/story/pete-buttigieg-revived-south-bend-with-tech-up-next-america/.

8 James Fallows, "How America is putting itself back together," *The Atlantic*, March 6, 2016. https://www.theatlantic.com/magazine/archive/2016/03/how-america-is-putting-itself-back-together/426882/.

9 Laura Lane, Ben Grubb, & Anne Power, "Sheffield City Story," CASEreport 103, May 2016, LSE Center for Analysis and Social Exclusion.

10 Mainstreet, "America's dying cities," *Newsweek*, January 21, 2011. https://www.newsweek.com/americas-dying-cities-66873.

11 Jorge Lopez, "Digital business is everyone's business," *Forbes*, May 7, 2014. https://www.forbes.com/sites/gartnergroup/2014/05/07/digital-business-is-everyones-business/#4952ea4b7f82. See also: https://knowledge.wharton.upenn.edu/article/every-business-digital-business/.

12 Jagdish Bhagwati, *In Defense of Globalization* (New York: Oxford University Press, 2007), p. 3.

13 Michael Spence, *The Next Convergence: The Future of Economic Growth in a Multispeed World* (New York: Farrar, Straus and Giroux, 2011), p. 15.

14 The G7 (Group of 7) represents the seven largest economies in the world as designated by IMF many years ago: Canada, France, Germany, Italy, Japan, United Kingdom, and the United States. (Some members of the G7 are no longer the world's largest economies.)

15 BRIC stands for Brazil, Russia, India, and China, an acronym devised by Jim O'Neill in 2001, then the Chief Economist of Goldman Sachs, to represent nations at a somewhat similar stage of economic development and on way to becoming developed economies.

16 Homi Kharas, "The unprecedented expansion of the global middle class, an update," Brookings Institution, February 2017. https://www.brookings.edu/wp-content/uploads/2017/02/global_20170228_global-middle-class.pdf.

17 Homi Kharas and Kristofer Hamel, "A global tipping point: Half the world is now middle class or wealthier," Brookings Institution, September 2018. https://www.brookings.edu/blog/future-development/2018/09/27/a-global-tipping-point-half-the-world-is-now-middle-class-or-wealthier/.

18 "General purpose technologies" (GPT) is a generic term, applicable not just to information technologies. For instance, B.J.G. van der Kooij has explored the GPT of Electricity that led to the Communication Revolution via the General Purpose Engines of the Telegraph, the Telephone, and the Wireless. https://pure.tudelft.nl/ws/portalfiles/portal/12555102/The_Invisble_Hand_of_Innovation.pdf.

19 Brynjolfsson and McAfee (2014).

20 Brynjolfsson and McAfee (2014, p. 81).

21 See samples of buildings and houses constructed by Apis Cor using 3D printing at: https://apis-cor.com/3d-homes/.

22 Teradata Press Release, "Global survey, Hyper disruption and digitization leading forces of change within business," Teradata, October 21, 2019. https://www.teradata.com/Press-Releases/2019/Adapt-or-Perish-The-New-Reality-in-a-Hyper-Digitized-World.

23 See Michael Porter's seminal books on *Competitive Strategy* (New York: The Free Press, 1980); and *Competitive Advantage: Creating and Sustaining Superior Performance* (New York: The Free Press, 1985).

24 In fairness to Prof. Porter, he does show the relevance of his theories to the digital economy and to what he calls the third IT revolution. See his March 2001 article, "Strategy and the internet" and his coauthored November 2014 article, "How smart, connected products are transforming competition", both in *Harvard Business Review*.

25 Services account for about 80% of the US economy, and about 70–80% of the economies of most other developed countries. Even developing countries are increasingly services-focused. For instance, the contribution of services to GDP in 2015 was 53% for China, 56% for India, 60% for Russia, and 67% for Brazil. https://en.wikipedia.org/wiki/List_of_countries_by_GDP_sector_composition.

26 Erik Brynjolfsson, Andrew McAfee, and Michael Spence, "New world order: Labor, capital, and ideas in the power law economy," *Foreign Affairs*, July/August 2014.

27 Carl Shapiro and Hal R. Varian, *Information Rules: A Strategic Guide to the Network Economy* (Cambridge, MA: Harvard Business School Press, 1998).

28 Erik Brynjolfsson, Andrew McAfee, and Michael Spence, "New world order: Labor, capital, and ideas in the power law economy," *Foreign Affairs*, July/August 2014.

Chapter 2

Paradox of Globalization

> What an extraordinary episode in the economic progress of man that age was which came to an end in August 1914! … The inhabitant of London could order by telephone, sipping his morning tea in bed, the various products of the whole earth, in such quantity as he might see fit, and reasonably expect their early delivery upon his doorstep; he could at the same moment and by the same means adventure his wealth in the natural resources and new enterprises of any quarter of the world …
>
> *John Maynard Keynes, The Economic Consequences of the*
> *Peace (London: Macmillan & Co., Ltd., 1919) p. 6*

This is how John Maynard Keynes (1883–1946), the renowned economist and man of quite a range of interests and influence, described globalization as it existed (for the upper classes in Britain) during the pre-World War I era—in some respects a bit akin to what exists today. His 1919 book, *The Economic Consequences of the Peace*, from which the above quotation was taken, made him a celebrity, well before he formulated Keynesian Economics and became famous.

The railroads, steamships, telegraph, and telephone—multinational communication networks—already existed by the year 1900. Prior to 1914, people, goods, and capital could move between countries much more easily than today—largely unimpeded by trade and investment barriers, visas, and such. Hence, a London inhabitant could indeed order on phone what he needed to purchase or invest his capital in any part of the world relatively easily.

So, what is globalization and when did it begin? And what is the paradox? It depends on whom you ask.

Views on globalization range from it being the root of all evil to a solution for many of the problems the world is facing. Perhaps there is some truth to both positions. However, there are many kinds of globalization, such as cultural, ecological, economic, and political. Even though these types are somewhat interconnected, economic globalization tends to be the most prominent and bears the brunt of criticism. Some people tend to ascribe anything and everything to (economic) globalization, without making distinctions among the different kinds of globalization.

In this book, we will mostly be concerned with *economic globalization*, defined as growing integration and economic interdependence among nations—via international trade and investment, and people, capital, and technology and data flows. The paradox centers on positive and negative forces impacting globalization, discussed later in this chapter.

DOI: 10.4324/9781003037446-3

Economic globalization derives its underpinnings from Adam Smith's *The Wealth of Nations*, published in 1776 during the early years of the first Industrial Revolution, which explored the role of free trade, specialization, division of labor, and markets in raising productivity and prosperity in nations. However, globalization actually preceded Adam Smith by thousands of years.

When Did Globalization Begin?

Well, if globalization implies growing integration and interdependence among nations, it truly began with the Silk Road and the Spice Routes some 4,000–5,000 years ago. The Silk Road was a network of international trade and cultural routes connecting China, India, Persia, and the Mediterranean and intermittently bringing together traders, merchants, pilgrims, monks, thieves, and soldiers from different countries. Claimed to have begun around 3,200 BC, the Silk Road lasted several millennia. Not just silk and cultural influences, many other goods, even disease, religions (e.g., Buddhism and Christianity), and technologies of the time traveled along the road— early signs of the growing integration of the world. The Silk Road followed land routes, but the Spice Routes were largely sea routes (Figure 2.1).

The map shows trading routes centered on the Silk Road, shown as thick lines mostly on land. Other trading routes are shown in thin lines on both land and sea, including the Spice Routes mostly on sea. Both these trade and cultural routes helped connect the East and the West.[1] According to a description of the Spice Routes on a UNESCO website:

> The principal and most profitable goods they traded in were spices... But precious goods were not the only points of exchange between the traders. Perhaps more important was the exchange of knowledge: knowledge of new peoples and their religions,

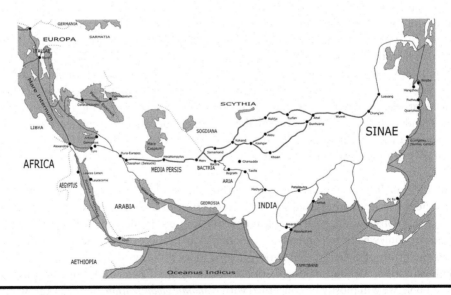

Figure 2.1   The Silk Road and the Spice Routes.

Source: The Silk Road and Spice Routes, 1st Century CE, https://commons.wikimedia.org/wiki/File:Transasia_trade_routes_1stC_CE_gr2.png.

languages, expertise, artistic and scientific skills. The ports along the Maritime Silk Roads (Spice Routes) acted as melting pots for ideas and information. With every ship that swept out with a cargo of valuables on board, fresh knowledge was carried over the seas to the ship's next port of call.[2]

More recently, explorers like Marco Polo (thirteenth and fourteenth centuries), Zheng He (fifteenth century), Christopher Columbus (fifteenth and sixteenth centuries), Vasco da Gama (fifteenth and sixteenth centuries), and David Livingstone[3] (nineteenth century) were some of the early torchbearers of globalization.

Marco Polo, for instance, traveled the Silk Road with his uncle and father eastward from their home in Venice in 1271, taking a somewhat different route from the one his uncle and father had taken 10 years earlier. While in China, Marco Polo served in the court of the Great Kublai Khan for 17 years, in various important, high-ranking positions, and traveled a great deal on official missions within China and even to Burma and India. Some of the places Marco Polo visited during his travels were not seen by the Europeans until centuries later. The Polos returned to Venice in 1295 with great wealth, singing tales of the wonders and the wealth of the Chinese civilization. Three years after his return to Venice, war broke out between Venice and the rival city of Genoa. Marco joined the army but was captured and spent a year in a Genoese prison. While in prison, he dictated the story of his travels to a fellow prisoner, a writer, who recorded his tales. The story turned out to be one of the greatest travelogues in history, *The Description of the World* or *The Travels of Marco Polo*, a "bestseller" in Medieval Europe. However, the book came to be known as *Il Milione* (*The Million Lies*), because no one believed that any country could actually be as rich and cultured as China. The book had a tremendous impact as Europeans began to learn more about the East, and future explorers, including Columbus, read it with interest. Much of what Marco Polo wrote was later verified by travelers in the eighteenth and nineteenth centuries. Even Chinese historians found the book of great value as it helped them better understand the thirteenth century China.[4]

Some of the "more recent" traders were the various East India Companies of the seventeenth to nineteenth centuries from Britain, the Netherlands, France, etc. For example, the British East India Company was chartered in Britain in 1600 to trade with the East Indies, and the Dutch East India Company was chartered in the Netherlands in 1602 with a 21-year monopoly to trade with Asia. Some have referred to the East India Companies as the first *multinational corporations* (MNCs).[5] Not really, they were indeed chartered to conduct trade, but they also carried armies with them, conquered lands, and subjugated native populations in those lands for hundreds of years. The British East India Company became involved in politics and acted as an agent of British imperialism in India from the early eighteenth to the mid-nineteenth centuries.[6] The company was also a catalyst for British imperialism in China. The Dutch East India Company was, in fact, given "quasi-government powers, including the ability to wage war, imprison and execute convicts, negotiate treaties, strike its own coins, and establish colonies."[7] They were no MNCs.

Zheng He, an Admiral during China's Ming dynasty, led an armada of the largest ships[8] in the world at the time exploring the Indian Ocean, including India, Ceylon (now Sri Lanka), Arabia, and East Africa, on seven voyages in the early 1400s. The armada had over 27,000 crew members and soldiers and 300 ships, the longest being 400 ft by 160 ft. (By comparison, in 1492, Columbus had 90 sailors on three ships, of which the longest ship, the *Santa Maria*, was 85 ft long.) The purpose of his voyages was apparently to obtain recognition and gifts for emperor Yongle from rulers of the lands he visited, rather than to conquer or colonize them. He did use force against those who refused to respect the emperor's wishes.

During the Age of Discovery, a period from the fifteenth to the eighteenth centuries, Europeans carried out many global explorations and discovered many ocean routes, such as to the West in 1492 when Christopher Columbus reached the Americas and to the East in 1498 when Vasco da Gama reached India. The conquistadors, professional warriors from Portugal and Spain, conquered the Americas, especially Mexico and Peru in the sixteenth century, and ruled the region for 300 years. European explorers also set up trading posts in Africa, Americas, and Asia for tradable *goods* such as spices, gold, silver, firearms, and slaves.

Angus Maddison (1926–2010), formerly Professor Emeritus at the University of Groningen, was a noted British economist who had specialized in measuring and analyzing economic growth and development during long periods of time in dozens of countries. His databases are important sources for analyzing long-term economic growth and are used by academic researchers and policy analysts worldwide. Table 2.1 presents excerpts from one of his databases highlighting how the different countries and regions of the world fared over the last 1,000 years.[9] Although China and India had the highest gross domestic product (GDP) in the world early on, they were overtaken by Western Europe by 1870 (not shown in the table), by the US by 1913, by the former USSR by 1950, and by Japan by 1973.

These data show the GDP in different countries and regions, but they do not show the extent to which these countries/regions were involved in trade. Table 2.2 presents Maddison's estimates of merchandise exports as a share of GDP for a selected group of countries, which give an indication of the extent to which they were involved in international trade from 1870 to 1998. The most active exporters throughout this period were the European countries included in the table, though Spain and France seem to have joined the club of big exporters of manufactured goods only in

Table 2.1 World GDP in 1990 Million International Dollars, 1000–2003 CE

Country/ Region	1000	1500	1700	1820	1913	1950	1973	2003
Western Europe	10,925	44,183	81,213	159,851	902,210	1,396,078	4,096,764	7,857,394
Former USSR	2,840	8,458	16,196	37,678	232,351	510,243	1,513,070	1,552,231
US	520	800	527	12,548	517,383	1,455,916	3,536,622	8,430,762
Japan	3,188	7,700	15,390	20,739	71,653	160,966	1,242,932	2,699,261
China	26,550	61,800	82,800	228,600	241,431	244,985	739,414	6,187,984
India	33,750	60,500	90,750	111,417	204,242	222,222	494,832	2,267,136
Total Asia (excl. Japan)	81,683	153,617	214,281	391,738	609,135	830,428	2,621,624	13,855,834
Africa	13,835	19,383	25,776	31,266	79,486	203,131	549,993	1,322,087
World	120,379	248,445	371,428	694,598	2,733,365	5,331,689	16,022,888	40,913,389

Source: Angus Maddison, Contours of the World Economy, 1–2030 AD: Essays in Macroeconomic History (London: Oxford University Press, 2007), p. 379.

Table 2.2   Merchandise Exports as Percent of GDP in 1990 Prices, Selected Countries, 1870–1998

Country	1870	1913	1929	1950	1973	1998
France	4.9	7.8	8.6	7.6	15.2	28.7
Germany	9.5	16.1	12.8	6.2	23.8	38.9
Netherlands	17.4	17.3	17.2	12.2	40.7	25.0
UK	12.2	17.5	13.3	11.3	14.0	25.0
Spain	3.8	8.1	5.0	3.0	5.0	23.5
US	2.5	3.7	3.6	3.0	4.9	10.1
Mexico	3.9	9.1	12.5	3.0	1.9	10.7
Brazil	12.2	9.8	6.9	3.9	2.5	5.4
China	0.7	1.7	1.8	2.6	1.5	4.9
India	2.6	4.6	3.7	2.9	2.0	2.4
Japan	0.2	2.4	3.5	2.2	7.7	13.4
World	4.6	7.9	9.0	5.5	10.5	17.3

Source: Angus Maddison, *The World Economy: A Millennial Perspective*, Vols. I and II, (OECD 2006), p. 362.

the 1990s. The US, on the other hand, had not been a big exporter throughout this period, partly because of its huge domestic consumption.[10]

According to Maddison's analysis, the causes for the ascent of the West compared to the rest of the world included higher population growth, dramatic progress in shipping and navigation, scientific progress, and technical innovations. For instance, population grew five-fold in the West between 1000 and 1820, somewhat less than four times in the rest of the world. Progress of Western shipping and navigation, a result of scientific discoveries and innovation, led to twenty-fold increase in world trade between 1500 and 1820. Table 2.3 shows that world trade had been growing much faster than the world GDP throughout the period shown in the table, except during 1913–1950 because of the two world wars and the near collapse of world trade and cross-border capital flows.[11]

What Is Behind the Growth of Globalization in Recent Periods?

In more recent periods, i.e., over the last 200 years or so, integration of the world was driven by technology and transportation—such as steam power, telegraphy, telephony, radio, television, shipping, and the airplane. Still more recently, i.e., over the last 70 years or so, economic integration of the world (globalization) has been driven by at least four forces—multilateral institutions, governments, multinational enterprises (MNEs), and information and communication technologies (ICTs).

Table 2.3   Globalization Ratio: Comparative Growth in the Volume of World Trade and GDP, 1500–2001 (Annual Average Compound Growth Rates)

	World Trade	World GDP	Col. 1/Col. 2
1500–1820	0.96	0.32	3.0
1820–1870	4.18	0.93	4.5
1870–1913	3.40	2.11	1.6
1913–1950	0.90	1.82	0.5
1950–1973	7.88	4.90	1.6
1973–2001	5.22	3.05	1.7
1820–2001	3.93	2.22	1.8

Source: Angus Maddison, *Growth and Interaction in the World Economy: The Roots of Modernity* (Washington, DC: The AEI Press, 2004), p. 22.

Multilateral Institutions

The devastation caused by the two world wars and most countries' desire to create a calmer world led to the creation of three multilateral institutions—the International Monetary Fund (IMF), the World Bank, and the General Agreement on Tariffs and Trade (GATT); GATT was later absorbed into the World Trade Organization (WTO) on January 1, 1995. Representatives from 44 nations met in Bretton Woods, New Hampshire in the US from 1944 to 1947 to try and develop international *institutions* that would help create stability in the world's economic, financial, and trading systems, and to help rebuild Europe. The idea behind the creation of these institutions was that they would help manage, regulate, and police the global marketplace, and provide financial assistance to countries when needed. They did and continue to do all of that—at least to some extent—and have had a major influence in helping to create an increasingly integrated and inter-dependent world.

Governments

Member countries must fulfill their obligations as members of the three multilateral institutions—obligations to which they had previously agreed at the Bretton Woods Conference and at later meetings and discussion *rounds*. Over the years, governments of individual countries have taken many actions in their own interest, though some of them also helped bring countries together economically, politically, and culturally. For instance, countries within certain regions (though not always in the same region) have formed economic integration agreements, such as the European Union (EU) and the US–Mexico–Canada Agreement (USMCA), which replaced NAFTA (North American Free Trade Agreement) in March 2020. Such agreements are designed to help countries benefit from free trade over and above what they could achieve as WTO members. There are many other such actions taken by country governments to foster their economic interests and have a greater say in world affairs, which also led to greater interaction among nations.

Multinational Enterprises

An MNC or an MNE is a firm that has manufacturing and/or service presence in two or more countries. As of 2018, there were an estimated 60,000 MNCs in the world, with about 500,000 subsidiaries worldwide.[12] Unlike a few decades ago, many of today's MNEs come from developing countries. Some MNEs are small- and medium-sized enterprises (SMEs) and some were even *born global*. The latter category includes companies that operate on the internet, such as Skype, Netflix, and Google, serving customers anywhere and everywhere. Netflix shows are available in dozens of countries, some in their own language and some dubbed or with subtitles, and with Google Translate, enabling people from throughout the world read foreign-language newspapers; it's often the MNEs that are now helping integrate the world.

Information and Communication Technologies

We discussed the role of technologies, including ICTs, in the first chapter. The ICTs have indeed made the world seem smaller—bringing people, companies, industries, and nations together more than any other technologies and at any time in the past.

These four forces are, of course, not the only factors behind recent growth of globalization, but they are the more important ones. Other major factors in globalization in the last few decades were the development of containers in shipping and NGOs (nongovernmental organizations or civil society organizations), which are set up by concerned citizens as not-for-profit entities. An NGO is often concerned with one or more specific issues and raises funds to work on those issues, over and above what governments do. Most NGOs typically work within the countries in which they are established, but many have cross-border charters, such as Greenpeace, CARE, and OXFAM. A discussion of NGOs is beyond the scope of this book.

Globalization Today

The result of the recent growth in globalization is that the world today is much more integrated and more interdependent than it was even a few decades ago, even taking into account growing trade tensions, protectionism, and move away from democratic and free market institutions. Furthermore, there is a growing convergence between the developed and developing worlds. However, the impacts of globalization extend much beyond that. We now observe trends depicting *role reversal* between developed and developing nations, which is redefining the rules of global competition.

Reversal of Attitudes toward Globalization

With the formation of GATT in 1947, developed countries began promoting the idea of liberalizing trade and investments in the 1950s and 1960s as a means of achieving prosperity for both rich and poor countries. The developing countries, however, had been fearful of integration and turned away from using trade and investments as instruments for development and growth.

Although developed countries in the 1950s/1960s were generally pro-globalization and developing countries antiglobalization, national sentiments seem to have reversed since then. For the last two to three decades, the antiglobalization sentiment has been running high in many of the developed countries, while the emerging and developing countries are beginning to see globalization as a positive force.

Table 2.4 Faith and Skepticism about Globalization, Views on Trade, 2014 and 2018

Views on Trade	US		Advanced Countries[a]		Emerging Countries	
	2014	2018	2014	2018	2014	2018
Trade is good	68%	74%	84%	87%	78%	83%
Trade creates jobs	20	36	44	47	52	56
Trade decreases prices	N/A	37	28	28	24	18
Trade raises wages	17	31	25	31	45	47

[a] Excluding the US.
Source: The 2014 and 2018 Global Attitudes & Trends Surveys, Pew Research Center.

Table 2.5 Views on Foreign Direct Investment, 2014

Country Category	Foreign Companies Building Factories in Our Country Is Good	Foreign Companies Buying Our Companies Is Good
Advanced	74%	31%
Emerging	70	44
Developing	85	57
Global median	74	45

Source: Global Attitudes and Trends.

The 2014 and the 2018 Global Attitudes Surveys conducted by the Pew Research Center,[13] a Washington, DC-based think tank, found that most countries believe that globalization is good for their country at least in some respects (see Table 2.4). However, respondents in advanced countries, especially in the US (and Japan and Italy, not shown in the table), seem to be ambivalent about its benefits on trade in matters relating to jobs and wages, whereas emerging countries are the strongest supporters of trade and globalization.

Foreign direct investment, the second pillar of globalization (the first being trade), is generally welcomed by countries, both advanced and emerging. More specifically, greenfield investment which involves creating a new business in a foreign country (e.g., building a new factory) as compared to executing mergers and acquisitions (M&As; taking possession of existing businesses) is generally preferred, because it can mean creation of new employment and dissemination of new technologies, new management methods, and other intangibles in the host market. Table 2.5 shows countries' contrasting views on greenfield investment versus M&As. A global average of 74% of the survey respondents approved of foreign firms building new factories in their countries, but only 45% said that foreign companies acquiring local enterprises was a good thing. The distinction is even more pronounced for advanced countries—74% approving building new factories compared to only 31% approving foreign acquisitions of domestic enterprises. However, the difference in public opinion between greenfield investment and M&A is less pronounced among emerging and developing countries. In developing countries, especially, 85% of the respondents

Table 2.6   Views on Foreign Direct Investment, 2019

Country	Foreign Companies Building Factories in Our Country Is Good	Foreign Companies Buying Our Companies Is Good
Israel	83%	60%
South Korea	76	27
Japan	57	33
Brazil	72	41
Mexico	73	51
South Africa	67	45
Nigeria	89	38
India	62	43
Indonesia	44	28
Turkey	46	24

Source: Global Attitudes and Trends Survey, 2019, Pew Research Center Survey, 2014, Pew Research Center.

thought that greenfield investment was good, but 57% said that foreign acquisitions of domestic enterprises was good.

Pew Research Center repeated the survey in 2019, but only for 15 selected countries. Of the G7 countries, only Japan was included in the survey. The results are generally in the same direction as for the 2014 survey, but with some significant differences. On an average, 72% of the respondents in the 15 countries surveyed said that foreign companies making greenfield investments in their countries was a good thing, while only 40% thought that foreign companies buying companies in their countries was a good thing. Table 2.6 shows differences of views in 10 of the 15 countries surveyed in 2019.

Reverse Innovation

General Electric's former Chairman and CEO, Jeffrey Immelt and Dartmouth College Tuck School professors, Vijay Govindarajan and Chris Trimble, coined and popularized the term *reverse innovation* in their 2009 *Harvard Business Review* article.[14] Reverse innovation, also known as trickle-up innovation, refers to any innovation developed for emerging markets that is then sold in developed markets. General Electric and most MNEs typically sold modified Western products in emerging markets (a process often called *glocalization*); reverse innovation, as the term implies, is just the reverse.

The best-known example of reverse innovation is GE MAC 400—an inexpensive, portable electrocardiogram (ECG) machine developed by GE Healthcare in Bangalore, India in 2007 for the rural market in India—that was later launched in the US as GE MAC 800. Another good example, also from GE, is the conventional ultrasound machine sold in sophisticated hospital imaging centers in China in 2002 for $100,000 and more. The local R&D team in China developed an inexpensive, portable ultrasound machine using a laptop computer that was sold for $30,000–$40,000 in 2002 in China. By 2007, cheaper models were selling at $15,000 and found a huge, growing market in China, the US, and elsewhere.

Other examples of reverse innovation include Procter & Gamble's Vicks Honey Cough, a remedy for cold and cough developed by the company in Mexico, which found success in America and Europe, and Coca-Cola's Minute Maid Pulpy, orange fruit juice with real orange pulp, popular in the Chinese market. Later introduced in other Asian markets and in New Zealand, Minute Maid Pulpy is the first billion-dollar Coca-Cola brand to emerge from China. Microsoft created an app for *dumb* (nonsmart) phones to allow their users in India and South Africa access to websites, such as Facebook and Twitter. The app has found new use as a low-cost cloud computing platform.

MNEs have been investing in R&D in emerging and developing nations for over two decades—primarily to develop products for local use, but also to arbitrage the cost and talent advantage of such nations for R&D work for developed nations. Now, with reverse innovation, some of the products developed by the MNEs in emerging nations find markets in developed nations.

Strategy &, the consulting arm of PwC, conducts the annual *Global Innovation 1000* study of the world's top 1000 R&D spenders. Since 2005, the study has been charting the pattern of innovation spending by these top spenders. In the 2015 *Global Innovation 1000* study, PwC reported that 94% of the world's largest innovation spenders conducted key elements of their R&D programs overseas, with Asia being the top destination, followed by North America and Europe. The top 1000 R&D spenders, for instance, spent a total of $28 billion in India in 2015, a 115% increase since 2007. Multinationals have been relocating R&D to India for a variety of reasons, with cost not necessarily being the most important. According to Denise Ramos, the CEO of the US-based ITT Corporation, "Our tech center in India gives us an around-the-clock capability to accelerate development work due to the time difference with the US... Highest priority was access to technical talent that was in close proximity to regional customers. The fact that some of the labor is lower cost was nice to have, but not a primary driver." As for moving R&D to China, 71% of the survey respondents mentioned proximity to high-growth market as their top reason for moving R&D to China, followed by proximity to key manufacturing sites (59%) and key suppliers (54%), and a cost advantage (53%).[15]

Reverse FDI

For too long, international investment between developed and developing countries was a one-way street, with investment flowing from the developed to the developing countries. In recent decades, however, we have been seeing a reversal, whereby developing countries have also been investing in developed countries. China, for instance, has been making substantial outward foreign direct investment (FDI) for many years—investing in both developed and developing countries—ranking as the #2, #3, or #4 largest foreign direct investor nation in the world; with state-owned enterprises (SOEs) accounting for a dominant share of Chinese firms' outward FDI. However, outward FDI from China has been declining since 2016 (when it was $196.149 billion, the second largest foreign direct investor nation in the world)—due to stricter government regulations against capital outflows, slowdown due to COVID-19, and security concerns in recipient countries due to Chinese companies' investments there.

The US had been the largest foreign direct investor nation for a long time but lost its top rank in 2018 as American MNEs began repatriating their foreign investments and earnings back to the US as a result of the Tax Cuts and Jobs Act of 2017. The US regained its status as the largest foreign direct investor nation in the world in 2020. Table 2.7 shows the list of the top five foreign direct investor nations during 2019–2021.[16]

Table 2.7   The Top Five Foreign Direct Investor Nations, 2019–2021 (US$ Billion)

2021		*2020*		*2019*	
US	403.101	US	234.919	Japan	232.627
Germany	151.690	China	153.710	Germany	137.293
Japan	146.782	Japan	95.664	China	136.905
China	145.190	UK	65.363	France	33.818
UK	107.741	Germany	60.624	US	28.596

Source: UNCTAD, World Investment Report, Various Years.

According to Sanford C. Bernstein, a Wall Street research firm, the Chinese are "increasingly aspirational and conspicuous consumers."[17] The same can also be said of Chinese corporates. For example, Chinese carmaker Geely acquired Volvo from Ford and took a 9.69% stake in Germany's Daimler AG. Lenovo acquired IBM's PC division with the right to use the IBM logo for 5 years. China National Chemical Corporation's (ChemChina's) wholly owned subsidiary China National Tire & Rubber Co. acquired Italy's tire maker Pirelli, while Dongfeng Motor took a 14% stake in France's PSA Peugeot Citroen. Chinese companies go to developed countries for a variety of reasons, including seeking new markets, global brands, advanced technologies, and global management expertise. With China's *going out* policy, companies often receive significant government support in their efforts to become world leaders in their respective industries. SOEs may especially be driven to be seen as *national champions* in the eyes of their government.[18]

Indian companies had been making investments abroad for much longer, though mostly in developing countries in the past. Since about 2000, however, some two-thirds of Indian MNEs' foreign direct investments have gone up-market—to highly developed countries such as the US, the UK, Germany, and France. India's Tata Steel acquired the British-Dutch steelmaker Corus, Tata Motors acquired Jaguar Cars and Land Rover from Ford, and Suzlon Energy acquired Germany's Repower. Other foreign acquisitions by Indian firms included HCL Technologies' acquisition of UK's Axon Group, an SAP consulting company, and Tata Consultancy Services' acquisition of the French IT services firm, Alti SA. The Indian-owned Mittal Steel Company acquired Arcelor (France, Spain, and Luxembourg) through a hostile takeover in 2006 and became the world's largest steel maker, ArcelorMittal SA, headquartered in Luxembourg city.

India Inc.'s investments in developed countries result from several factors, including Indian companies' ability to arbitrage their cost advantage; India's human capital, both technical and managerial; a huge domestic market with cut-throat competition in many industries; well-developed institutions (compared to many other emerging markets); business acumen resulting from deeply embedded entrepreneurial traditions; and a long exposure to Western and Japanese multinationals and their management practices.[19]

In addition to the Chinese and Indian MNEs, companies from other emerging and developing countries have also been investing in advanced countries. When Mexico's cement firm, CEMEX, decided to go global in 1992, it acquired two cement firms in Spain, Valenciana, and Sanson, for reasons of cultural and linguistic affinity. Much of the investment between Spain and Latin America had been a one-way street for decades. Reversing two decades of Spain's acquisition spree into Latin America, Latin American firms spent more on acquiring Spanish firms for the first time in 2013 than the other way around. In fact, Mexican firms were the biggest acquirers of Spanish firms from Latin America in 2013. Charoen Pokphand of Thailand purchased the South-East Asia operations of Britain's TESCO, one of the largest supermarket chains in the world—the biggest ever takeover by a Thai firm.

With regard to international Joint Ventures (JVs), in decades prior to the 2000s, a JV was typically between a company from a developed country taking a majority share, and a company from a developing country taking a minority share, with the two being at different stages of the global value chain for their industry. For example, the developed-country partner in a JV could be a manufacturer and the developing-country partner a distributor. With the emergence of global players from many developing countries, there has also been role reversal in how some JVs are established and the functions they perform. Now and in the recent past, we see several cases where the controlling partner is from a developing country and the minority partner is from an advanced country, with the two being at a similar stage of the global value chain in their industry, even direct competitors.

In September 2014, Movile from São Paulo, Brazil, entered into a 50.02:48.98 JV with Just Eat of Britain. According to the press reports, Just Eat, Britain's online food-ordering giant, decided to join its competitor in Brazil rather than to continue fighting it. The JV, called IF-JE Participações S.A., operates under Movile's iFood brand. In September 2013, Haier from China formed a 51:49 JV with the Fagor Group of Spain to establish a refrigerator manufacturing plant in Poland. In 2005, India's automotive maker Mahindra & Mahindra entered into a 51:49 JV with America's commercial vehicle leader Navistar to form Mahindra Navistar Automotive Limited. This was followed by another JV between the two global automotive leaders in 2007. The two JVs produce diesel engines and an extensive line of trucks and buses in India. In 2013, Mahindra & Mahindra acquired Navistar's full stake in both JVs.

Reverse Outsourcing/Offshoring

Multinationals from developed countries have been outsourcing production work to developing countries for decades, with the emergence over time of East Asia as a choice location for the outsourcing of intermediate and final production in most industries. In the 1990s, they also began to outsource (offshore) a variety of corporate services functions to developing and middle-income countries, such as India, China, and countries in Central and Eastern Europe—countries that offered highly skilled workers at low cost. There have been many instances of role reversal between firms from developed countries and those from developing countries, especially in the last 10–15 years. Many developing-country firms have gone from being outsourcees in earlier decades to now being outsourcers to developed-country firms—a trend likely to continue and accelerate in the coming decades.

Embraer, the maker of small- and mid-sized jet planes in Brazil, pioneered the use of reverse outsourcing in the 1990s and 2000s. It does the high value-added design and assembly work itself, but outsources the making of parts to leading companies from advanced countries—parts such as jet engines from GE and avionics from Honeywell, both from the US, wing stubs and pylons from Kawasaki of Japan, door and fuselage parts from France, Spain, and Belgium, and so on (Figure 2.2). With reverse outsourcing, Embraer benefits from alliances with companies at the forefront of technology, speedy development, and lower costs compared to its fully integrated competitors.[20]

One of the most far-reaching reverse outsourcing deals between a developing-country firm and a developed-country firm was negotiated by India's largest telecom operator at the time, Bharti Airtel, with IBM Global Business Services (and other foreign IT companies) in 2004. Under this 10-year deal, valued at over $2 billion, IBM took responsibility for supplying, installing, and

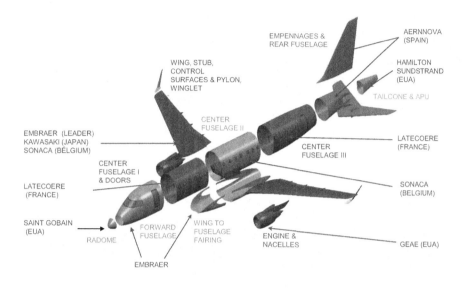

A Worldwide Partnership Project
EMBRAER 170/175 Suppliers

Figure 2.2   Embraer's risk-sharing partnerships for the ERJ 170/190 program.

Source: Embraer Company. Reprinted with permission.

managing Bharti Telecom's end-to-end IT infrastructure, integrating a wide range of customer-facing and back-office processes. All client-specific investments in the infrastructure and its management were made by IBM, allowing Bharti to focus its energies on marketing and branding. In return, IBM was paid a share of Bharti's telecom revenues. (Bharti renegotiated its agreement with IBM in 2014, bringing some IT tasks in-house and giving some to other IT service vendors in India, with a deal value of $400–$500 million over 5 years. In May 2019, the deal was further extended temporarily until a new deal was negotiated.)

Along with the outsourcing of the IT infrastructure to IBM, Bharti Airtel negotiated outsourcing agreements with Ericsson, Nokia, and Siemens in 2004 to obtain network capacity and a full range of managed services, such as network design, optimization, operation, and field maintenance. Payment for network capacity to the vendors was to be made only when the capacity was actually used by Bharti's customers. Bharti was not responsible for paying for unused capacity at any time, even though the ownership of the assets created by the vendors providing that capacity rested with it.[21]

Globalization Today versus in Earlier Eras

Well, if globalization has been evolving for thousands of years, what makes it different today from globalization in earlier eras? We have already seen how today's world is much more integrated than what it was just 10 or 15 years ago through the processes of globalization and convergence—aided by technologies, networks, and information. In this section, we attempt to see how else today's world is different from that in earlier time periods, which may also provide a window into what might be expected in the future.

A McKinsey Global Institute[22] study on cross-border flows of trade, finance, and people shows how connected the world is now compared to, say, 10 or 20 years ago. According to the study, although cross-border trade and investment flows had been behind the growth of globalization since the earliest periods, cross-border exchanges today have exploded in scope and complexity. In addition to the globalization forces discussed earlier, the study highlights two major forces that are accelerating the growth of cross-border flows. They are *increasing global prosperity* and the *growing pervasiveness of internet connectivity and spread of digital technologies*. Some key findings of the study are presented below.[23]

The knowledge-intensive portion of global flows now increasingly dominates the capital- and labor-intensive flows (such as trade in physical goods and services) and is growing faster than they are. In the past, global flows were dominated by labor-intensive, low-end manufacturing, and commodity flows. Now, knowledge-intensive cross-border flows account for half of all global flows, and the percentage is growing larger. Cross-border flows are enabled by digitalization and by the consequent reduction in the marginal cost of production and distribution. Once the preserve of governments and major MNEs, now companies of all size, entrepreneurs, and individuals have the opportunity to participate in the global economy. Today, even the smallest company and individual entrepreneur can be a *micro-multinational* enterprise that sources, produces, and sells its products, services, ideas across borders, courtesy of digital technologies. And this trend is accelerating with the growth of the global–digital economy.

The Paradox

Globalization trends of the most recent past, however, present a paradox. There is indeed growing integration among nations, but there are also signs of breakup represented by growing trade tensions, protectionism, terrorism, even a move away from democratic and free market institutions. The same global trends that suggest a difficult near future for globalization, however, also portend considerable opportunities for firms and nations able to take advantage of them. Dealing with issues like protectionism, terrorism, cyberattacks, disease (such as COVID-19), and climate change requires much greater collaboration among nations, not less, with MNEs and others playing a key role.

> The achievements of the industrial and information ages are shaping a world to come that is both more dangerous and richer with opportunity than ever before... the most powerful actors of the future will draw on networks, relationships, and information to compete and cooperate.[24]

Notes

1 For an even earlier perspective on the history of globalization, starting with the period when humans began moving out of Africa and dispersing throughout the world, see Nayan Chandra, *Bound Together: How Traders, Preachers, Adventurers, and Warriors Shaped Globalization* (New Haven, CT: Yale University Press, 2008).

2 UNESCO, "What are the spice routes." https://en.unesco.org/silkroad/content/what-are-spice-routes. For an history of spice trade, including his own family's history as spice traders, from 3000 BC to the present, read University of Arizona professor Gary Paul Nabhan's book, *Cumin, Camels, and Caravans: A Spice Odyssey* (Berkeley, CA: University of California Press, 2014).

3 David Livingstone, of the "Dr. Livingstone, I presume?" fame, was a Scottish medical practitioner, missionary, and antislave crusader who traveled though Africa for almost 30 years until his death in 1873. He was an explorer, the first European to visit certain areas in Africa, who received much fame after the publication of his travelogue—somewhat in the tradition of Marco Polo who traveled to the East in the thirteenth century. In addition to his scientific research and missionary work, Livingstone was a proponent of trade and commerce, believing that if a country had legitimate trade, it would not need to trade in slavery.

4 Based on the description of Marco Polo's travels at the Silk Road Foundation website http://www.silk-road.com/artl/marcopolo.shtml. See also Francis Wood, *The Silk Road: Two Thousand Years in the Heart of Asia* (Berkeley, CA: University of California Press, 2004) for a fascinating account of history and survey of the Silk Road over several thousand years.

5 See, for example, Pankaj Ghemawat, *World 3.0: Global Prosperity and How to Achieve It* (Boston, MA: Harvard Business Review Press, 2011); BBC, "The world's most powerful corporation," March 30, 2016, https://www.bbc.com/worklife/article/20160330-the-worlds-most-powerful-corporation.

6 The British East India Company ruled large parts of India from 1757 to 1858, when the British Crown assumed direct control of India as one of its colonies. British rule in India ended in 1947.

7 See specific references in Wikipedia: http://en.wikipedia.org/wiki/Dutch_East_India_Company.

8 The largest ship in the armada was believed to be over 400 ft long and 150 ft wide. By comparison, Christopher Columbus's largest ship, the *Santa Maria*, was 90 ft long and 30 ft wide and carried about 90 crew members and soldiers.

9 Angus Maddison, *Contours of the World Economy, 1–2030 AD: Essays in Macroeconomic History* (London: Oxford University Press, 2007).

10 Angus Maddison, *The World Economy: A Millennial Perspective*, Vols. I and II (OECD 2006).

11 Angus Maddison, *Growth and Interaction in the World Economy: The Roots of Modernity* (Washington, DC: The AEI Press, 2004).

12 Multinational corporations, September 28, 2018. https://espace-mondial-atlas.sciencespo.fr/en/topic-strategies-of-transnational-actors/article-3A11-EN-multinational-corporations.html.

13 The Pew Research Center, a prominent thinktank in Washington, DC, conducts public opinion surveys worldwide on a range of subjects, including trade and investment. The 2018 Global Attitudes Survey included some 200,000 face-to-face and telephone interviews in 57 countries.

14 Jeffrey R. Immelt, Vijay Govindarajan, and Chris Trimble, "How GE is disrupting itself," *Harvard Business Review*, October 2009.

15 Barry Jaruzelsky, Kevin Schwartz, and Volker Staack, "Innovation's new world order," *Strategy-Business*, Winter 2015.

16 UNCTAD, "FDI outflows." https://view.officeapps.live.com/op/view.aspx?src=https%3A%2F%2Functad.org%2Fsystem%2Ffiles%2Fnon-official-document%2FWIR2022_tab02.xlsx&wdOrigin=BROWSELINK.

17 Quoted in *The Economist*, January 25, 2014, p. 19.

18 Joel Backaler, "5 Reasons why Chinese companies go global," *Forbes*, May 6, 2014.

19 Excerpted from Vinod K. Jain and Kamlesh Jain, *How America Benefits from Economic Engagement with India*, (Washington, DC: India-US World Affairs Institute, Inc., 2010), p. 10.

20 Antoine van Agtamael, *The Emerging Markets Century: How a Breed of World-Class Companies Is Overtaking the World* (New York: Free Press, 2007).

21 Various sources including Bharti Airtel, IBM, and Ericsson websites and Everest Group research reported in LiveMint, an online publication: http://www.livemint.com/Companies/v0BPytPnOJ-MAalnMRWRDAM/Bharti-Airtels-evolving-outsourcing-strategy.html.

22 The McKinsey Global Institute is the business and economics research arm of McKinsey & Company. It was established in 1990 to develop a deeper understanding of the evolving global economy.

23 McKinsey Global Institute, "Global flows in a digital age: How trade, finance, people, and data connect the world economy," McKinsey Global Institute, 2014. https://www.mckinsey.com/capabilities/strategy-and-corporate-finance/our-insights/global-flows-in-a-digital-age.

24 National Intelligence Council, *Global Trends: Paradox of Progress*, (Washington D.C.: National Intelligence Council, January 2017), ix. https://www.dni.gov/files/documents/nic/GT-Full-Report.pdf.

Chapter 3

Digital Business: Technology at Warp Speed

The computer makes no decisions; it only carries out orders. It's a total moron, and therein lies its strength. It forces us to think, to set the criteria. The stupider the tool, the brighter the master has to be…

Peter Drucker, "The manager and the moron," McKinsey Quarterly, 1967, No. 4.

On October 15, 1997, San Francisco-based Charles Schwab Corporation's entire management team, 120-strong, walked across the Golden Gate Bridge, each wearing a gold-trimmed navy blue jacket with the words CROSSING THE CHASM across the back—symbolizing the full-service brokerage firm's changeover to an online, discount brokerage that allowed its customers to trade stocks online at $29.95 per trade.[1] In the early years of the changeover, Charles Schwab adopted a hybrid model integrating its core full-service business with eSchwab, its online business. A customer seeking to trade stocks could visit one of Charles Schwab's 360+ offices for a face-to-face meeting with an investment specialist, call a customer service representative on the phone, consult with one of the 5,800 independent, fee-based investment advisors, or trade online at eSchwab anytime, anywhere.[2]

Charles Schwab has been a disruptor in the brokerage business ever since the launch of the firm in 1970. The firm became one of the first *discount* brokers in 1975, shortly after the SEC (Securities and Exchange Commission) deregulated brokerage commissions—switching commissions from fixed to negotiable. While some brokerages increased their commission rates, Schwab became a discount broker. In 1979, Schwab became the first discount brokerage firm to automate their back-office settlement processes, leading to the first-ever online order entry system in the market. In 1989, the firm introduced TeleBroker®, an automated telephone brokerage service. Schwab introduced trading on the internet in 1996 (a year before *crossing the chasm*), allowing customers to trade listed and over the counter (OTC) stocks as well as check balances and order status online. With technology in its DNA, Schwab continues to make industry-leading innovations, even disrupting itself on occasion, and reducing online trade commissions in 2019 to $0.[3] (Currently, Charles Schwab charges zero commission for online stock trades, the same as charged by its competitors like E*Trade, Merrill, and Vanguard.)

DOI: 10.4324/9781003037446-4

The seventh largest investment services firm in the US, Charles Schwab now has 360 branch offices with 33,400 employees, 7,500+ independent, registered investment advisors, and $8.5 trillion in client assets as of February 2022. Schwab's net revenue for the 12 months ending December 31, 2021 was $18.52 billion and net income was $5.9 billion.[4]

Since the dot-com boom of the late 1990s, millions of (legacy) companies worldwide have crossed the chasm as they began digitalizing their businesses—physical businesses treading cautiously, sometimes with only a hazy idea of what might work, into the digital world. Other companies have been *pure play* digital businesses from inception. Both kinds of players are creating hybrid ecosystems spanning the physical and digital worlds.

This chapter discusses the economics of digital business, some of the key technologies firms use, risks arising from digital disruption, and how digital businesses create and capture value. In the digital arena, my focus will be on applications of technology, not on technology itself. I look at technologies such as artificial intelligence (AI) through the lens of business capabilities and applications, not technology *per se*.

Economics of Digital Products

Chapter 1 distinguished among three kinds of products—physical, digital (e.g., software or an eBook), and smart machines (e.g., a manufacturing robot). The economics and strategy of each kind of products are different from that of the others. This is so because several core economics concepts, such as diminishing returns to scale and resource scarcity, do not apply to digital products. The strategy for digital products derives from their economic properties (see also Chapter 7).

Digital products are intangible, meaning they do not have a physical presence. They have at least five important characteristics that distinguish them from physical products—zero marginal cost, nonrivalry, network effects, no need for inventory, and customizability. While it is costly to produce the first copy of a digital product, it costs little or nothing to produce it again and again. First, not just *zero marginal cost* of production, but also zero marginal cost of delivery to a customer (via the internet). Consider Microsoft's Office Professional 2021, which probably cost Microsoft a billion dollars or more to develop, test, and make user-friendly over its many incarnations. Office Professional 2021 can be downloaded for $439.99 from Microsoftstore.com for use by one person on one PC. However, making and shipping another copy of the software for a customer costs Microsoft practically nothing (actually, nothing if the customer downloads it from Microsoftstore.com).

Second, digital products are *nonrival* in the sense that any number of individuals can own and use the same product at the same time. (Physical products are rival; no two persons can use the exact same product at the same time). Digital products are intangible, so any number of individuals or organizations can use the exact same product and because the additional (marginal) cost of producing another copy of the same product is zero or negligible. Even the additional cost of delivering a digital product to a customer, on the internet, is zero. Most intangible products are nonrival, but not all. For example, a specific domain name, an intangible product, is a rival product—no two individuals or organizations can own the same domain name. Like tangible products, it can be owned by only one individual or organization at a time.

Third, many digital products exhibit *network effects*, meaning the value of a digital product (to the users and to the owner) increases as the number of users increases—alternatively stated, digital products exhibit increasing returns to scale. This is also known as the Metcalfe's law (named after the inventor of the Ethernet, Robert M. Metcalfe), whereby the value of a network grows exponentially as the number of the network's users increases. Network effects combined with learning-curve effects (the more units are produced in a factory, the lower the average cost of production due to learning or experience effects) can lead to a *winner-take-all* market. Physical products, by contrast, do not exhibit network effects. Instead, they exhibit diminishing returns to scale.[5]

Gordon Moore, Intel Corp. founder, suggested in 1965 that about every 18 months to 2 years, it is possible to double the number of transistors on a computer chip without a corresponding increase in cost; it came to be known as the Moore's law. Ever since, computers have been becoming more and more powerful over time, with no increase in cost—a characteristic of increasing returns to scale. According to futurist Ray Kurzweil, Google's Director of Engineering and cofounder of the Singularity University in Silicon Valley, "once a technology becomes digital—that is, once it can be programmed in the ones and zeros of computer code—it hops on the back of Moore's Law and begins accelerating exponentially." Practically all of the technologies discussed in this chapter, and more, have followed the Moore's law in their dramatic evolution and growth.

Fourth, a digital product cannot be used up (though it can become obsolete) and thus *need not be stocked in a firm's inventory*. It follows that the supply of a digital product is inexhaustible—no product scarcity. The quality of a digital product does not deteriorate as time passes, as more copies are produced, and one can *ship* digital products internationally without worrying about cost, Customs controls, and transportation problems. (However, if a digital product, such as Office Professional 2021, is shipped to another country in a physical package, it will incur cost and be subject to Customs and other issues.) Even the smallest company can play in the global market for digital products. But because such products are subject to network effects, the company might have to compete with a dominant player in a winner-take-all or a winner-take-most market, forcing it to seek a market niche.

Finally, digital products are relatively easy to *customize* or modify; the functionality of a digital product can be changed by simply changing some (or many) lines of code in its software. A recent story at slate.com, an online magazine, was titled, "The Lines of Code that Changed Everything," referring to codes for such functionalities as jpeg, the first popup ad, and the addition of the *Like* button at facebook.com.[6] Digital products are therefore extremely customizable, permitting the digital firm to offer differentiated products to different market segments—even personalizable for individual customers—and allowing the firm to charge different prices to different customers. Pricing of digital products is often based on the value customers expect to derive from the product or on their willingness to pay, rather than the cost of production and distribution. Like an extremely durable product, the quality of a digital product does not deteriorate over time; therefore, someone who buys such a product is unlikely to buy another copy of the same unless the firm selling the product makes frequent updates to its software code. Brad Smith and Carol Ann Browne suggest in their highly readable 2019 book, *Tools and Weapons: The Promise and the Peril of the Digital Age* (Penguin Press, p. 169), "a tech company is only as good as its next product."

Physical products, on the other hand, have significant marginal cost and are rival products. The same physical product cannot be used by more than one individual at the same time. They do not exhibit network effects, are not easy to modify, and have diminishing returns to scale.

Smart (or **intelligent**) **machines** are physical products with digital technologies (e.g., software and sensors) embedded into them *and* connected to the internet. Smart machines, also known as the Internet of Things (IoT), can perform a variety of physical and intellectual tasks. An important characteristic of IoT devices is that they can communicate with their network and **act** on commands *independently of human action*. Examples include Amazon's digital assistant Alexa, cars that can parallel park themselves, a delivery drone, or a chatbot like Replika that *becomes you*. Replika creates a digital representation of the person it is designed to replicate, and one can actually *chat* with it.[7] By 2025, the number of smart machine (connected devices) is estimated to be about 31 billion, compared to 13.8 billion in 2021.[8]

Table 3.1   Core Characteristics of Physical Products, Digital Products, and Smart Machines

Characteristics	Physical Products	Digital Products	Smart Machines
Zero marginal cost		✓	
Nonrivalry		✓	
Network effects		✓	✓
Inexhaustible supply		✓	
Customizability		✓	✓

The economics and strategy of smart machines are quite different from the economics and strategy of digital products. For example, the marginal cost of producing a smart machine, because it is also physical, is not zero and is generally much larger than the marginal cost of its physical equivalent. In fact, of the five characteristics of digital products, only two are potentially applicable to smart machines, namely network effects and customizability. See Table 3.1 for distinctions among the three kinds of products with respect to the economic characteristics of each. Such distinctions have implications for strategy-making for different kinds of products discussed in Chapters 5 and 7.

Technologies

Some of the information technologies that underpin the digital economy are discussed in this section: AI, robotics, 3D printing, cloud computing, blockchain, and 5G. Other than AI, these other technologies are discussed very briefly.

Artificial Intelligence

AI is perhaps the hottest technology today. Work on AI can be traced as far back as 1956 when an AI conference (the Dartmouth Summer Research Project on Artificial Intelligence) was held at the Dartmouth College in the US. Its progress over the years, especially during the last decade, has been literally life-changing. It is beginning to encroach on all aspects of human experience and has been termed more important than any other innovation since the first Industrial Revolution. And, for organizations, AI is changing how they operate and create and capture value.

The main lesson of thirty-five years of AI research is that the hard problems are easy and the easy problems are hard. The mental abilities of a four-year-old that we take for granted—recognizing a face, lifting a pencil, walking across a room, answering a question—in fact solve some of the hardest engineering problems ever conceived... As the new generation of intelligent devices appears, it will be the stock analysts and petrochemical engineers and parole board members who are in danger of being replaced by machines. The gardeners, receptionists, and cooks are secure in their jobs for decades to come.

Steven Pinker, *The Language Instinct* (New York: William Morrow & Co., 1994)

So, let us take a look at what AI is and what it can accomplish. Consulting firm McKinsey & Company defines AI as a machine's ability "to perform cognitive functions that we associate with human minds (such as perceiving, reasoning, learning, and problem solving) and to perform physical tasks using cognitive functions (for example, robotics, autonomous driving, and manufacturing work)."[9]

Cognition—a distinctly human trait requiring intelligence—is essentially the kind of activity we expect AI to undertake. The specific cognitive tasks we might expect AI to perform range from "trivial to substantive to life changing."[10] Here are some tasks that AI can perform under each of these categories:

Trivial: For example, picking someone in a crowd (facial recognition), and the ability to read traffic signs.

Substantive: Self-driving cars, movie recommendations on Netflix, writing magazine-quality prose without human assistance, and Gmail's *smart compose* feature that recommends the next word or phrase one might use in an email message.

Life-changing: Controlling a wheelchair by thought, helping doctors better diagnose a patient's illness, and even creating a Rembrandt indistinguishable from an actual painting by one of the greatest visual artists who ever lived.

A portrait created in 2016 by J. Walter Thompson, an advertising holding company, and Microsoft for ING, a Dutch banking and financial services company, was definitely identified as a Rembrandt by museum visitors, though someone who ran a leading art museum in Australia couldn't recall seeing this specific painting before. It was not, of course, a real Rembrandt. The portrait was created using AI based on 168,263 scans of Rembrandt's known 300 paintings and printed in 13 layers of paint-based UV ink on a 3D printer in a way that closely imitated the master's brushstrokes (Figure 3.1).[11]

Amazon's speech-driven AI, Alexa, similar to iPhone's Siri, is *trained* to answer questions posed to it and perform a variety of tasks. Amazon devices like Echo, Echo Dot, Echo Show, and

Figure 3.1   The Next Rembrandt.

Source: https://commons.wikimedia.org/wiki/File:The_Next_Rembrandt_1.jpg.

Fire TV are needed to interact with Alexa. Currently, Alexa has some 130,000 skills, i.e., actions it can perform with voice commands, created by a large number of independent developers. They range from simple tasks like finding the population of Helsinki to substantive tasks like ordering pizza at dominos.com or paying bills with Capital One mobile banking app. Some time ago, there was an interesting case of a child doing homework by asking questions to Alexa. Recently, I happened to say "OK" in response to something at home, when I happened to be close to my iPhone. I was shocked to hear Siri come alive and say, "I am OK, are you OK?"

Several technologies have fueled the evolution of AI to its current status. These include big data and data science, cloud computing, computing power, graphics processing units (GPUs), and computers' ability to reason and learn (cognition). Some of these technologies are discussed in the following pages.

Machine learning (ML), a subset of AI, uses statistics to find patterns in massive amounts of data, where data can be words, numbers, images, songs, videos, and even clicks—practically anything that can be digitized. Once digitized, data can be fed into machine-learning algorithms to make, for example, product recommendations. Companies like Netflix and Spotify use ML to recommend movies and music, respectively, to their subscribers, Amazon uses ML to make product recommendations to customers, and so on. The idea behind ML is that the company using ML collects as much data about you as possible—about your likings, past purchases, and the links you clicked on—to make educated guesses about what you might like next. Over time, massively large amounts of data (*big data*) become available to *train* AI-based systems, which, using data science, help find connections in unstructured and structured data.

McKinsey & Company's third Global Survey, "The State of AI," in 2021 indicated that AI adoption in companies continues to grow, leading to significant benefits—reduced costs and improved profits.[12] However, during the COVID-19 pandemic's first year, cost savings were more significant than profit improvement. The online survey was carried out during May–June 2021 and had 1,843 respondents representing the full range of regions, industries, company sizes, functional specialties, and tenures.

- A total of 56% of the respondents said that their organization had adopted AI in at least one function.
- AI adoption had increased in most of the companies headquartered in emerging economies, which include China, India, the Middle East and North Africa, compared to the 2020 survey; across regions, the adoption rate was highest at Indian companies, followed closely by those in Asia-Pacific.
- The business functions where AI adoption was most common were service operations, product and service development, and marketing and sales, though the most popular use cases spanned a range of functions.
- A total of 27% of respondents reported that at least 5% of earnings before interest and taxes (EBIT) was attributable to AI, up from 22% in the previous survey.
- Respondents reported significantly greater cost savings from AI than they did previously in every function, with the biggest year-over-year cost savings from using AI were in product and service development, marketing and sale, and strategy and corporate finance.

A Previous McKinsey Global AI Survey identified some specific ways companies use AI, given below. This is not a comprehensive list of potential uses of AI, just those identified in the McKinsey's 2019 global survey[13]:

- Marketing and sales—customer-service analytics, customer segmentation, channel management, prediction of likelihood to buy, pricing and promotion, closed-loop marketing, marketing budget allocation, churn reduction, and next product to buy.
- Product and service development—product-feature optimization, product-development-cycle optimization, and creation of new AI-based enhancements.
- Supply chain management—logistics-network optimization, sales and parts forecasting, warehouse optimization, inventory and parts optimization, spend analytics, and sales and demand forecasting.
- Manufacturing—predictive maintenance and yield, energy, and throughput optimization.
- Service operations—service-operations optimization, contact-center automation, and predictive service and automation.
- Strategy and corporate finance—capital allocation, treasury management, and M&A support.
- Risk management—risk modeling/analytics and fraud/debt analytics.
- HR—performance management and organization-design, workforce development, and talent-management optimization.

James Wilson and Paul Daugherty further identified how some specific companies use AI in their operations, including[14]:

- In auto manufacturing, Mercedes-Benz uses assembly robots to customize cars.
- In banking, HSBC uses AI for fraud detection—flagging questionable credit and debit transactions for human intervention.
- In healthcare, Roche uses AI to aggregate patient data from disparate sources to speed up collaboration among scientists.
- In financial services, Morgan Stanley uses robo-advisors to make investment recommendations to clients based on real-time market information.
- In fashion retail, Stitch Fix uses AI to analyze customer data to make individualized styling recommendations to customers.

Robotics

Peter Drucker's opening quote to this chapter about computers being *total morons* was written in 1967, when even Drucker could not have visualized how technology might evolve in the coming decades. Now, 50 years later, IoT devices can perform tasks that previously only humans could perform, they are called smart or intelligent machines.

Robots are autonomous things in the same class as self-driving cars and drones that use AI to perform tasks previously performed by humans. Sci-Fi movies have long used robots—from flying cars to humanoids—hinting what we might expect in the future. However, robots are here and have been here for quite a long time—one hopes not as deadly as the cyborg in *The Terminator* or as defiant as the supercomputer HAL 9000 in *2001: A Space Odyssey*.

The term *robotics* was coined by Isaac Asimov, professor of biochemistry and author of popular science and science-fiction books, in 1941, and since then robots and robotics have become part of the business lexicon. Today, robots are extensively used in manufacturing as well as in most other sectors of the economy, including construction, agriculture, and healthcare. Automotive manufacturers, like Honda and General Motors, electronic assembly companies,

Figure 3.2   Robots in automotive manufacturing.

Source: Photo by Lenny Kuhne on Unsplash.

like Foxconn (maker of iPhone), and online retailers, like Amazon, have replaced thousands of jobs with robots. Robots are also used for work that is dirty, dull, and dangerous, as well as for disaster relief, as in Haiti after Hurricane Sandy in 2012. Robots are being put to newer and newer uses, including assisting with heart bypass surgery, filling prescriptions, spotting sharks, assembling cars, even managing a hotel front desk, or conducting a Buddhist funeral in Japan.[15] Figure 3.2 shows robots in automotive manufacturing.

Companies like Amazon and UPS are planning package delivery via drones; Amazon expects to start delivering packages by drones by the end of 2022. However, Wing, a subsidiary of Alphabet (parent of Google), has been delivering small packages via drones to homes and businesses since 2014. Operating autonomously, Wing drones use advance vision to understand their surroundings, and the company's flight planning and navigation systems plan delivery routes. Orders placed using the Wing app can be delivered to customers in as little as 15 minutes, wherever the service is available. Wing has operations in the US, Australia, and Finland—working with local businesses and major global partners to deliver food, goods, medicines, and parcels. Customers order products using the Wing app, wherever this service is available.

John Seabrook's article, "The age of robot farmers," in *The New Yorker* magazine of April 8, 2019 offered interesting details and examples of how robotics is being used in farming—uses such as picking strawberries in a field. Such applications are based on converging technologies, including robotics, AI, big data, GPS, machine vision, and materials science.

Isaac Asimov introduced his three Laws of Robotics in 1942 in a short story, "Runaround." These are[16]:

1. A robot may not injure a human being or, through inaction, allow a human being to come to harm.
2. A robot must obey the orders given to it by human beings, except where such orders will conflict with the First Law.
3. A robot must protect its own existence as long as such protection does not conflict with the First or Second Laws.

Asimov created the laws 80 years ago when life and technology were very different from what they are today—presumably for use in his sci-fi stories and books. Today, robots are involved in literally most aspects of our lives and work. There are many situations where Asimov's Laws might conflict with practice. For example, if a human orders a robot to kill a terrorist (as has happened many times in the past), it should refuse to follow the order, with the First Law taking precedence over the Second Law. (The 2004 movie, *I, Robot*, highlights some of the ethical and philosophical issues involved in the Three Laws.)

3D Printing

Three-dimensional (3D) printing, which has been around since the 1980s, has lately been experiencing much development, innovation, and applications. It is now the technology of choice in dozens of industries for dozens of different applications. It involves *additive* manufacturing—building a three-dimensional object from a digital model (software) one layer at a time—as compared to traditional (*subtractive*) manufacturing, which takes a piece of solid material and uses processes such as cutting, drilling, and machining to remove material from it to make the object. Recall the *Next Rembrandt* that was created on a 3D printer with 13 layers of paint-based UV ink, placed one over the other.

Unlike traditional manufacturing, which has different machines—some costing millions of dollars each—performing different functions, 3D printing uses a single piece of equipment, a 3D printer, to print (make) solid objects based on instructions given to it by software; one needs to only change the software and the raw materials (the feedstock) being used. Over the years, the capabilities of 3D printers have been improving, while their cost has been coming down. Today, a simple 3D printer can be purchased for as little as $500, though more complex printers are substantially more expensive. One can find 3D printers in many public libraries in the US and many other countries and there are companies, such as the UPS Stores in the US, that offer 3D printing services for a fee.

A 3D printer can *print* (make) a vast variety of goods, ranging from jewelry, footwear, and industrial components to highly complex items like prosthetic limbs, circuit boards, and most parts that go into GE's advanced turboprop jet engine. The GE advanced turboprop engine has 855 individually milled parts, which, with 3D printing, now requires only 12 individually milled parts, the rest being 3D printed.[17] During the COVID-19 pandemic in the spring of 2020, Voodoo Manufacturing, a 3D printing startup, made thousands of nasal swabs and Origin (origin.io), a maker of 3D printers, pivoted to begin making nasal swabs. SmileDirectClub, a direct-to-consumer maker of 3D-printed teeth straightening kits, began making face shields for hospital workers. All such applications show the flexibility that 3D printers enjoy.

The materials used for 3D printing range from plastics and metal to glass, concrete, and even organic materials like leather, cells, and chocolate.

There is little wastage in 3D printing because it is an additive process. Traditional manufacturing results in much wastage when a specific part or component is carved out of a piece of metal or made through plastic injection molding. Because 3D printing is on-demand manufacturing, there is generally no need to stock finished goods in an inventory—with major implications for supply chain management. In fact, the manufacturing process using a 3D printer can often be performed close to the place of consumption. An extreme example is Made in Space, Inc., which makes 3D printers for use in microgravity (micro-g) environments, such as on a spaceship. Made in Space's Zero-G printer has already been in use at the International Space Station since 2014.[18] See Figure 1.2 in Chapter 1 for the example of a house printed (constructed) with 3D printers.

The 3D printers can be used in regular manufacturing, but because they create one piece at a time by depositing feedstock layer-by-layer, they are much more time-consuming and costly than traditional manufacturing and are thus not appropriate for mass production. A new product can usually be designed and made on a 3D printer in 1 or 2 days, depending on the complexity of its design. Traditional manufacturing of a new product requires preparatory work, such as setting up plant and machinery and making tools and molds, before manufacturing could begin. The lead time for producing something with traditional manufacturing, when plant and machinery are already available, can take from a couple of weeks to a couple of months before the first items can start coming off the production line. Especially ideal for prototyping and small-scale manufacturing, 3D printing allows extreme customization (personalization) to meet the needs of individual customers.

Cloud

With the explosion of data, ever more data, we need a filing system large enough to be able to store it all. Recall that data can be words, numbers, images, songs, videos, and clicks—literally anything that can be digitized. Data can be stored on one's computer, in a data center, or in cloud, among other possible storage devices. *Data centers* are physical locations that store a company's data, typically nondescript buildings, or sets of buildings, with tall walls and no windows. A specific data center can be only a few buildings, or, like Microsoft's two data center campuses in Quincy, Washington, with more than 20 buildings and measuring 2 million square feet.[19] Data centers are like fortresses where no one (no outsider) is allowed to enter without permission. (Northern Virginia, where the author resides, is considered the data center capital of the world (see Figure 3.3).)

The *cloud* is the digital infrastructure (containing servers and storage) that stores data. Think of it as a huge filing cabinet for data storage on the internet. The cloud can be public or private. In a *public* cloud, the cloud infrastructure is owned and operated by a third party, a cloud service provider like Microsoft Azure, Amazon Web Service, Google Cloud Platform, and IBM Cloud Services. Many different client organizations, the *tenants*, typically use the same public cloud to access their data and services. Storing data in a public cloud is often a good option for companies with limited budgets and for startups, because they get immediate storage capacity without the need to make a huge upfront investment to create cloud storage of their own. A *private* cloud, by contrast, is used by a single organization—owned by it or hosted by a third-party provider for its exclusive use. Private clouds are often used by mid- to large-size organizations with business-critical needs, seeking enhanced control over their cloud environment. Storing data in a cloud is also a good disaster-recovery strategy.

Cloud computing is on-demand processing and analysis of data stored in a cloud. Public clouds offer cloud computing services like data storage, databases, networking, software, and analytics

Figure 3.3   A data center in Loudoun County, Northern Virginia.

Source: Photo by the author.

performed over the internet (*the cloud*). Such services fall into four broad categories: infrastructure as a service (IaaS), platform as a service (PaaS), serverless computing, and software as a service (SaaS). The market for public cloud services has been growing by double digits annually.[20] During the COVID-19 pandemic, as many brick-and-mortar stores were closing down, Etsy, the online sales platform, saw its traffic double, helped by cloud computing to handle the surge.

Blockchain

A blockchain is a database (ledger) that records transactions and tracks assets in a network. The *assets* can be tangible (real estate, clothing, raw materials, etc.) or intangible (intellectual property, bitcoin, brand, etc.). The database or ledger is an open, secure, and decentralized record of transactions between two or more parties. Transactions are authenticated and then entered in the ledger with a time stamp; they cannot be changed or erased. Records and transactions in the ledger are accessible to all members of the network, and once entered in a database, they are a permanent, verified record. Blockchain information is instantly accessible to members of the network.

Blockchain technology is being used in hundreds of organizations. For instance, in audits, because the blockchain is essentially a permanent record of transactions, it is an ideal means of examining an organization's time-stamped paper trail of verified transactions. The auditor doesn't have to gather records from different sources and then to try and make sense of them. In supply chain management, an organization's blockchain can track goods, containers, etc. throughout the supply chain—from supplier to manufacturer to wholesalers and retailers. Blockchain technology was invented for use in Bitcoin, the most popular cryptocurrency. Unlike physical currencies, cryptocurrencies are digital currencies that use encryption techniques to control the creation of monetary units and to verify transfer of funds. Blockchain is the underlying technology on which cryptocurrencies operate.

5G

The fifth-generation cellular communication network (5G) is currently being slowly deployed in dozens of countries by their cellular phone companies, replacing the existing 4G technology standard. The three main differences between 4G and 5G networks are speed, bandwidth, and latency (the lag time between the server and the device being used). A 5G network can be up to 100 times faster than a 4G network. For instance, downloading a two-hour movie on 4G takes about seven minutes, but it could take as little as ten seconds on 5G. However, actual speeds achieved on both 4G and 5G depend on the serving network, how busy it is, and the end device—in addition to other factors.

These 5G networks also have massive capacity and ultra-low latency, implying virtually imperceptible lag time (which, for example, might be required by a military drone needing constant, real-time communication between the drone and the operator on earth). All kinds of IoT devices, telemedicine, public safety, and gaming requiring real-time communication benefit greatly from 5G availability.

Building the 5G infrastructure is hugely expensive and requires billions of dollars in annual spending. According to Qualcomm, 5G has already been deployed in more than 60 countries around the world and major smartphone manufacturers have been upgrading their phones to 5G.[21]

Exponential Characteristics of Information Technologies

As discussed previously, information technologies are general-purpose technologies that can be used in multiple industries in multiple ways, thus creating opportunities for value creation and value capture across a spectrum of industries. The fact that information technologies are exponential derives not only from their general-purpose characteristics, Moore's law, and Metcalfe's law of network effect, but also from increasingly cheaper computing power, cheaper data storage, and cheaper hardware.

Moore's law stated differently means that computing power doubles every 18 months to 2 years at the same cost. We are paying less and less as computing power increases. For example, Apple's "M1 Max chip," which powers its high-end laptops, has an incredible 57 billion transistors. Technology has kept advancing to shrink the size of chips: Tens of thousands of transistors can fit in an area no wider than a human hair. Smaller transistors, which are also faster and cheaper, have enabled exponential progress in computing power and boosted productivity."[22] In the age of AI, computing power has been increasing much faster than Moore's law would predict, in fact, faster by orders of magnitude. Researchers at Stanford University found that, as of 2019, computing power for AI was doubling every 3.4 months. Computing power between 2012 and 2018 increased 300,000-fold, Moore's law would have predicted only an eight-fold increase in computing power.[23]

Similarly, the cost of data storage has been coming down, though with so many variables involved in pricing, it is hard to make a general statement about the cost of storage. As for the cost of IT hardware, it has been on a downward trend, though different hardware products have different pricing trends. For instance, the cost of sensors, a critical component in IoT devices, has been declining. The average cost of a sensor was $1.30 in 2004, which came down to $0.38 by 2020.[24]

Digital Disruption

The iPhone announced by Steve Jobs on January 9, 2007 at the Macworld Expo in San Francisco and launched by Apple Inc. on June 29, 2007, is one of the greatest digital disruptors of all time.

The iPhone, which now accounts for about 52% of Apple's total annual sales, made Apple what it is today—America's first 3-trillion-dollar company on January 3, 2022 (though briefly), tripled its market capitalization in less than 4 years. As of March 31, 2022, Apple was the most valuable company (based on market capitalization) as well as the most valuable brand in the world. By now, of course, there are several competing brands in the smartphone category, with Samsung's Galaxy having the largest unit sales among all brands, though iPhone continues to have the highest profitability among all smartphone brands.

The futurist Ray Kurzweil said in 2012, "a kid in Africa with a smartphone has access to more information than the President of the United States did 15 years ago."[25] The iPhone helped create billion-dollar corporations, like Uber and Airbnb. A smartphone is typically the first device we look at when we get up in the morning and the last device we see before going to sleep. With a smartphone, everyone is a photographer now! And, with WhatsApp, Snapchat, Instagram, and other social media platforms, millions of people worldwide seem to have found their voice and inherent creativity. For instance, smartphones completely transformed the business of photography and activities related to photography to a scale quite unimaginable just a decade ago. In 2022, 54,400 photos were taken every second or 1.72 trillion per year.[26] These are stored in the cloud managed by Google, Facebook, WeChat, and others, as well as on users' smartphones. Approximately 90% of the people who have ever taken a photograph did so on a smartphone, not having ever owned a conventional camera.

In emerging and developing nations, the smartphone has perhaps had a much greater impact on millions of people who previously did not even have access to a landline, a cellular phone, a computer, or the internet. They now use it as their telephone (and computer).[27] According to a 2016 World Bank study, more people in low- and middle-income countries had access to mobile phones than to water and electricity.[28]

iPhone's voice-activated digital assistant Siri is *trained* to perform such tasks as answer queries, control devices, check email, send text messages, schedule wakeup calls, and even read bedtime stories. It can understand and speak in 20 languages and is available in 30 countries. In 2016–2017, when I was a visiting professor at Rutgers Business School, Newark and New Brunswick, I was surprised to find that some undergraduate students came to class without paper, pen, or a laptop, doing much of their work on smartphones. Recently, while driving on Virginia State Route 28, the GPS on my iPhone warned me, "speed check ahead," and sure enough there was a police officer on a motorbike stopped by the side of the highway checking vehicle speeds on radar.

With over $900,000 worth of applications embedded into it, the iPhone has disrupted several industries, including photography, healthcare, telecommunication services and devices, gaming, PC and laptop, GPS, news media, and many others. As shown in Table 3.2, several technologies that were once considered luxuries come standard in the iPhone. It even disrupted Apple's own iPod, a portable music player, which itself—along with iTunes—had previously disrupted the digital music industry. At the time of iPhone's introduction in 2007, iPod was a $5 billion business for Apple. Steve Jobs cannibalized it by introducing iPhone despite internal objections to the idea.

Apple launched its App Store in July 2008, which allowed millions of independent software developers to build and sell software (apps) to smartphone owners. According to *Wired*, a monthly magazine that focuses on emerging technologies and their impact on culture, economy, and politics, "[T]he App Store will almost certainly stand as Apple's most important contribution to both the tech industry and society in general, even more than the phone itself."[29] With the launch of Android's Google Play in October 2008, mobile phone users now have access to some 5.7 million apps in the two app stores as of the second quarter of 2022—with 3.5 million apps in Google Play and 2.2 million in App Store.[30]

Table 3.2   Over $900,000 Worth of Applications in a Smartphone (as of 2011)

	Application	$ (2011)	Original Device Name	Year[a]	MSRP	2011s $
1	Video conferencing	Free	Compression Labs VC	1982	$250,000	$586,904
2	GPS	Free	TI Navistar	1982	$119,000	$279,366
3	Digital voice recorder	Free	Sony PCM	1978	$2,500	$8,687
4	Digital watch	Free	Seiko 35SQ Astron	1969	$1,250	&7,716
5	5 Mpixel camera	Free	Canon RC-701	1986	$3,000	$6,201
6	Medical library	Free	e.g. CONSULTANT	1987	≤$2,000	$3,988
7	Video player	Free	Toshiba V-8000	1981	$1,245	$3,103
8	Video camera	Free	RCA CC010	1981	$1,050	$2,617
9	Music player	Free	Sony CDP-101 CD player	1982	$900	$2,113
10	Encyclopedia	Free	Compton's CD encyclopedia	1989	$750	$1,370
11	Videogame console	Free	Atari 2600	1977	$199	$744
	Total	**Free**				**$902,065**

[a] *Year of launch*
Source: Peter H. Diamandis & Steven Kotler, *Abundance: The Future is Better Than You Think* (New York: Free Press, 2012), p. 316

In the business world, the smartphone has not been the only source of industry disruption. In fact, disruption is almost as old as business itself, associated with technological innovation, business model innovation, and emergence of new markets.

Technological innovation. We saw earlier how the 3D printer technology is set to disrupt several industries. In fact, technological innovation is often the cause of disruption, digital or otherwise.[31] In addition to products, several services such as retailing, financial services, healthcare, movie rental, and education have suffered (or are suffering) from digital disruption. This process, which Joseph Schumpeter called *creative destruction*, is "the essential fact about capitalism." Schumpeter, writing in 1934, powerfully suggested that capitalism or the free-market system is an evolutionary process of innovation, entrepreneurial activity, and creative destruction. Industries contain the seeds of their own destruction through incursions by both new and established firms using innovative products and strategies to destroy incumbents' advantage.[32] In today's hypercompetitive digital world, Schumpeter's seminal insights are truer than ever before. This is because the digital representation of any analog object is infinitely scalable, replicable, and transmittable at zero—or near zero—marginal cost, thus permitting a digital upstart to destroy the competitive advantage of incumbents. For instance, digital representation completely transformed the business of photography and activities related to photography, to a scale quite unimaginable just a decade or so ago.

Kodak (Eastman Kodak Company) is a classic case of industry disruption caused by the iPhone (and other smartphone brands). A 130-year-old US company, Kodak was once a household name for its film business and, as of 1990, had 145,000 employees and $19 billion in annual

Table 3.3 Eastman Kodak Company—Some Metrics

Year	Revenue ($Billion)	Net Income ($Million)	# Employees
2021	1.150	24	4,200
2020	1.029	−541	4,500
2019	1.242	96	4,922
2015	1.803	−80	6,400
2010	5.993	−687	18,800
2007	10.301	676	26,900
2005	11.396	−1,261	51,100

Source: https://www.macrotrends.net/stocks/charts/KODK/eastman-kodak/revenue.

revenues. Kodak's film business got disrupted as new technologies and new competitors emerged. With the advent of digital photography, the company, hesitant to cannibalize its cash-cow film business, moved into digital photography only in the late 1990s. (Ironically, it was Steven Sasson, a Kodak engineer, who invented the first digital camera in 1975.) Kodak's performance has since been on a downward spiral (Table 3.3). It filed for bankruptcy in January 2012, emerged from it in September 2013, but serving only niche markets and selling nothing directly to consumers. By December 2021, it had only 4,200 employees and $1.15 billion in revenues. Although Kodak's performance had been declining since the 1990s as analog photography was being disrupted by digital photography, true disruption happened with the emergence of the iPhone in 2007, social network firms like Facebook (especially WhatsApp), Google, and Tencent, and cloud storage.

Business model innovation. Industries are getting increasingly disrupted through *business model innovation* by both startups and established firms. New and innovative business models have disrupted incumbents and industries through improved offerings, lower prices, and better service. Let us look at just two business models that have had disruptive impact on incumbents—online business platforms and subscription business model. (See Chapter 6 for detailed discussion of these and other digital business models.)

Business platforms. The Uber platform disrupted the taxi industry, while the Amazon platform decimated thousands of small and big retailers. Major US retail chains like J.C. Penney, Neiman Marcus, and Brooks Brothers declared bankruptcy in spring and summer of 2020—impacted by the Amazon effect and aggravated by factors like COVID-19. In Britain, the online fast fashion retailer, Boohoo, acquired the 243-year-old high street fashion retailer, Debenhams, in late 2020 for £55 million ($75.4 million)—along with all its IP assets (e.g., brand names), customer data, selected contracts, and related business information, but not the physical stores or any employees. Debenhams had been in trouble since 2019, with COVID-19 adding to its misfortunes in 2020. Boohoo, a leading multibrand ecommerce platform, had been on an acquisition spree since 2017—acquiring fashion brands like PrettyLittleThing, Nasty Gal, and Karen Millen.

Price comparison platforms (price comparison websites or PCWs) that help online shoppers find the best deals for products and services they want to buy have also contributed to the disruption of brick-and-mortar and other sellers. Google Shopping, BizRate, and many other price comparison platforms offer the same facility to shoppers. At BizRate.com, for instance, a prospective customer can search for a variety of product deals, and even set price alerts. For automobile insurance in the US, there are several PCWs that offer price quotes from numerous insurance companies within a few minutes; these include Insurify.com, TheZebra.com, and Compare.com.

Subscription model. The subscription model is intended to lock in customers for the medium or long term. Amazon offers a subscription service for everyday consumables, like detergents and cosmetics, delivering them to subscription customers at regular intervals. In the market for women's clothing and accessories, a number of new subscription businesses, such as *Rent the Runway*, have started in the last few years. In November 2019, Le Tote, a women's clothing rental subscription startup, acquired Lord & Taylor, one of the most iconic department store chains in the US, for $71 million. In August 2020, Le Tote (along with Lord & Taylor) filed for Chapter 11 bankruptcy and was later acquired by The Saadia Group in October 2020 for $12 million. Companies in both physical and digital worlds have been selling their products and services for a long time on a monthly or annual subscription. Companies offering their products or services on subscription are assured of recurring, predictable revenue for the duration of the subscription, while customers benefit from not having to tie up capital for what they need and be assured of automatic supplies replenishment, and product updates for digital products, generally without any additional cost. The subscription model also helps create deeper customer engagement, compared to direct selling, and provides the company with data on customer behavior and purchase patterns that it can use to improve its offerings or monetize in some other manner.

Emergence of a new market. New markets do not actually *emerge*, they are created through the actions of one or more innovative firms offering a new product or service for which there is no existing or latent demand. Several products and services launched in the last few decades satisfy this condition, including the Apple iPhone, Google search, and micropublishing by Twitter. The creation of a new market, by definition, disrupts or at least seriously hinders the prospects of an existing market. It takes away at least some customers from incumbents to completely decimating their market. The iPhone did that to its smartphone competitors, such as BlackBerry and Nokia N95.

Value Creation and Capture with Technology

In 2003, Nicholas Carr, a former Executive Editor of the *Harvard Business Review* (HBR), wrote an article in HBR titled "IT Doesn't Matter." He claimed that the evolution of IT had followed a pattern similar to that of earlier technologies, like electricity and railways, which are now essentially commodities. In his view, "the opportunities for gaining IT-based advantages are already dwindling. Best practices are now quickly built into software or otherwise replicated. And as for IT-spurred industry transformations, most of the ones that are going to happen have likely already happened or are in the process of happening."[33] Further, Carr claimed that IT is no longer a source of competitive advantage for firms. Any advantages that IT might bestow upon a firm are available to every firm that makes the same investment. The article generated a great deal of discussion—some for, but mostly against, Carr's prognostication. Joe Weinman, a former senior executive at AT&T, HP, and Bell Laboratories, put it plainly, "pork bellies may be a commodity but a Michelin three-star restaurant extracts more value out of them than the average corner diner does."[34]

The world's most profitable companies are, by and large, those that directly derive their competitive advantage through IT or through innovative applications of IT. Here's the list of the ten most profitable companies in the world as of August 2022. The list includes not only hi-tech companies, but also four Chinese banks that make extensive use of information technologies.

The ten most profitable companies in the world (August 2022) are as follows:

1. Apple
2. Microsoft
3. Industrial and Commercial Bank of China
4. China Construction Bank
5. Alphabet
6. Agricultural Bank of China
7. JP Morgan Chase
8. Alibaba Group Holdings
9. Bank of China
10. Intel

Source: Matthew Johnston, "10 most profitable companies in the world." Investopedia, August 27, 2022. https://www.investopedia.com/the-world-s-10-most-profitable-companies-4694526.

As discussed in Chapter 1, a company creates value through one or more of at least four approaches: cost reduction, creating a new market, innovation, and increasing customers' willingness to pay. This section explores how digital technologies (IT) help companies create and capture new value.

Cost reduction. Companies attempt to reduce costs through greater efficiency in operations—to improve profitability and free up resources to reinvest in the company's growth. For digital products, as observed earlier, the marginal cost of producing (and delivering) another copy of a product is zero or almost zero. One cannot reduce costs more than that! Research by Erik Brynjolfsson and Lori Hitt confirmed that companies that were the heaviest users of IT were dramatically more productive than their competitors.[35]

Besides, in the digital world, companies don't just try and improve existing processes, they use new technologies like AI, machine learning (ML) and robotics to improve productivity, reduce costs, and strengthen their market position. The Intel Corporation, for instance, uses AI to optimize its time-consuming product-validation process by automating and augmenting human validation capabilities. In addition to improving the process itself, AI helps Intel reduce cost and accelerate time to market. ChristUS Health, an international Catholic, faith-based, not-for-profit health system with about 350 services and facilities, has automated up to 80% of its preregistration tasks, such as inputting patients' health history—resulting in productivity enhancement of 60%, while reducing human errors. It also uses chatbots and digital assistants for customer service, enabling customers to reach these AI helpers 24/7. Servion, a global customer experience solutions provider, has predicted that AI will power 95% of customer interactions by 2025.[36]

According to Deloitte's second global cost survey in 2019, while the traditional methods of reducing costs are still important, more and more companies are investing in digital technologies to reduce cost, improve performance, and strengthen competitive advantage.[37] The survey of over 1,200 executives and leaders in global corporations found that the use of AI, ML, and automation is expected to more than double from the current level over the next 24 months in view of the expected benefits.

Creating new markets. This can range from expanding the existing market to capturing new markets within their existing industry, in adjacent industries, in completely new industries, and even creating a new category. However, most companies are happily trying to expand their existing market or attempting to enter adjacent markets. Relatively few explore completely new markets or attempt creating a new business category.

Irrespective of what approach a company decides to follow, IT always has a major role to play in the expansion. Uber and Airbnb both created *new business categories*, as did Dropbox for file storage and sharing, Apple with iPhone, WhatsApp Inc. with WhatsApp, Spotify with legal music streaming, and many others.

Although smartphones existed before iPhone and instant messengers before WhatsApp, both of these companies essentially created new business categories by offering significantly enhanced features and services. How did people communicate on the internet before WhatsApp? Well, there were services like mIRC, Microsoft's Internet Relay Chat introduced in 1995, AOL Instant Messenger introduced in 1997, and Yahoo! Messenger introduced in 1998. WhatsApp, initially launched in February 2009 by WhatsApp Inc., was acquired by Facebook 5 years later for $19 billion. WhatsApp users can send text and voice messages, make audio and video calls, and share documents, images, etc., on their smartphones—internationally. WhatsApp is now the most popular mobile messenger app in the world, with over 2 billion active users monthly.

Expanding into an adjacent line of business, and using its core strength, namely some 3.9 million Uber drivers worldwide, Uber launched UberEATS, a food delivery service in the US in 2016. Currently, UberEATS is available in over 6,000 cities in 45 countries. From selling books online, Amazon expanded into adjacent lines of business including eBooks, digital content, magazine distribution, publishing, and eBook readers. Once Amazon entered retailing, sky was the limit for the company to expand into dozens of adjacent markets.

None of these and other expansions would have been possible without extensive use of critical information technologies.

Innovation. Information technologies are behind most of the innovations we see today in practically all fields of human endeavor, and their progress has been exponential as suggested by Moore's law and Metcalfe's law of network effects. Unlike physical goods, digital goods and smart machines exhibit increasing returns to scale (because of their exponential characteristics) and can even lead to a winner-take-all or a winner-take-most market.

Increasing customers' willingness to pay. Getting customers to pay for the products they purchase is how companies capture value created by their products. Customers' willingness to pay for a product or service depends on several interrelated factors, such as how precisely the product meets customers' needs, price, brand image, perceptions of quality and durability, availability of close substitutes, the product's value proposition, after-sale service (if relevant), the context of where the product is to be purchased, the type of product, and other factors. Customers are generally willing to pay more for products that have the features they value and that meet *their* specific needs. Information technologies have permitted companies to customize their products relatively easily to meet the needs of specific customers and customer groups precisely; sometimes it is just a matter of changing some lines of code to create different versions of a product. Using data analytics, companies can better understand customer needs, which will help create and capture more value for the products they sell.

Different customers (or customer groups) have different levels of willingness to pay for the products they purchase—implying that they are in different market segments that require differential pricing. Microsoft 365, for instance, is a Microsoft Office software product line—available for outright purchase or on annual subscription—separately for home, business, and enterprise—each with a range of pricing plans. For business, Microsoft offers four subscription plans ranging from $5 per month per user for Microsoft 365 Basic to $20 per month per user for 365 Business Premium. Once the 365 software has been developed, it costs Microsoft practically nothing to sell another copy of 365. Such pricing flexibility is easier to implement for digital products and smart machines than for purely physical products.

Notes

1 The phrase "crossing the chasm" was popularized by Geoffrey Moore's 1991 bestselling book of the same title, published by Harper Business. The book is about the marketing of a fundamentally new technology product, with strategies a company could use to present the product to the marketplace. Moore's Technology Adoption Life Cycle describes five stages in the life of such a product: innovators, early adopters, early majority, late majority, and laggards. As a product begins to gain traction in the marketplace, it comes across a big gap (the *chasm*) between *early adopters* and *early majority*. To be able to succeed in its marketing efforts, the firm must close the gap (cross the chasm) by moving from early adopters to early majority in its life cycle. The book offers strategies for crossing the chasm. Charles Schwab invoked the phrase to signal the company's move to a digital business model, the chasm being the gap between physical businesses and digital businesses.

2 Brian J. Slywotzky and David J. Morrison, with Karl Weber, *How Digital is Your Business* (New York: Crown Business, 2000). See also: Paul J. Lim, "Schwab, Merrill plans blur industry's lines," *Los Angeles Times*, November 28, 1999.

3 For company history, visit https://www.aboutschwab.com/history.

4 Source, company websites, including schwab.com.

5 Carl Shapiro and Hal R. Varian, *Information Rules: A Strategic Guide to the Network Economy* (Boston, MA: Harvard Business School Press, 1999).

6 Slate, "The lines of code that changed everything," October 14, 2019. https://slate.com/technology/2019/10/consequential-computer-code-software-history.html.

7 For more information on Replika, visit https://www.youtube.com/watch?reload=9&v=yQGqMVuAk04.

8 Statista, "IoT and non-IoT internet connections worldwide, 2021–2025," September 6, 2022. https://www.statista.com/statistics/1101442/iot-number-of-connected-devices-worldwide/.

9 McKinsey Analytics, "Global AI survey: AI proves its worth, but few scale impact," McKinsey & Company, November 2019, p. 2 (end notes).

10 Erik Brynjolfsson and Andrew McAfee, *The Second Machine Age: Work, Progress, and Prosperity in a Time of Brilliant Technologies* (New York: W.W. Norton & Co., 2014) p. 91.

11 Marco Iansiti and Karim R. Lakhani, *Competing in the Age of AI: Strategy and Leadership When Algorithms and Networks Run the World* (Boston, MA: Harvard Business Review Press, 2020). See also https://www.nextrembrandt.com/.

12 McKinsey 2021 Global Survey, "The State of AI," December 8, 2021. https://www.mckinsey.com/capabilities/quantumblack/our-insights/global-survey-the-state-of-ai-in-2021.

13 McKinsey Global AI Survey, 2019, November 22, 2019. https://www.mckinsey.com/featured-insights/artificial-intelligence/global-ai-survey-ai-proves-its-worth-but-few-scale-impact.

14 H. James Wilson and Paul R. Daugherty, "Collaborative intelligence: Humans and AI are joining forces," *Harvard Business Review*, July–August 2018.

15 Emily Matcher, "Nine tasks that robots can do that may surprise you," September 5, 2017. https://www.smithsonianmag.com/innovation/nine-tasks-robots-can-do-that-may-surprise-you-180964729/?page=5.

16 Brynjolfsson & McAfee Op. cit., pp. 27–28.

17 Peter H. Diamandis and Steven Kotler, *The Future Is Faster Than You Think: How Converging Technologies Are Transforming Business, Industries, and Our Lives* (New York: Simon & Schuster, 2020).

18 Wikipedia, "Made in Space, Inc." https://en.wikipedia.org/wiki/Made_In_Space,_Inc.

19 For an interesting exploration of Microsoft's data center campuses, see Brad Smith and Carol Ann Browne, *Tools and Weapons: The Promise and the Peril of the Digital Age* (New York: Penguin Press, 2019).

20 Azure, "Invest with purpose." https://azure.microsoft.com/en-us/.

21 Qualcomm, "Everything you need to know about 5G." https://www.qualcomm.com/5g/what-is-5g#:~:text=5G%20can%20be%20significantly%20faster,traffic%20capacity%20and%20network%20efficiency.

22 Jacky Wong, "Is it the end of the road for computing power," *Wall Street Journal*, March 4, 2022. https://www.wsj.com/articles/is-it-the-end-of-the-road-for-computing-power-11646389802.

23 Cliff Saran, "Stanford University finds that AI is outpacing Moore's Law," December 12, 2019. https://www.computerweekly.com/news/252475371/Stanford-University-finds-that-AI-is-outpacing-Moores-Law.

24 Mario Honrubia, "Industrial IoT is booming thanks to a drop in sensor prices," 2021. https://www.ennomotive.com/industrial-iot-sensor-prices/#:~:text=The%20cost%20of%20sensors%20is,decisions%20at%20a%20lower%20cost.

25 Andrew McAfee and Erik Brynjolfsson, *Machine Platform Crowd: Harnessing the Digital Future* (New York: W.W. Norton & Company, 2017) p. 308.

26 Matic Broz, "Number of photos (2022): Statistics, facts, and predictions," August 27, 2022. https://photutorial.com/photos-statistics/#:~:text=Photo%20Statistics%20(Top%20Picks),or%204.7%20billion%20per%20day.

27 An earlier version of this iPhone case study appeared in my blog on June 29, 2022, iPhone's 15th anniversary. https://www.vinodjain.com/post/iphone-at-15.

28 Malaka Gharib, "Surprising charts about smoking, unemployment and mobile phones, January 14, 2017. https://www.npr.org/sections/goatsandsoda/2017/01/14/509137225/surprising-charts-about-smoking-unemployment-and-mobile-phones.

29 David Pierce and Lauren Goode, "The WIRED guide to the iPhone," December 7, 2018. https://www.wired.com/story/guide-iphone/.

30 Statista, "Number of apps available in leading app stores as of 2nd quarter 2022." https://www.statista.com/statistics/276623/number-of-apps-available-in-leading-app-stores/.

31 Disruption is not the domain of only digital technologies. Disruption can be caused by any new "technology" of the time, such as in the wet shave market by Harry's, the online seller of shaving products, which, in 2019, disrupted the duopoly of P&G's Gillette and Edgewell's Schick and Wilkinson Sword brands.

32 Joseph A. Schumpeter, *The Theory of Economic Development* (Cambridge, MA: Harvard University Press, 1934).

33 Nicholas Carr, "IT doesn't matter," *Harvard Business Review*, May, 2003.

34 Joe Weinman, *Cloudonomics: The Business Value of Cloud Computing* (New York: Wiley, 2012).

35 Erik Brynjolfsson and Lorin Hitt, "Paradox lost: Firm level evidence on the returns to information systems," *Management Science*, 42, no. 4 (1996).

36 Finance Digest, "AI will power 95 percent of customer interactions by 2025." https://www.financedigest.com/ai-will-power-95-of-customer-interactions-by-2025.html.

37 Deloitte Cost Survey, Press Release April 23, 2019: https://www2.deloitte.com/us/en/pages/about-deloitte/articles/press-releases/deloitte-launches-cost-survey-report.html.

STRATEGY

Chapter 4

Entering Foreign Markets

I believe it is a mistake to open a factory overseas without first having a sales and market-ing system established and knowing the market very well. My view is that you must first learn about the market, learn how to sell to it, and build up your corporate confidence before you commit yourself. And when you have confidence, you should commit yourself wholeheartedly.

Akio Morita, Co-founder, Sony Corporation (1921–1999)

On December 31, 2010, Bobbie Johnson, then the European editor for GigaOm—a media com-pany with a focus on technology—wrote a piece about Netflix at gigaom.com with the title: "Will Netflix go global in 2011? Maybe, but it won't be easy."[1] The US-based Netflix had just entered Canada in September 2010 and had hinted about global expansion in the years to come. Johnson was questioning whether Netflix would be able to enter other foreign markets.

He outlined three reasons why Netflix's global expansion will not be easy. First, Netflix is going to face entrenched local competition in its target markets. For example, in Britain, it would face LoveFilm,[2] a successful DVD rental firm that had been preparing defensively against Netflix's pos-sible entry into the country by launching its own streaming services and making deals with major movie studios and the retailer, Tesco. (LoveFilm was acquired by Amazon in 2012.) Second, it will face a lot of red tape in each country it tries to enter. Finally, Netflix's biggest issue going abroad will be cultural divide, considering that several US firms, such as Craigslist and Yelp, had faced difficul-ties in foreign markets. Johnson concluded, "None of this is to say that Netflix can't succeed, just that it will certainly not be an easy ride … global expansion requires a sales operation, a backbone and an infrastructure." Some of the readers at gigaom.com suggested other issues that Netflix might face such as the need to localize its content and services for each foreign market.

Fast forward to the second quarter of 2022. Netflix is the world's leading streaming entertainment service with 220.67 million paid subscribers in over 190 countries, of which 65% are in the US and Canada. They can watch TV series, documentaries, and feature films across a wide variety of genres and languages, all without commercials.[3] (Netflix is still not available, however, in Mainland China and countries where the US government restricts US companies from doing business, such as Syria, Crimea, and North Korea.) Netflix offers DVD video rental as well as online streaming services in the US, but only the online streaming service in foreign markets. It streams its own original con-tent, such as its currently successful TV series, *Squid Game*.

DOI: 10.4324/9781003037446-6

Figure 4.1 Netflix Headquarters Building in Los Gatos, California.

Source: https://upload.wikimedia.org/wikipedia/commons/1/18/100_Winchester_Circle.jpg.

It also licenses content from other media companies, such as Disney, Sony, Turner Broadcasting, Warner Brothers Television Group, and DreamWorks Animation (owned by Comcast since 2016). Securing content from these and other content owners is Netflix's biggest expense, projected at $19 billion for 2022, an increase of 13% over 2021.[4] In 2022, over half of the Netflix shows are of American origin. (In EU, streaming companies are required to have at least 30% of their content from within the EU bloc.) In 2021, Netflix had $24.9 billion in revenues, 23.6% more than in the previous year, and operating profit of $5.1 billion, 85% more than in 2020 (Figure 4.1).

With COVID-19 vaccine roll out and lifting of pandemic restrictions in most parts of the world as well as increasing competition from other streaming services, Netflix lost 200,000 global subscribers in the first quarter 2022 and 1 million in the second quarter. By June 14, 2022, Netflix shares had fallen to $167.54, a loss of 72% compared to a high of $597.37 on January 3, 2022.

In its internationalization journey, Netflix faced and surmounted practically all the challenges highlighted in the gigaom.com article. It succeeded because it followed a phased program of foreign-market entries, learned as it proceeded from country to country—applying the learnings from earlier entries to later entries—and built technological and operational capabilities and content needed for success in diverse markets. It also partnered with local companies in different markets, such as cellphone and cable operators, and forged global licensing deals with major studios so that their content is available to not only local viewers, but also to viewers everywhere on the Netflix platform.

Some of the selection criteria Netflix used for entering foreign markets at the start of its internationalization journey included a prospective market's degree of attractiveness based on shared similarities (with the US), presence of affluent customers, and broadband availability.

In addition to localizing its marketing materials for each major market, Netflix personalizes its offerings for individual subscribers based on user-specific choices, including language, viewing behavior, and taste preferences. To localize its content, Netflix dubs its shows in 34 languages, subtitling them in a few more.

Use of technology, such as machine learning, is paramount in all these processes. To illustrate the kinds of technology skills the company seeks, here is a list of three of the dozens of job openings on the day I visited the Netflix website (October 9, 2022): Sr Data Scientist—Data Science and Engineering, Experimentation; Software Engineer—Streaming Algorithms; and Research Scientist.

After entering its first foreign market, Canada, in September 2010, Netflix entered other markets in quick succession—Latin America in September 2011, the UK and Ireland in January 2012, Nordic countries in October 2012, the Netherlands in September 2013, and so on.

How could an editor at a respected research firm be so wrong about a company's globalization prospects? Well, it was not the first time and will not be the last. Predicting the future is a very risky business.

Why did Netflix adopt such an aggressive approach to internationalization? As it was for Airbnb, global expansion had become a strategic imperative for Netflix by 2015—for reasons such as the need to continue to grow, to become more efficient, and to source content for its streaming services from throughout the world.[5] By December 2014, its growth in the US domestic market—where it derived three-fourths of its total worldwide revenues—had begun to slow down. At the same time, its international growth was rising. For instance, Netflix signed up more subscribers internationally in the third quarter of 2013 than it did in the US for the first time since its launch in the UK and Ireland in January 2012. Content providers typically licensed Netflix to stream their content on a country-by-country basis, which is very expensive and time-consuming. So, to gain efficiencies as its global network expanded, it needed to be able to license content on a global basis. It was essential for Netflix to have new and varied content, especially for local markets worldwide, in order to hold on to its existing subscriber base and continue adding new subscribers in its existing and new markets—enabling it to benefit from network effects.[6]

Foreign Market Selection

Foreign market selection is a critical step in any firm's internationalization, whether it is starting out on its internationalization journey or planning to enter a new market after having been abroad for some time. Oftentimes, firms' first foreign forays are into markets for reasons of proximity and/or cultural affinity. Netflix's first entries, for example, were into Canada and Latin America. When Walmart decided to go global in the early 1990s, it entered the largest markets in Latin America—Mexico (1991), Brazil (1994), and Argentina (1995). The same also was true for French retailer Carrefour, whose first international entry in 1973 was into Spain. Similarly, when the Mexican cement giant, CEMEX, decided to go abroad, it chose Spain for reasons of cultural and language affinity.

Other major factors in country selection for Netflix were market size as judged by the extent of internet adoption and the availability of fast broadband speeds. Accordingly, Western European countries including Britain, Germany, France, and the Nordic countries were among the first foreign markets outside North America that Netflix entered. All had large and growing internet populations and fast broadband speeds. See also mini case study on Costco e-commerce (Box 4.1).

The PRISM Framework

The PRISM framework of foreign market selection—proposed by the author in 2016—uses the PRISM mnemonic device to convey an understanding of the differences between nations and how they might impact decisions relating to foreign market selection and entry.[8] It offers

BOX 4.1   COSTCO E-COMMERCE

Costco Wholesale Corporation is a US-based membership warehouse club offering a huge variety of goods and services in the US and 11 foreign countries, including Canada, Mexico, the UK, Japan, Taiwan, South Korea, France, Spain, Iceland, Australia, and Mainland China (since 2019). As of January 2023, Costco had 848 warehouse stores worldwide, including 264 outside the US and Puerto Rico, 120.9 million paid members, and $222.7 billion in FY 2022 revenues.[7]

Although Costco had been selling online in the US and Canada, it did not begin to explore the possibility of selling online in other foreign markets until early 2012. Costco management was concerned about the challenges the company might face in foreign markets, the additional cost of selling online, whether online operations might cannibalize warehouse sales, whether it might distract local managers from growing their warehouse business, regulatory issues, and so on. The Costco Internet Business Solutions Group (IBSG) was given the responsibility of exploring the online business opportunity, analyzing key countries' online markets, and prioritizing country rollout.

As part of its research, the IBSG interviewed several global e-commerce pioneers, major retailers, consulting firms, and suppliers to understand the best practices in e-commerce rollout and management. These expert interviews revealed that Costco should prioritize its country rollout based on the size of its existing business, and the overall size and maturity of the e-commerce market, in prospective countries.

Based on IBSG's findings, Costco decided to launch its e-commerce operations in the UK in October 2012. It did so for four main reasons: (1) Costco already had high sales and membership in the country, with presence since 1993; (2) as of 2012, the UK was the second largest e-commerce market in the world and growing very fast; (3) the UK had a sophisticated e-commerce infrastructure, which, along with its supplier network, could be leveraged relatively easily; and (4) having e-commerce operations located in the UK could help Costco reach out to online customers on the continent as had been the experience of some other UK-based retailers.

Costco's entry into online retailing has been slow relative to the expansion of its physical warehouses worldwide. After its entry into Britain's online market, it began selling online in Mexico, adding other foreign markets to its e-commerce portfolio over the years. As of the end of 2019, Costco operated e-commerce sites in the US, Canada, the UK, Mexico, South Korea, Taiwan, Australia, and Japan. During FY 2019 (ending in September), Costco's online sales represented about 6% of its total net sales and were growing faster and were more profitable than warehouse sales.

This case study is based on the information taken from the company website and FY 2022 corporate profile, https://investor.costco.com/corporate-profile-2/.

a comprehensive and systematic approach to decisions relating to choosing foreign markets for entry. However, no single framework, no matter how comprehensive, can incorporate every possible factor relevant for foreign market selection for every firm. The PRISM framework incorporates the most important factors relevant in a large variety of situations.

The PRISM framework of foreign market selection (Figure 4.2 and Table 4.1) has the following five elements: **P**olitical economy, **R**esources, **I**nstitutions and infrastructure, **S**ociety and culture, and **M**arket potential. The PRISM framework does not include *risk* as a specific factor because risk can arise from any of the five factors (P, R, I, S, and M). While evaluating the PRISM dimensions, one should always assess the risks posed by each.

THE PRISM FRAMEWORK OF FOREIGN MARKET SELECTION

Figure 4.2   The PRISM framework.

Table 4.1   The PRISM Framework

Factor	Description
P	Political economy: Political and economic systems, along with the formal institutions embedded within them
R	Resources: Basic and advanced resources
I	Institutions: Formal and informal institutions Infrastructure: Physical, telecommunication, energy, and broadband infrastructure
S	Society and culture
M	Market potential: Market size and growth rate, industry structure, competition, capacity utilization, exports/imports, etc.

P: Political Economy

The term political economy refers to interdisciplinary studies incorporating political science, economics, and law to explain how political and economic systems and legal institutions in a nation influence each other. All of these are key factors in evaluating the suitability of a foreign market for entry. Under **P** here, we are concerned with political and economic systems in a country. The legal institutions are contained in the **I** (Institutions) of the PRISM framework.

Political Systems

A *political system* describes the form of government in a nation, such as the formal and informal structures representing a nation's sovereignty (power) over its territory and people.[9] A nation's political system shapes its economic and legal systems, and all three systems present opportunities and risks for businesses operating in the nation. We can classify the political system of a nation by the degree to which it is democratic or totalitarian.

Democratic. A democratic form of government implies a system in which the nation is governed by the people through elected representatives. A *social democracy* is a system whereby a nation attempts to achieve socialist goals through democratic means (as opposed to through authoritarian means as in communism). In a *representative democracy*, the government is run by the people through their elected representatives. In a representative democracy, most businesses are privately owned and managed. In a democracy, citizens generally enjoy a number of constitutionally guaranteed rights, such as the right to free speech, free media, and limited terms of elected representatives.

Totalitarian. The freedoms enjoyed by citizens in democratic societies are typically denied to citizens in totalitarian regimes. Under totalitarianism, one person, a group of people, or a political party exercises total control over all aspects of human life, and opposition political parties are not allowed. In a *communist* form of government, for example, the people in power believe that socialist goals can only be achieved through violent revolution (that is how they came into power) and an authoritarian regime. During the late 1970s, more than half of the world's population lived under communist rule. Today only a few countries, such as China, North Korea, Vietnam, and Cuba practice communism. There are also other forms of totalitarian regimes, such as theocratic regimes as in Saudi Arabia and Iran.

Economic Systems

An *economic system* is a structure for the production and consumption of goods and services as well as the allocation of resources in a nation. The economic systems prevalent in the world today range from *(free) market economies* to *command economies*, with an intervening position taken by *mixed economies*. Economic systems can be visualized as a continuum, shown in this diagram:

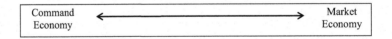

In a *market economy*, all economic decisions (such as what to produce, how to produce, how much to produce, for whom to produce, and what prices to charge) are made by private entrepreneurs and corporations—based on an interplay of market forces. All business is privately owned.

In a *command economy*, the government makes all economic decisions, generally guided by central planning. This is why a command economy is also referred to as a centrally planned economy. All businesses are owned by the state and run as state-owned enterprises (SOEs)—in the interest of the people—and all property is owned by the state.

In a *mixed economy*, some sectors of the economy are state-owned and some are privately owned. Today, there is no *pure* market economy or *pure* command economy. All economies are mixed economies, though the balance between private and public sectors varies widely. In some countries, such as the US, much of the economic activity is controlled by private interests. This fact places the US toward the far right of the continuum shown in the diagram, as effectively a free-market economy. Although the government in China has been giving a good deal of economic freedom (but not political freedom) to its citizens, it still largely controls the economy. As a result, China belongs near the left side of the continuum, though no longer at the extreme left.

R: Resources

Why do so many multinational firms set up manufacturing plants in China or in-house IT service centers in India? They do so partly because of the availability of specialized human resources (not simply any human resources) and talent there. The *mantra* for smart companies today is "we go where the talent is," not just "we go where the market is." California's Silicon Valley has been a magnet for IT firms from throughout the world for over two decades. It offers many of the resources that IT firms need, such as talent (the IT workforce in the Silicon Valley region), capital (most of the prominent venture capital firms have operations there), technology, and premier research and higher education institutions (Stanford University and University of California at Berkeley, to name just two) that are a continuing source of technology and talent.

The resources available in a nation can be classified in many ways; for our purpose, the classification suggested by Michael Porter[10] is preferred: basic and advanced resources.

The *basic resources* in a nation include its demographic and natural resources, whereas its *advanced resources* are resources created through the efforts of governments, industries, firms, and individuals. While exploring the potential of different markets, looking at demographics (e.g., population and socio-economic indicators) and natural resources is not quite enough; skilled labor, technology, research and higher education institutions, and other *man-made* resources must be considered as well. The kinds of resources to be assessed in PRISM analysis depend on the industry in which the firm operates. For instance, a firm in the automotive industry would want to know whether the country or region being targeted has the kinds of skilled shop-floor manpower and engineering talent it would need, high-quality engineering schools, certification agencies, and other kinds of human resources needed for an automotive-industry firm. The firm would, of course, also need business development, sales, marketing, finance, and many other professionals, which are often more readily available than engineers.

In performing PRISM analysis, it is useful to list the specific resources (e.g., talent, technology, capital, and research and higher education institutions) available in a prospective host market, especially those sought by the entrant.

I: Institutions and Infrastructure

Institutions, the first **I** of the PRISM framework, provide the context for individual and corporate behavior in societies and nations and must be considered while making foreign-market-selection decisions. Institutions are the *rules of the game* often devised by people in positions of power or authority, such as a nation's parliament or the ruling political elite. They may incorporate economic incentives so that people (and organizations) are encouraged to follow them, as well as penalties to discourage people from violating them. Thus, institutions both enable and constrain behavior. They tell prospective entrants how to conduct business in a host market and provide them with definitive information on what they might expect there.

Institutions arise, for example, in politics (*rules* codified in a nation's constitution), economics (property rights and contract enforcement), and law (various laws and regulations). Clearly, a firm doing business in a foreign market must familiarize itself with, and follow, the rules, laws, and regulations there.

Institutions can be *formal* (rules codified into laws and regulations, such as laws against corruption) or *informal* (unwritten rules or folkways). Formal institutions (codified rules) are central to the functioning of a society, and violations can invite serious consequences. Informal rules or folkways, on the other hand, are the unwritten conventions of everyday life in a society, such as dress code and social manners.

Tarun Khanna and Krishna Palepu of the Harvard Business School proposed an innovative definition of *emerging markets*. According to them, an emerging market is one that does not have strong institutions, or where institutions are not adequately enforced—a nation with *institutional voids*. The existence of factors such as corruption, excessive red tape, inability to enforce contracts, and inability to enforce one's intellectual property (IP) rights, can lead to persistent difficulties in doing business in a host market. On the other hand, "in developed markets, a range of specialized intermediaries provides the requisite information and contract enforcement needed to consummate transactions."[11]

It is essential for a company planning to enter a foreign market to know its institutional environment and the opportunities and risks it might entail. For instance, a firm whose core competence is its IP should think hard before entering a country which has a poor record of safeguarding foreign companies' IP rights or perhaps enter using an entry mode (such as greenfield investment, rather than a joint venture (JV) or licensing) that poses lesser risk of loss of IP.

Infrastructure in a proposed host market, the second **I** of the PRISM framework, is also very important and includes the usual dimensions, such as transportation and communication networks, utilities, and telecommunication networks, that are critical for the success of most businesses. In specific situations, a firm should be concerned about the availability of the infrastructure elements important to it. For example, a company selling fast-moving consumer goods or machine tools will want to know whether a prospective country has adequate road, railroad, and port infrastructures. A company like Netflix is concerned about the availability of fast broadband in prospective foreign markets. A company wanting to locate its data center in a foreign market is concerned about the continuous availability of sufficient electric power there because data centers consume huge amounts of electric power.

S: Society and Culture

A country's social fabric and culture (or cultures) are important factors in foreign market selection since they have a major impact on entering firms' business practices and their competitive and growth strategies there. Cross-cultural and cross-national understanding *and* sensitivity are crucial for global business, as they are in fact for any business anywhere in today's global–digital world.

The term *culture* represents "a system of values and norms that are shared among a group of people and when taken together constitute a design for living."[12] More broadly, culture consists of values, norms, customs, attitudes, and the beliefs of a group of people, which distinguish it from other groups. A *society* is a group of people who share the same culture.

There is no one-to-one correspondence between society and nation state. A nation may contain a single society or several societies, and a specific society may span several nations. For instance, we may talk about the Arab society, which exists across most countries in the Middle East. Similarly, a country may have several societies within its borders. In the US, for instance, there are German-Americans, Irish-Americans, Chinese-Americans, Indian-Americans, Mexican-Americans, and so on, each representing a specific social group.

To describe the social and cultural context of a nation, it is useful, especially from a business perspective, to identify a nation as having a *high-context* or a *low-context* culture.[13] Some cultures are high-context cultures, like Chinese, Arabic, Slavic, and Spanish, while some are low-context cultures, like Anglo-American, German, and Scandinavian. Most countries can be placed somewhere along the high context–low context continuum shown below.[14]

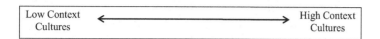

This is a very broad-brush distinction, however, and not everyone and every interaction in a particular culture could be described by the kinds of characteristics (stereotypes) described in the next section. Besides, a culture may have both high-context and low-context elements.

High-context cultures. A high-context culture evolves when a group of people have had a very long history together, forging close connections over long periods of time, so much so that not everything in their daily interactions needs to be explicit. Most people know how to behave and what to expect of others from years of interactions with each other, as if they have been living in a small town where everyone knows everyone else. In other words, they can *read between the lines*. History, tradition, and language are important in high-context cultures. In high-context cultures, written contracts and formal agreements are of lesser importance; the culture itself provides alternative enforcement mechanisms ("Russian culture, for example, uses shame, fear, personal friendship, honor, loyalty, and obligation to enforce agreements.").[15]

Low-context cultures. In a low-context culture, people have also had many connections, but of shorter duration, and some could indeed be impersonal in nature. People tend to play by the rules, which are often explicit and public—with the task being often more important than relationships. They think of the present and the future, rather than of the past. Written agreements and contracts are more important than verbal agreements, and, in fact, form the basis for most transactions between companies from different countries.

A nation with low-context culture may be easier to enter for a company than a nation with high-context culture because an outsider can get on with the task at hand rather than first trying to develop deep relationships. For instance, in a high-context culture like in France or Japan, business dealings are often preceded by much wining and dining. In China, a high-context culture, the role of *guanxi* (connections or relationships) is pre-eminent in business dealings. In a low-context culture like Germany or the US, business can be done without first getting to know each other very much (though it is always a good idea to get to know prospective partners or customers before beginning to interact with them).

There are other ways to classify a society's or a nation's culture, such as Hofstede's cultural dimensions; they are beyond the scope of this book.[16]

M: Market Potential

No firm can expect to enter and be successful in a market without first having an in-depth understanding of market potential and market dynamics in the host nation. Measures to assess the market potential of a prospective foreign market include market size and growth rate, industry structure, competition and rivalry, level of economic development, capacity utilization, exports/imports, inward and outward foreign direct investment (FDI), and so on.

It is appropriate to use a country's population size or gross domestic product (GDP) to measure its market potential for some products. However, for a lot of goods and services, the market size must be defined differently. For instance, for a company selling machine tools, market size could be defined as the number of companies in the foreign market that could potentially use its machine tools in their own production processes. Official statistics in many countries provide such information. As we saw earlier, market size could be defined as the number of internet users in a country for companies like Costco e-Commerce and Netflix. Along with market size, it is also important to know how fast the market is growing in the host country. (See Box 4.2 for a mini case study of Mary Kay Cosmetics' (MKC's) entry into Japan and China.)

BOX 4.2   MARY KAY COSMETICS INC.

In 1992, Mary Kay Cosmetics Inc. (MKC) was a billion-dollar company, with about 11% of its annual revenue derived from foreign markets, compared to 55% of the $3.6 billion in revenue for its major competitor, Avon Products Inc., which also relied on the direct selling method. MKC executives were evaluating further expansion into Asia, specifically entry into Japan and/or China. (The company had previously entered Thailand in 1988 and Taiwan in 1991.) Japan was an established market for cosmetics but growing at only 3% a year, while China represented a very small but rapidly growing market for cosmetics. Japan's population in 1992 was 124 million with high purchasing power, compared to China's 1.139 billion with very low purchasing power. The total market size for cosmetics in Japan was $9.3 billion versus $825 million in China. Avon was the only direct-selling company that had entered China by then, and its sales had doubled from $4 million in 1991 to $8 million in 1992. In addition to market size and growth rate, MKC executives also considered other factors in foreign-market-selection decisions, such as competition, cost of entry, and the acceptance and potential success of their party plan method of direct selling[17]. Based on much analysis, MKC decided to enter both Japan and China, entering Japan in 1994 and China in 1995.

By 2008, China had become Mary Kay Inc.'s (MKI's) second-largest national market. MKI exited the Japanese market in 2001 because of legal restrictions, cultural mismatch, the need to reformulate (customize) its products, and because low prices did not quite appeal to the Japanese market. (Avon also exited the country for somewhat similar reasons, but in 2010.) When the Chinese government banned direct selling in 1998, MKC was the only direct-selling company to survive the ban (which was lifted in 2005)[18]. The moral of the story is: market size and growth rate are both important in foreign-market-selection decisions, and a country's population and GDP are often poor indicators of market potential.

In 2015, MKI started offering nutrition products in the Chinese market—going beyond its traditional focus on cosmetics—in the belief that nutrition products will have a huge potential in China, possibly surpassing the company's cosmetics sales there. In 2017, MKI invested $143 million in its Asia-Pacific center in Hangzhou, Zhejiang Province to strengthen its manufacturing and distribution operations. And, in 2018, it invested $50 million in the Mary Kay Science & Technology Center in Shanghai's Zhangjiang National Science & Technology Center, known as China's *Medicine Valley*, to develop nutrition and health products.

Industry Structure

The term *industry structure* refers to the number and size distribution of firms in an industry in a nation. The number of firms in an industry may run into hundreds, thousands, or more. If all firms in an industry are small in size, relative to industry size, it is a *fragmented* industry. If a few firms control a large share of the industry's output or sales, it is a *consolidated* (or *concentrated*) industry, often referred to as an oligopoly. Industry structure between *fragmented* and *consolidated* can be visualized as a continuum, with different industries positioned at different points on the continuum. On the extreme left side of the continuum are industries with literally hundreds or thousands of firms, each taking a negligible share of the market; these are referred to as *perfectly competitive* industries or markets.[19] On the extreme right side of the continuum are industries dominated by a single seller, or monopolies. Oligopolies are industries positioned toward the right end of the continuum dominated by two, three, or a few major sellers.

A good, intuitive measure of industry structure is the *four-firm concentration ratio*, denoted by CR4, which is the combined share of market held by the four largest firms in the industry. A CR4 of 40% or higher represents a consolidated industry, an oligopoly. The larger the value of CR4, the more consolidated the industry.

Another measure of industry concentration is the *Herfindahl-Hirschman Index* (HHI), which provides a better measure of industry concentration than CR4. The HHI is computed-based on the sum of squares of the market shares of all firms in an industry, typically of the largest 50 firms in the industry. The HHI ranges from zero to 10,000 points, with a score of zero for a completely fragmented industry (a perfectly competitive market), and 10,000 for a monopoly. It is the measure used by the US Federal Trade Commission and the Department of Justice to decide on merger and acquisition applications in the US. Their objective is to make sure that, with the combination of two competing firms, the industry structure does not get so consolidated that the combined firm could hurt consumer or competitor interests. These agencies generally consider markets in which the HHI is between 1,500 and 2,500 points to be moderately concentrated, and markets with HHI in excess of 2,500 points to be highly concentrated.[20]

A CR4 of 60% or more (HHI of 2,000 or more) represents a tight oligopoly with significant opportunities for dominant firms to exercise their market power. A CR4 of 90% or more (HHI of over 8,000) represents a highly consolidated industry, with one firm being effectively the market leader.

In the US, the US Census Bureau does an economic census of industries every 5 years and publishes concentration ratios (for example, CR4 and CR8) and the HHI (based on the largest 50 companies) for all industries—such as manufacturing, trade, and services. Such measures may also be available for many other countries. Table 4.2 shows a sampling of manufacturing industries and their concentration ratios as well as the HHI for the latest available year.

Analyzing the structure of an industry reveals a good deal about competition, rivalry, entry barriers, and other aspects of competitive dynamics in that industry. For instance, the type of competition in fragmented industries is generally very different from that in consolidated industries. Consolidated industries are often mature industries with a few dominant firms and high entry barriers.

Table 4.2   Concentration Ratios and HHI for Selected Manufacturing Industries, 2007 (Based on the Value of Shipments)

NAICS Code	Industry Description	No. of Companies	CR4 (%)	CR8 (%)	HHI (50)
311	Food manufacturing	21,355	14.8	22.8	102.1
311111	Dog and cat food manufacturing	199	71.0	83.5	2,325.1
311230	Breakfast cereal manufacturing	35	80.4	91.9	2,425.5
339	Miscellaneous manufacturing	30,934	10.1	15.4	52.4
339920	Sporting and athletic goods manufacturing	1,808	27.0	37.7	253.4
339992	Musical instruments manufacturing	580	32.2	49.4	404.6

Source: 2007 Economic Census of the US, accessed from https://www.census.gov/econ/concentration.html.

Note: The NAICS Codes are based on the industry classification system used in North America.

Market potential in a country depends on market size, growth rate, industry structure, who the actual competitors are (domestic, foreign, and SOEs), the values of imports and exports of the industry in question, inward and outward FDI, capacity utilization, and other relevant factors.

A Systematic Approach

The PRISM framework is a systematic and comprehensive approach for analyzing foreign markets. It can be customized for use in practically any industry and for any host-home country pair. Firms that explore foreign markets systematically, prior to entry, have a greater chance of success than those that do not.[21]

Given how comprehensive the PRISM framework is, no firm would want to use it as a preliminary step in its search for markets to enter. A three-step process for identifying such markets is a better approach.

Step 1: Perform initial screening—designed to narrow down the number of prospective markets to two or three countries to be included in Step 2 (PRISM) analysis. Possible approaches include brainstorming within the management team, learning from the experiences of other industry firms that went abroad, participating in industry trade association activities, and attending international trade fairs (see also "Learning about Foreign Markets" section later in the chapter).

Step 2: Apply the PRISM framework to the countries identified in Step 1, compare them with the home country, and rank them in terms of market potential and risk in each.

Step 3: Since foreign market entry is a very costly and often risky decision, the final step should ideally involve actual visits to the shortlisted countries, and matching company resources and capabilities with the market opportunities and risks presented by them.

Learning about Foreign Markets

As Akio Morita says in the opening quote of this chapter, a firm must learn much about a foreign market before making a commitment to it. Entering and succeeding in foreign markets is a race to learn; the firm that learns the most and the fastest has a better chance of success. So, how can a firm embark on a learning journey about a foreign market of interest to it?

One of the best ways to learn about a prospective host market is to go on a trade delegation or attend a trade fair there. This offers an opportunity to see what exists there and, if you wish, even an opportunity to talk to competitors, wholesalers, and others *incognito*.

Much information about a host market can also be gained from trade magazines and online sources such as trade association websites in the host market, as well as other online sources. Joining an international trade association or a bilateral chamber of commerce in the home country can also be an excellent means of learning about specific foreign markets.

The commerce departments in the home country at the national, state, and local levels are usually excellent sources of information about foreign markets. The US Department of Commerce, for instance, is perhaps the world's most valuable resource for US companies interested in exploring foreign markets. The US Commercial Service, a unit of the Commerce Department, offers excellent services to US exporters at a relatively low cost. Services are available to US companies through 100 offices within the US and over 70 offices worldwide. Some examples of the services the USCS offers include International Partner Search, Gold Key Service, Single Company or Location Promotion, Featured US Exporters, Trade Show Representation, Virtual Fairs, and Virtual Introduction. One of the services which my clients have used is the Gold Key Service. Under this service, USCS provides US companies with matchmaking appointments with five interested and vetted partners at a low cost when they are traveling to an overseas market. Visit the USCS website for details of this and other services for US companies.[22]

Another approach to learning about a foreign market is to engage a consultant to research the foreign market for its products or do its own research and analysis. The company should also try to learn what its home-based competitors are doing in the foreign market of interest to it.

Entering Foreign Markets

Finally, we come to the topic of entry strategy for foreign markets. The possible entry mode choices available to a prospective entrant are exporting/importing; licensing; franchising; FDI; and strategic alliances. Exporting/importing, licensing, franchising, and strategic alliances are nonequity modes of foreign market entry (a company going abroad through such an approach does not necessarily have to invest in physical assets in the host market). Foreign direct investment, whether a JV or a wholly owned subsidiary, by definition implies investment in physical assets abroad. It is the costliest and the riskiest means of doing business abroad, because it can take a significant amount of time to accomplish it and anything can potentially go wrong during that time, and because such investments are typically large and nonreversible. Each approach has its pluses and minuses, discussed briefly in the next section.

Exporting/Importing

This is often the first approach many companies take when they begin their internationalization journey. It is a cost-effective, low-risk approach to internationalization and it offers opportunities for a firm to get its feet wet in a foreign market to start learning the nitty-gritty of doing business there. It is a nonequity entry mode, unless the firm decides to invest in setting up its own branch office, a buying office, or a servicing operation in a foreign market. If successful, it can set the stage for further commitment to the market. Exporting/importing is beneficial when the value-to-weight ratio of a product is high and when there are low trade barriers (in the host market for imports and the home market for exports). For digital products, this is an ideal way to do business abroad.

Companies sometimes engage agents and distributors to sell abroad, known as indirect exporting or importing. One disadvantage of exporting/importing through agents or distributors is that the firm may have little control over their actions. Host-country regulations regarding international trade, such as tariffs and local-content requirements, can also pose challenges for foreign firms.

Licensing

A cross-border licensing agreement gives a foreign company the right to produce and sell the licensor's goods in its market. Under licensing, a company (the licensor) grants the rights to its IP (patents, trademarks, copyrights, designs, etc.) to another company (the licensee) for a certain period of time in return for royalties. The royalties can be payable as a one-time lump sum or as a percentage of sales by the licensee during the term of the license. A licensing agreement typically specifies the geographic area where the licensee can sell the products manufactured under license and using the licensor's brand name. Since it does not necessarily involve an investment by the licensor, it can be an easier, less risky means of foreign market entry for some products. This is especially true if a host market restricts inward FDI, if the company does not have the managerial, organizational, and financial resources to invest in foreign markets, or for other strategic reasons.

Licensing can pose serious risks for the IP owner if a licensee misuses the IP granted to it by the owner or produces a shoddy product giving the brand a bad name. The licensor cannot often keep tight control over the actions of foreign licensees. There is also always a risk that by licensing its IP, a company might be creating a future competitor. For these reasons, licensing is not advisable for companies whose core competence is technology and know-how. Box 4.3 has the interesting case of Volkswagen acquiring Rolls-Royce in 1998, but, unwittingly, without the Rolls-Royce brand name and logo.

Imagination Technologies, a UK-based technology company whose software is used in billions of phones, cars, homes, and workplaces worldwide, signed a multiyear license agreement with Apple in January 2020, replacing its earlier multiyear license agreement of February 2014. Apple had previously advised Imagination Technologies in February 2017 that it would stop using their software in its products, which drove Imagination Technologies' stock price down by 64% in a single day. After ensuing dispute resolution and intense renegotiations between the two companies, they signed the new license agreement giving Apple access to a wider range of Imagination Technologies' IP in exchange for license fees.

Franchising

While licensing typically involves manufacturing, franchising is almost always done for services. Under franchising, a franchisor sells its intangible property to another company (the franchisee) for an initial franchise fee and a certain percentage of its sales during the period of the franchise agreement. A franchise agreement often includes the obligations of both parties to the agreement with the franchisor agreeing to offer a variety of continuing services to the franchisee, such as advertising support and fulfilling its supply chain needs, and the franchisee agreeing to follow the operating policies (the business model) of the franchisor. Franchising, like licensing, also allows

BOX 4.3 VOLKSWAGEN AND BMW SPAT OVER ROLLS-ROYCE

The Rolls-Royce PLC of the UK was the manufacturer of aircraft engines (the second largest in the world), luxury cars, and equipment for the marine and energy industries during the late 1990s. The cars were made by its Rolls-Royce Motor subsidiary in its legendary factory in Crewe, England. In 1998, Volkswagen (VW) of Germany purchased Rolls-Royce Motor Cars Ltd., along with its two luxury brands, Rolls-Royce and Bentley, and the Crewe factory for $917 million, for which BMW had also unsuccessfully bid. However, the VW deal did not include Rolls-Royce's valuable assets, the *Rolls-Royce* brand name and the *RR* logo, which by some quirk of fate had previously been sold by the Rolls-Royce aircraft company to BMW for $78 million. Now, even though VW could make cars that looked and performed like Rolls-Royces, it could not call any car it made a Rolls-Royce (Figure 4.3).

After protracted negotiations between VW and BMW, the latter allowed VW to use the brand name and logo on its cars for a significant sum of money, though only until December 31, 2002. Now, VW makes the Bentley at the Crewe factory, and BMW makes the Rolls-Royce in West Sussex, England.

Figure 4.3   The Rolls-Royce logo.

Source: Photo by 777 S on unsplash.com.

a company to expand abroad without necessarily making much (or any) investment. Some disadvantages of franchising include the possibility of poor quality control at a franchisee's location, and potential legal problems if a franchisee fails to meet the terms of the franchise agreement. Enforcing such agreements in foreign countries can be very expensive and time-consuming, especially in countries that may lack strong contract enforcement mechanisms. Even in a highly developed market such as the US, a foreign company interested in franchising its business model in the US faces challenges such as a highly regulated business environment, fierce competition, diverse demographics, and generally high investment requirements. Yet, dozens of foreign companies have found franchising success in the US, including Kumon, an education company from Japan.

In the technology industry, there are companies offering franchises for equipment repair, IT services, and the like. For example, CPR Cell Phone Repair repairs cell phones, MP3 players, game consoles, laptops, tablets, etc. and, as of February 2018, had 571 franchises, including 73 outside the US. TeamLogicIT offers IT support services to smaller companies for business continuity (keeping systems up and running), cybersecurity, cloud services, data backup, and so on. It had 176 franchises by February 2018, of which only one was outside the US.

Foreign Direct Investment

As indicated earlier, foreign market entry via direct investment is the costliest and the riskiest means of doing business abroad; it is also the second most popular means of entering foreign markets after exporting/importing. It is the costliest because it necessarily involves creating physical presence in a foreign market and all that it entails. It is the riskiest not only because of the significant investment involved, but also because FDI can take one, two, or more years before becoming fully operational, and anything can happen (government regulations, political change, competition, etc.) during the intervening period. However, FDI also has advantages for the company making the investment, such as the ability to have tight control over foreign operations, ability to transfer its organizational routines and core capabilities relatively quickly to the foreign subsidiary, ability to better serve local customers by being close to them, lesser risk of losing technological competence to others, and learning in the host market. A company can make FDI via a partly owned enterprise such as a JV or a wholly owned subsidiary via greenfield investment or mergers and acquisitions (M&As).

A *joint venture* is an arrangement whereby two (or more) companies invest financial and other resources to set up a new legal entity in the home or host market. The new entity, a JV, can be set up with equal investment by both parties, as in a 50:50 JV, or a majority JV where one of the partners invests more than 50% of the total investment needed. A JV allows a company to leverage its partner's knowledge, relationships, and expertise; share the cost and risk of developing and commercializing new technologies and new products; and even reduced political risk in a foreign market. However, the risks of entering into a JV with a foreign partner are also not insignificant. The company risks losing its technology to a JV partner and even creating a future competitor. Yet, JVs and strategic alliances are popular means of entering foreign markets (see also discussion on strategic alliances next).

The autonomous vehicle (AV) industry has lately been experiencing many JVs and partnerships between carmakers and technology firms, between two or three carmakers, between carmakers and ride-sharing firms, and even between suppliers and suppliers to carmakers. Examples of JVs include the Ford-Google JV to equip Ford AVs with Google self-driving software; the GM-Lyft car-rental JV to supply Lyft drivers with GM-connected cars; a JV between German carmakers Daimler, BMW, and Audi that acquired the Dutch digital mapping service firm Here Technologies, with minority investment by tech firms; and a 50:50 JV between Audi and Ford that invested $7 billion in Argo AI, Ford's autonomous driving platform.[23]

A *wholly owned* foreign subsidiary is one where a firm sets up a new 100%-owned legal entity in a foreign market. It can do so through M&A by acquiring or merging with an existing enterprise in the foreign market or by establishing a greenfield enterprise from the ground up. For example, Honda of America Manufacturing, Inc. is a wholly owned subsidiary of Honda of Japan in the US, set up as a greenfield entity starting in 1977. Google has over 50 foreign subsidiaries, including bruNET Schweiz GmbH of Switzerland that offers management consulting services and Google Payment Singapore Pte Ltd that offers commercial services. A wholly owned enterprise set up as a greenfield operation offers the best opportunity for a firm to learn the most about the foreign market.[24]

Strategic Alliances

A *strategic alliance* is a partnering arrangement between two or more companies sharing resources in the pursuit of a common goal, *while remaining independent*. A strategic alliance can be formed with suppliers, customers (a foreign distributor, for example), universities, government agencies, and even with direct competitors,[25] and is generally intended to enter new markets, strengthen a specific skill, share the cost and risk of a major project, develop technology, and so on. A strategic alliance may or may not involve equity investment by either or both parties. If equity investment is involved and the two parties form a new legal entity, it is a JV.

As indicated previously, the AV industry has had numerous partnerships (and JVs) in the last decade. For instance, Uber has an R&D partnership with Carnegie Mellon University to develop AV driving technology, and the GM-Honda R&D partnership for developing hydrogen fuel cells has now expanded its scope to include self-driving technology, IT, and electrification.

This chapter presented the approaches that companies might use to select and enter foreign markets. However, that is just the beginning. The next chapter presents strategies for competing and growing in foreign markets—for digital businesses.

Notes

1 Bobbie Johnson, "Will Netflix go global in 2011? Maybe, but it won't be easy," Gigaon.com, December 31, 2010. https://gigaom.com/2010/12/31/netflix-global-expansion/.
2 LoveFilm was later acquired by Amazon in 2011.
3 From the company website https://ir.netflix.net/ir-overview/profile/default.aspx.
4 Lauren Forristal, "Report: Top streaming companies will spend $140.5 billion on content in 2022," January 18, 2022. https://thestreamable.com/news/new-data-shows-top-9-media-and-tech-companies-will-spend-140–5-billion-on-content-in-2022.
5 In their January 2015 letter to shareholders, as part of the company's Q4 earnings report, Reed Hastings, CEO, and David Wells, CFO, stated: "Our international expansion strategy over the last few years has been to expand as fast as we can while staying profitable on a global basis… With the growth of the Internet over the next 20 years, there will be some amazing entertainment services available globally. We intend to be one of the leaders." https://www.sec.gov/Archives/edgar/data/1065280/000106528015000003/nflx-123114xex991.htm.
6 Several sources, including the company website.
7 In 2015, MKI started offering nutritional products in the Chinese market—going beyond its traditional focus on cosmetics—in the belief that nutrition products will have a huge potential in China, possibly surpassing the company's cosmetics sales there. In 2017, MKI invested $143 million in its Asia-Pacific center in Hangzhou, Zhejiang Province to strengthen its manufacturing and distribution operations. And, in 2018, it invested $50 million in the Mary Kay Science & Technology Center in Shanghai's Zhangjiang National Science & Technology Center, known as China's *Medicine Valley*, to develop nutrition and health products.
   This case study is based on information taken from the company website and FY 2022 corporate profile, https://investor.costco.com/corporate-profile-2/.
8 Vinod K. Jain, *Global Strategy: Competing in the Connected Economy* (New York: Routledge, 2016), Chapter 4.
9 Charles W.L. Hill, *International Business: Competing in the Global Marketplace*. 9th Edition. New York: McGraw-Hill/Irwin, 2013, Chapter 2, and R.J. Rummel, *Understanding Conflict and War: The Conflict Helix*. v.2. New York: John Wiley & Sons, 1976. Chapter 31. Accessed from https://www.hawaii.edu/powerkills/TCH.CHAP31.HTM#31.2.
10 Michael Porter, *The Competitive Advantage of Nations* (New York: Free Press, 1990).
11 Tarun Khanna and Krishna G. Palepu, *Winning in Emerging Markets: A Roadmap for Strategy and Execution* (Boston, MA: Harvard Business School Press, 2010), p. 14.

12 Hill, 2013, p. 101.
13 This distinction was suggested by Edward T. Hall in *Beyond Culture*. (New York: Anchor Books, 1976).
14 Much of this discussion in this subsection is adapted from Maria Carlson, "Culture and History Matter: Russia's Search for Identity After the Fall" (Lecture at the University of Kansas, April 10, 2007). https://kuscholarworks.ku.edu/bitstream/handle/1808/1368/halllecturecarlson10Apr07.pdf? sequence=3.
15 Maria Carlson, "Culture and history matter: Russia's search for identity after the fall" (Lecture at University of Kansas, April 10, 2007). https://kuscholarworks.ku.edu/bitstream/handle/1808/1368/ HallLectureCarlson10apr07.pdf.
16 Geert Hofstede, *Culture's Consequences: International Differences in Work-Related Values*. Newbury Park, CA: Sage Publications, 1980.
17 John A. Quelch, Nathalie Laidler, "Mary Kay Cosmetics: Asian Market Entry (A)," Harvard Business School Publishing Case Study, 1994 (Revised June 2009). Product Number: 9-594-023.
18 John A. Quelch, "Mary Kay Inc.: Asian Market Entry (B)," Harvard Business School Publishing Case Study, 2009. Product Number: 9-509-067.
19 In economics, a perfectly competitive market is one that has many sellers, each taking a negligible share of the market, and many buyers, each taking a negligible amount of the market's output. Some other characteristics of perfectly competitive markets are the existence of a homogenous product, free entry and free exit, perfectly available market information to all market participants, and so on.
20 Source: The US Department of Justice: https://www.justice.gov/atr/herfindahl-hirschman-index.
21 George S. Yip, Javier G. Biscarri, and J.A. Monti, "The role of internationalization process in the performance of newly internationalizing firms," *Journal of International Marketing*, 2000 (8), pp. 10–35.
22 International Trade Administration, "Services for exporters." https://www.trade.gov/services-current-exporters.
23 More information on these and other joint ventures and partnerships is available at: https://www.cbinsights.com/research/autonomous-driverless-vehicles-corporations-list/.
24 Vinod K. Jain, *Evolution of International Investment Strategy: The Case of Foreign MNEs in the United States*. Unpublished Ph.D. dissertation, University of Maryland, College Park, 1994.
25 Strategic alliances between direct competitors from different countries are generally allowed by the parent countries' antitrust laws, but not between direct competitors from the same country without the permission of the country's antitrust authority (e.g., the US Department of Justice and the FTC in the United States).

Chapter 5

Global Strategy for Digital Businesses

You have no choice but to operate in a world shaped by globalization and the information revolution. There are two options: adapt or die.

Andrew S. Grove, former COO, CEO, and Chairman, Intel Corporation

Strategy is concerned with (1) how companies create and capture value and (2) how they establish and sustain competitive advantage. A firm is judged by its stakeholders for the value it creates for them. Different stakeholders of course have different expectations of the firm in which they have (or claim to have) some stake. From a *customer* perspective, a firm creates value when it satisfies their needs efficiently and effectively. And, from a *shareholder* perspective, a firm creates value when it makes an economic profit to be able to offer its shareholders good returns on their investment (see Chapter 7 for more on value creation and value capture).

Chapter 4 was about how firms enter foreign markets; this chapter is about how firms, especially digital firms, compete in foreign markets. It presents strategies a digital business might employ to create (and capture) value through international operations.

But, first, what's a digital business? One often sees references to such terms as *digital*, *digital company, software company*, and *technology company*. There are even articles in respected publications with titles like, "Every business is a digital business," "Every company is a software company," and so on.[1] Irrespective of how it is defined, people instinctively know what a digital business is (*I know it when I see it*). It's not surprising therefore that the term *digital business* has been defined differently by different consulting firms, though with some commonalities. According to Accenture, "Digital businesses create competitive edges based on unique combinations of digital and physical resources."[2] For Gartner, "Digital business is the creation of new business designs by blurring the digital and physical worlds."[3] And, according to McKinsey & Company, "digital should be seen less as a thing and more a way of *doing* things."[4]

In this book, I use the term *digital business* to include companies with two characteristics:

First, a digital business is one that digitalizes its processes. Using the terminology introduced in Chapter 1 and shown in Figure 5.1 (types of products—physical, digital, and smart machines),

DOI: 10.4324/9781003037446-7

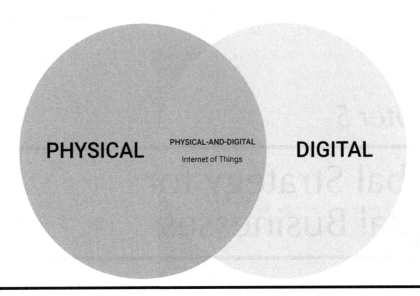

Figure 5.1 Types of products.

this includes companies that sell *digital products* as well as *smart machines* (also known as the Internet of Things or IoT). For example, companies that sell digital products include Spotify, Netflix, Uber, Airbnb, Salesforce, and thousands of other companies whose businesses are built around software and algorithms. Companies that sell smart machines or IoT products include Nest that sells connected thermostats and other home-security products; autonomous vehicle companies such as Waymo; and industrial IoT companies such as Bosch that sells networked parking-space sensors, among other products.[5] Such products are both physical and digital and connected to the internet (Figure 5.1).

Second, a digital business harnesses digital technologies (AI, robotics, cloud computing, etc.) to create and capture value. Notice that this definition focuses on *how* (digitalization of processes and harnessing of digital technologies) more than on *what* (products). For example, Amazon uses AI and machine learning to make product recommendations to customers and to power its smart products like Alexa. Peloton is a connected stationary exercise bike with an integrated tablet that displays fitness programming. Peloton users, who purchase the bike and pay a monthly subscription fee, have access to thousands of digitally streamed fitness classes and can even connect with other users taking the same class at the same time somewhere in the world.

Despite the somewhat restrictive definition of digital business used here, the strategies included in this chapter are largely applicable to most technology businesses, not just information technology (IT) businesses. Box 5.1 distinguishes between digitization, digitalization, and digital transformation.

We begin our exploration of global strategy for digital businesses with two illustrative examples—one a purely digital product (Spotify) and the other a smart machine (Peloton). Both are involved in digital business—succeeding with network effects and innovation and using software, data, analytics, and digital technologies such as AI. Each disrupted a traditional industry and created a new business category, thus transforming its industry. We explore their operations and strategy to create and capture value in the home market and in foreign markets.

**BOX 5.1   DIGITIZATION VERSUS DIGITALIZATION
VERSUS DIGITAL TRANSFORMATION**

There is often confusion when these terms are used in media, even in professional and scholarly journals; sometimes they tend to be used interchangeably.

Digitization is the conversion of something from an analog source (such as data, WORD documents, images, or sound) into a series of zeros and ones so it can be deciphered by computers; it is a bridge between the analog and the digital worlds. The analog content can be text from a printed book converted into an e-book. It can be a musical score (a printed manuscript) or a phone conversation (physical sound) converted into a digital file. Digitization converts analog content into digital content without making any changes to the underlying process itself. Changing the process is what *digitalization* does.

Digitalization is the process of moving to digital business; it cannot occur unless the different elements involved in a process have first been digitized. Digitalization thus involves transforming business processes using digital technologies. It makes processes easier to perform and more efficient. It is ubiquitous in our daily lives, so much so it is hard to visualize a world without digitalization. Many decades ago, managing customer relationships involved Rolodex and other forms of maintaining records of customer interactions. Now, we have customer relationship management (CRM) software that helps companies record and manage customer interactions—a transformed business process using digital technologies like data analytics.

Digital transformation typically requires the use of digital technologies in the conduct of business as well as any needed organizational changes to make digital transformation successful. Salesforce offers a good workable definition of digital transformation: It is "the process of using digital technologies to create new – or modify existing – business processes, culture, and customer experiences to meet changing business and market requirements." It is a reimagining of the business for the digital age.[6]

Digital businesses are already digital by definition; it is the nondigital businesses that need digital transformation before digital strategy can be implemented.

Spotify

Spotify (Spotify Technology S.A.) is a quintessentially digital, born-global Swedish company with executive offices in Luxembourg that operates worldwide in the online music streaming business. It was founded in 2006 to create a legal music streaming platform—in response to the growing Internet piracy of music since the early 2000s. (Remember Napster, a peer-to-peer file-sharing service started in 1999 but shut down by court order in 2001.) The Spotify platform offers listeners access to 82 million songs, the biggest collection of music in history, as well as to podcasts and video content; about 1.8 million songs are uploaded each month to the Spotify platform. With 11 million artists and creators on its platform as of September 2022, Spotify is available to listeners in 182 countries. Spotify has 433 million monthly listeners, including 188 million paid (premium) subscribers.

In 2021, Spotify achieved revenue of €9.67 billion, compared to €1.94 billion in 2015.[7] Its biggest competitors are Apple Music (founded in 2001, with 100 million songs available to 90 million paid subscribers in 2022) and Amazon Music (founded in 2007; all 200 million subscribers to Amazon Prime have free access to Amazon Music with 100 million songs; Amazon Music Unlimited, available to Prime members at $8.99 per month, has 100 million songs).

Spotify Technology launched its initial public offering (IPO) on April 3, 2018 on the New York Stock Exchange at a reference price of $132 per share; the share price grew $364.59 on February 15, 2021, its highest-ever level. (Spotify's share price on October 11, 2022 was $83.13, with market cap down to $16.797 billion.)

Spotify's two-sided platform boasts a massive network of 11 million content creators (artists) and almost 433 million active users. Using the freemium subscription model, Spotify permits anyone to instantly listen to music on its platform free of cost, though with advertisements and requiring an Internet connection. By contrast, its Premium service offers higher quality, ad-free listening, and subscribers have the ability to download songs on any device using the Spotify app for later listening. Spotify Premium costs $9.99 per month in the US ($15.99 per month for families). Spotify began offering access—to both free and paid subscribers—to (audio) podcasts in 2015 and video podcasts in July 2020.

Spotify's success can, at least partially, be traced back to 2008 when its founders convinced record labels to license their music to its platform in return for a share in the company's revenue. Spotify pays out about 52% of its revenue to record labels, who in turn pay their artists 15–50% of what they receive from Spotify. An artist whose song is streamed on Spotify receives about $0.00318 every time their song is streamed (compared to $0.00563 per stream paid out by Apple Music and $0.01196 by Amazon Music). A million streams on Spotify would earn an artist about $3,200. Spotify paid over 7 billion dollars to artists in 2021, the biggest payout among all streaming services. Over 1,000 artists received at least 1 million dollars each in Spotify royalties in 2021, and over 50,000 received at least $10,000 each in royalties that year.

In September 2018, Spotify began allowing artists to upload their music directly on its platform, for which they receive 50% of the net revenue generated by the song; this allows artists access to potential listeners without going through record labels.[8]

How Spotify Creates Value

Network effects. Spotify leverages the full power of network effects through its vast network of artists and users. Its scale of operations allows greater artist discovery, enabling artists to connect with more listeners, who in turn have access to more artists, thus creating a positive feedback loop. This network effect enhances the value created for both artists and listeners. Artists on the Spotify platform receive analytics (e.g., number of listeners, new listeners, conversion rates, and even intent of streaming an artist in the future), listener identities, and promotional tools. Listeners benefit from access to curated playlists, such as a *discover weekly* playlist tailored to listeners' tastes (see Figure 5.2), *mood playlists* for different times of the day, and *on repeat* playlists based on the songs a listener listened to multiple times during the last 30 days. The Spotify platform currently has over 4 billion playlists, of which about 3,000 were curated by it.

Spotify creates curated playlists for specific occasions and allows listeners to create their own playlists. For instance, some parts of Southeast Asia suffer from forest and agricultural fires every year, typically starting in Indonesia. The fires create a haze that clouds skies in several countries in the region, including Malaysia and Singapore. In September 2019, Spotify curated a tongue-in-cheek playlist, called *Hazed & Confused*, containing 69 songs that reflected the situation in Singapore. Here are some of the songs included in Hazed & Confused[9]:

- We Didn't Start the Fire (Billy Joel)
- Smoke Gets in Your Eyes (The Platters)
- Breathe Easy (Blue)

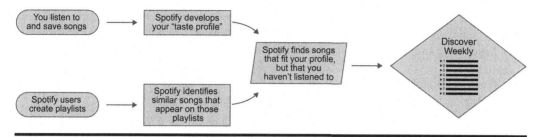

Figure 5.2 **How Spotify recommends songs and creates a discover weekly Playlist for each listener.**

Source: Based on: Adam Pasick, "The magic that makes Spotify's Discover Weekly playlists so damn good," December 21, 2015. https://qz.com/571007/the-magic-that-makes-spotifys-discover-weekly-playlists-so-damn-good/.

- Burnin' Up (Jonas Brothers)
- Burn (Usher)
- I See Fire (Ed Sheeran)
- Oxygen Mask (Eisley)

Technology. The algorithms that Spotify employs use big data, AI, machine learning, blockchain, and more to offer enhanced services to both artists and listeners. In addition to offering artists analytics and other tools, Spotify uses these technologies to generate playlists for listeners and correctly pay artists. Even though its competitors (Apple and Amazon) have much better technologies, Spotify has had first-mover advantage in creating auto-generated playlists for subscribers using their streaming history. The millions of listeners accessing music on Spotify every minute of the day generate huge amounts of data, such as which songs are played most often, when, by whom, the devices being used to listen to the music, and so on. Spotify uses such data to *train* its machines to predict what a listener might like to hear next (Figure 5.2). Through their own Discover Weekly playlist, listeners receive personalized playlist every week containing songs that align with their listening tastes and preferences and which they had not listened to before. Big data and data analytics are used for creating the Discover Weekly and other playlists for listeners.

Its app, Spotify for Artists, provides mobile access to analytics to artists, which they can even use while on a tour bus to help better plan their tours.

The company has lately been on something of an acquisition spree to strengthen its technology capabilities and enter new markets (such as podcasting). Here are three of Spotify's acquisitions in 2017 to strengthen its technology capabilities:

- French startup, Niland, "a music technology company that provides music search & discovery engines based on deep learning & machine listening algorithms."[10]
- New York City-based startup, Mediachain, to ensure, using blockchain technology, that the right artists are paid every time their tracks are streamed.
- British startup, Sonalytic, the maker of audio-detection technology featuring mashups and remixes of content and audio clips, even identifying copyrighted tracks before they are played.

These are just technology companies Spotify acquired over 5 years ago. It has also acquired companies to enter adjacent markets, such as podcasting, audiobooks, and video streaming. Here is a quick list of some audio and podcast-related acquisitions Spotify made in recent years.[11]

- Findaway, a digital audiobook distribution platform.
- Podsights, a podcast advertising measurement service.
- Chartable, a podcast analytics platform.

Innovation. Spotify is on *Fast Company* magazine's 2022 list of the ten most innovative media companies in the world, [12] an honor the company has had in the past also. For instance, it was Number 15 on *Fast Company* magazine's 2020 list of the 50 most innovative companies in the world, among all companies, not just media companies.[13] As indicated in the previous section, Spotify uses technologies to create innovations for artists and listeners alike. It also uses innovative technologies in marketing, advertising, and other business functions. For instance, Spotify uses innovation in brand building through outdoor ads targeting local users on specific occasions, like Valentine's Day. In 2018, its outdoor promotion created billboard ads like, "Dear Person who played 'Sorry' 42 times on Valentine's Day: What did you do?" Another 2018 billboard ad[14] showed unusual or unexpected statistics from its user base:

"God is a man" vs.
"God is a woman"
According to fan-made playlists:

"Man -9 playlists"
"Woman -28,802 playlists"

Spotify offers other companies a powerful addition to their own marketing strategy. For instance, Unilever wanted to improve awareness for its AXE Global Products in Germany. So, Unilever used Spotify's *video takeover ad experience* and sponsored sessions—allowing its target audience to listen to thirty minutes of ad-free music so long as they also watched a Unilever brand video. Spotify developed an *American Road Trip* campaign during the launch of the BMW 320i model. A Spotify-branded app for the campaign enabled users to select specific music for different regions along selected routes, resulting in the creation of some 14,000 playlists.

Spotify's use of technology throughout the enterprise enables it to perform various functions which might not have been possible without the use of advanced information technologies or perform them at a substantially higher cost.

How Spotify Captures Value

By offering customers a legal and convenient means of listening to music, Spotify helped discover an audience willing to pay for music and, with unlimited on-demand streaming, shifted consumer behavior from a transaction-based model (such as purchasing a music CD) to an access-based model (listening to music anytime, anywhere, without owning it). Spotify makes money from premium subscriptions and advertising, with about 90% of its revenue coming from subscriptions and the balance from advertising. As indicated earlier, subscribers to its premium service have access to high-quality, ad-free music and podcasts online and offline, whereas subscribers to its freemium service can only access music and podcasts online, interspersed with ads. Also, as indicated earlier, much of the value it creates is captured by record labels (and subscribers), leaving Spotify in a perennial loss. In 2021, the company posted a net income of –$0.04 billion compared to a net income of –$0.664 for 2020.

Spotify helped increase customers' willingness to pay for music through data-driven personalization, price discrimination (different price levels for individuals, families, and students), ad-free listening, and ease of filtering songs by genre, album, and artist—on demand. Personalization, ease of operation, and user-generated content (playlists) further helped with customer retention. Allowing listeners to share their playlists with friends—Spotify now houses over 4 billion user-generated playlists—helps increase switching cost from Spotify to other networks. In addition, Spotify aggressively integrated with social networks like Facebook (in 2011), video game consoles like PlayStation (2014), and platforms like Uber (2016) that also helped increase willingness to pay. Video game players on PlayStation, for example, can listen to music of their choice while gaming without the need for an additional device. A rider on Uber can use Spotify Premium to play music from the Uber app throughout travel. Spotify continues to enhance customers' willingness to pay through entry into new and adjacent markets (such as podcasting in 2015, video podcasts in 2020, and audiobooks in September 2022).

Spotify's Global Strategy

Starting in Europe in 2008, Spotify entered the UK in 2009, the US in 2011, Australia in 2012, Mexico in 2013, Brazil in 2014, and so on. Spotify entered 13 countries in the Middle East and North Africa (MENA) and Southeast Asia in 2018. Spotify entered India in early 2019 and Russia and 12 other countries in 2020, bringing the total number of countries served to 92 by July 2020. By now, Spotify is available to listeners in 182 countries.

Spotify uses essentially the same strategy to compete worldwide as it does in its home base, Europe, such as leveraging network effects, big data, technology, and innovation. In addition, it has been a first mover (or a fast second) in many foreign markets, localizes its content and marketing approaches in individual foreign markets, and signs up partnerships and license deals there.

A fast-second strategy. Compared to some other music streaming platforms, like France's Deezer which expanded aggressively to over 180 countries, Spotify has often followed a fast-second strategy[15] in foreign markets. For instance, when it entered Mexico, Deezer was already there, but it overtook Deezer and every other direct competitor there in short order. By 2016, Spotify had a 64% share of the music streaming market in Mexico, compared to, for example, Apple Music at 8%. Globally, Spotify has a 31% share of market, well ahead of competitors, including Apple Music at 15%, Amazon Music at 13%, and YouTube Music at 8%.

Localization. Spotify often goes to the extreme to localize its music and marketing strategy for individual foreign markets. It partners with local labels and artists and develops a strong local music catalog even before entering a market. It attempts to engage local listeners through local social media channels, local trends and news, as well as local users' concerns. (Recall the *Hazed & Confused* playlist it curated in Singapore.) Its apps, website, and other content are translated into local languages. Some examples of Spotify's hyper-localization:

Given India's rich music heritage and dozens of languages, Spotify created a custom-built user experience on entering India. Among some of the approaches it used are multilanguage music recommendations, playlists made specifically for India (e.g., Punjabi 101, Bollywood Butter, and Namaste Love) as well as top hits in major languages, playlists featuring the best songs from popular Bollywood movies, and city-focused playlists that tracked trending topics in key cities. To achieve this level of localization, Spotify worked closely with local teams of researchers, engineers, and cultural ambassadors. According to Cecilia Qvist, Spotify's Global Head of Markets, "A fundamental piece of that (overall growth) strategy is staying connected to global culture while allowing room for local adaptation, and we've certainly achieved that with our India launch."[16]

When Spotify entered the MENA region, it created a new Arabic hub and numerous playlists, supporting right-to-left text in its apps. Its TV and print ads in Japan featured humorous scenes from everyday life there.

Spotify's individual subscription for access to Premium content is also adjusted to cost of living in foreign countries. For instance, Spotify Premium costs 119 rupees ($1.45) per month in India, 169 rubles ($2.65) in Russia, and 100 pesos ($5.00) in Mexico—compared to $9.99 in the US (as of October 12, 2022).

Partnering. In addition to partnering with—and licensing music from—record labels and artists, Spotify partners with telecom companies in each foreign market it enters, often signing partnership deals with them well before entering the market. As of 2018, music streaming services had partnerships with telecom companies in over 60 countries, typically involving product bundles for a fixed price.[17] A bundle of telecom and music streaming services often includes phone, data, messaging, and streamed music. Such deals help the telecoms retain existing and lure new customers and, for streaming services, it is a means of acquiring new listeners and converting them into paying customers over time.

In the US, for instance, Spotify's partnership is with AT&T, which offers seven *premium entertainment* options (such as Spotify, Pandora, HBO, and Showtime) to its customers of "AT&T Unlimited & More Premium" service at no additional cost. In France, Bouygues Telecom subscribers can add Spotify on one bill = *c'est magique* (it's magic) that includes a free 6-month trial for Spotify Premium. In Australia and the UK, Spotify is partnered with Vodaphone, in Philippines with Globe, and in Malaysia with Maxis.

Partnering not just with record labels and telecoms, Spotify has also partnered with top retailing companies such as Magazine Luiza ("Magalu") in Brazil and with content aggregator and distributor Shemaroo in India. In Japan, Spotify is partnered with the country's top messaging app, Line, which allowed it to share its music over Line's mobile app. And, since 2018, Spotify has had a partnership with Samsung—becoming the phone company's exclusive music streaming service. In July 2022, Spotify entered into a partnership with FC Barcelona (Futbol Club Barcelona), becoming a Title Partner to the FC Barcelona stadium. The partnership also means that Spotify will appear on the front of men's and women's football shirts and training kits for 4 years, starting with the 2022/2023 season, and many other promotional opportunities.

Peloton

While Spotify offers a purely digital product (music), Peloton is a smart machine—a product that is both physical and digital and connected to the internet—an IoT device. Peloton Interactive, Inc. is an American company, headquartered in New York City, in the *connected fitness* business category that it helped create (Box 5.2). Peloton took a 200-year-old product, the stationary bike, and transformed it by adding digital elements to it and connecting it to the internet. In the process, Peloton also transformed the fitness business—from a studio- and gym-based business relying on rigid timetables—to one not constrained by time, place, or capacity.

BOX 5.2   CONNECTED FITNESS

It's a new category of fitness products like treadmills and stationary bikes that include a connected touchscreen mounted on the handlebar allowing users to join virtual workouts at home with performance tracking. Connected fitness companies typically offer live-streamed classes as well as a library of hundreds or thousands of prerecorded classes from which users can select classes that meet their specific fitness needs. In some cases, users can compare their performance with other users taking the same class at the same time somewhere in the world. The COVID-19 pandemic, with work-from-home and shelter-in-place regulations in many countries, was a boon to companies selling connected fitness products, though Peloton benefited from the increased convenience of working out at home even before the pandemic hit.

This is a fast-growing business category, with a number of established fitness-equipment companies joining the *connected fitness* model (for instance, NordicTrack) as well as VC-funded startups (such as Tonal, Mirror, and several others). Mirror is being acquired by Lululemon, a retailer of athletic apparel, while ICON Health and Fitness, the parent of NordicTrack, raised $200 million in 2020 to strengthen its connected offerings. Even major players like Apple and Amazon are entering the connected fitness market. In late 2020, for instance, Apple introduced the Apple Fitness+ app, a new fitness service powered by Apple watch. Users have access to thousands of video and audio exercises and guided meditations. Apple watch users are able to access workouts in several categories offered by expert trainers, somewhat similar to Peloton's categories, that are transported from the watch to other Apple devices—iPhone, iPad, and Apple TV. The app integrates the user's personal health metrics (such as heart rate and calories burned during a workout) along with Apple music and makes them visible on the device screen. The app costs $12.99 per month and Apple watch owners can share it with up to five family members.

While Peloton created the digital fitness category, some of its competitors have gone further with product and software enhancements. For example, NordicTrack offers a swivel screen (now also offered by Peloton) and the instructor in a live class can adjust a user's settings for things like incline and resistance depending on the user's performance.

The Peloton bike, introduced in 2014 in the US, costs $1,445 (or $2,495 for Bike+), including delivery and setup (Figure 5.3). Buyers of the bike also purchase all-access membership at $44 per month offering them access to daily live workouts by elite instructors, thousands of on-demand classes, curated training programs, and music playlists. The users access workouts, classes, and music on an integrated 22″ or 24″ touchscreen monitor through which they can select classes, track their performance, connect with other users, and even high-five others taking the same class at the same time. Users can take live classes in the company's studio in Manhattan, New York and Chelsea, London, UK. Live-streamed classes are conducted by elite instructors, some of whom have become celebrities in the Peloton world, and attended by a few hundred to over 10,000 members sweating simultaneously. (The largest reported turnout for a live class, with instructor Robin Arzon, was 23,000 on April 22, 2020.)

Peloton sessions are available across 11 categories, such as cycling, strength, dance cardio, running, and even yoga and meditation. Currently, the company has over 128 showrooms in the US, Canada, the UK, Australia, and Germany. A recent addition to the Peloton library is the Peloton Artist Series, featuring over 70 artists, with workouts built around famous artists and their music. For instance, over 1 million members completed their workouts with Beyoncé's music during one quarter.

Figure 5.3   A Peloton connected bike.

Source: Photo by the Author at a Peloton Showroom.

Peloton's mobile app, Peloton Digital, offers cheaper access to Peloton classes and programming, without owning the equipment. The app, priced at $12.99 per month, can be accessed through several devices, including Apple TV, Amazon's Fire TV, Android TV, Roku TV, Apple watches, smartphones, and tablets. In 2017, Peloton entered an adjacent market, the treadmill, with the Peloton Tread. In addition to its equipment and app, Peloton's range of products includes athletic clothing, shoes, and yoga and exercise accessories. As of June 2021, Peloton had 5.9 million members, including 2.3 million paid subscribers. It had annual revenue of $4.021 billion in 2021 (FY ending June 30), suffering a loss of $189 million.

Peloton Interactive launched its IPO on September 26, 2019 on NASDAQ at an offering price of $29 per share. However, the price tumbled to $27 on the first day; Peloton raised $1.16 billion, with the company being valued at $8.1 billion. The highest ever share price achieved by Peloton was $162.72 on December 24, 2020 at about the height of the COVID-19 pandemic, falling consistently since then to $7.24 on October 14, 2022 as the number of pandemic cases declined.

Peloton's declining performance led to several actions by the company. It laid off 2,800 employees globally in February 2022, and another 800 in July 2022, and began to outsource some positions and roles that were previously performed by company employees. Also in February 2022, John Foley, Peloton co-founder and CEO, stepped down from his position and took the role of Executive Chairman, eventually departing from the company in September 2022. In March 2022, Peloton adopted a rental business model under which customers would pay a one-time delivery fee plus a monthly equipment rental fee for the equipment and all workout classes. In August 2022, Peloton announced that it would start selling its equipment through amazon.com

Peloton had started out as a vertically integrated enterprise with the intention of keeping control over all its operations—manufacturing most of its equipment in its own manufacturing plant in Taiwan, shipping to customers through its own supply chain, and with delivery and installation by its own employees at customer locations. In July 2022, Peloton announced plans to stop in-house manufacturing and expand its current relationship with Rexon Industrial of Taiwan to manufacture all its equipment.

How Peloton Creates Value

Peloton's initial phenomenal success was based on strategies somewhat similar to those employed by other successful digital companies, such as Spotify and Netflix, and led partly be the COVID-19 pandemic that kept people mostly home.

First-mover advantages. While stationary bikes for homes had existed for decades and live exercise classes (such as those offered by SoulCycle) had also existed prior to Peloton, Peloton's innovation was to combine them and create an engaging user experience through digital streaming of live and on-demand content accessible at home anytime. In the process, Peloton disrupted the fitness industry, becoming an aspirational brand among home-workout aficionados. The company leveraged its first-mover status to build its brand, lock in customers before competition emerged, and benefit from economies of scale as its sales grew. It has also accumulated valuable knowledge related to customer needs and preferences, as well as product and process technology, which helps with product and service enhancements as well as better service for users.

The Peloton bike and treadmill are *experience goods* whose characteristics, such as features and quality, can be ascertained only after consumption or use (as compared to *search goods* whose characteristics can be ascertained prior to purchase). Hence the company's decision to open a storefront in a luxury mall in New Jersey in 2013 on a 4-month lease, where prospective customers could try out the product. This turned out to be one of the best 4 months for sales in Peloton's history. By now, the company has over 128 retail stores in the US, Canada, the UK, Australia, and Germany—102 in the US and Canada, 23 in the UK and Germany, and 3 in Australia.

Network effects. Peloton's performance benefits from network effects as more people purchase its equipment or the Peloton Digital app. Peloton attracts some of the most sought-after instructors by paying them more than they earned elsewhere, which in turn leads to more users signing up for membership. This attracts more elite instructors to Peloton, thus growing the network and creating more value for all participants. Also, with more people working out simultaneously, they develop a sense of camaraderie with each other. The social and community aspect helps with subscriber retention—92% after 1 year of membership and 80% after 3 years of membership.[18]

Technology. Technology is at the core of Peloton business, which enables the *connected* aspect of its connected fitness model. Peloton offers its members technologically advanced fitness products, immersive wellness content, and software to improve member experience and, thus, retention. The software analyzes millions of workouts every month to develop new software features and new wellness content.

The digital technologies employed by Peloton allow a user to connect to complementary apps (such as Fitbit and Apple Health), social networks (Facebook and Twitter), and devices such as heart rate monitors and smart watches. The company collects extensive user data, including class type, length, workout frequency, heart rate, taste in music, and social network engagement. Using AI and analytics, the company analyzes the data so collected to make personalized class recommendations, develop new products, and optimize its service offerings.[19]

Peloton equipment has sensors that collect resistance and revolutions-per-minute information and transmit it to the user's bike's (or treadmill's) touchscreen, where, along with other metrics, it shows the user's performance. In live-streamed classes, the performance is visible to the user as well as to other users taking the same class at the same time. The instructor can also see the data and even speak with individual remote users to comment on their performance or to make a suggestion in real time. For instance, a member in a yoga class at her home in San Francisco could get a shout-out or a birthday greeting from the instructor in New York. However, the ability of instructors to interact with individual users is possible only when the class has a few dozen users, not the hundreds or thousands of users typical for most live classes. (With over 10,000 members cycling together, Peloton set a Guinness World Record for the "largest live cycling class" in November 2017.)

Peloton offers curated music playlists to members via their own proprietary music platform that contains over 2 million songs. It is the largest audiovisual-connected fitness music catalog in the world.

Innovation. Peloton has been on *Fast Company* magazine's list of Most Innovative Companies since 2016 in one category or another. For instance, in 2021, it was #42 on *Fast Company's* list of the Most Innovative Companies and #1 on the list of the ten Most Innovative Wellness Companies in the world.[20] In its September 2019 IPO prospectus, Peloton declared itself as a full-fledged innovation company. So what makes Peloton an innovative company?

Many people buy treadmills and stationary bikes for their homes, but after an initial period of a few weeks, the equipment sometimes remains unused in the basement or garage. Others buy gym membership in January but may stop going there after the initial excitement dies down. Life gets in the way! Peloton management's innovation was to get people excited about owning an expensive bike or treadmill for their homes and then using it at their convenience, while remaining engaged with other users around the world and instructors. When offered access to live and on-demand streamed workouts, users can exercise without the constraints of time and place. Essentially, Peloton has been able to align people's lifestyles with technological fitness trends in a creative manner. Other elements of its business model, like compatibility with third-party devices, glamorous instructors, a proprietary music platform, and community all go to strengthen the company's bond with users. Peloton's R&D labs are based in Secaucus, NJ, and Taichung, Taiwan.

How Peloton Captures Value

Peloton captures value through multiple revenue streams—equipment sales, connected-fitness subscriptions, app (Peloton Digital) subscriptions, and accessory sales. In addition, Peloton charges $35 for members joining a live, filmed class at its New York City studio and £25 at the London studio. Peloton has experienced 100% revenue growth each year for the last 6 years, though it is still unprofitable. However, its losses declined from $915 million in FY2019 to $189 million in FY 2021.

Peloton employs a number of approaches to increase customers' willingness to pay, hence value-capture opportunities. These include in-home convenience, unlimited use by family members on the same subscription, elite instructors offering instruction in several health and wellness categories, creative programming, and community support. It has been able to create an engaged, global community of health and wellness enthusiasts. With literally millions of workouts each month, the company uses data analytics to create new wellness content and features to help improve member experience. Some of the programming involves goal-based challenges to keep members motivated. Programming to instill a competitive spirit among members has been shown (elsewhere[21]) to act as a top motivator to keep people exercising. Customers get locked-in to Peloton once they purchase a Peloton bike or treadmill; the high cost of the equipment could partly explain the company's high retention rates. Members may stop using the equipment after the initial excitement is over by ceasing to pay the monthly subscription fee, yet they may be unwilling to invest in a different brand.

Peloton's Global Strategy

First-mover strategy. Peloton has been the first mover in the digital fitness category. With entry into Canada, the UK, Germany, and Australia, Peloton has also been a first mover in these foreign markets, with many of the attendant first-mover advantages.

Localization. Like Spotify, Peloton's strategy for foreign markets includes most of the strategic elements they use for domestic business as well as some localization. For global markets, they develop local content. For example, their London studio has both British and German instructors.

Pricing also differs from country to country. For instance, Peloton membership in Canada costs C$55 per month (cheaper than in the US at the exchange rate of $1.00 = C$1.39 on October 16, 2022), whereas the Peloton Digital app costs C$16.99 per month. In the UK, membership costs £39 per month, and Digital Peloton app costs £12.99 per month, whereas in Germany membership costs €58 per month, and the app costs €12.99 per month. Membership costs in the UK and especially in Germany are higher than in the US.

As Peloton continues to expand abroad, it plans to offer classes in local languages as well as with subtitles for English-language programming. Music for foreign countries is typically licensed from local collecting societies representing publishers or directly from publishers.

Partnering. Like Spotify, Peloton also employs an artist- and publisher-centric partnering strategy for music. In addition, Peloton's partnership with Spotify and Apple Music allows members to play songs from their streaming service during workouts. And, because it is also a physical product, Peloton Interactive has numerous partnering arrangements with component suppliers, contract manufacturers, and logistics operators. For instance, its network of last-mile logistics operators is responsible for in-home delivery of Peloton equipment, setup, customer education, and ongoing in-home service.

The Globalization–Localization Dilemma

Companies competing internationally want to be both global and local—to have the reach and the power of a global company but also the flexibility to serve the needs of customers in individual foreign markets as a local company. According to Theodore Levitt, writing in the *Harvard Business Review* in 1983, "the world's needs and desires have been irrevocably homogenized. This makes the multinational corporation obsolete and the global corporation absolute."[22] This meant that companies could design and produce standardized products (because customers' needs and desires the world over were becoming essentially similar), produce them in one, two, or a few optimal locations to derive economies of scale, and export them worldwide.

Levitt was ahead of his time in 1983 to suggest that all business had become global business. Even in the twenty-first century, his prognostication does not quite hold for many products and services and is not even an important consideration for many digital products and smart machines. This is because for digital products and smart machines, it is *relatively* easy to customize a product to serve the needs of customers in local markets, even to personalize a product for individual customers. This is achieved by potentially changing some lines of code, producing different versions of the same product, and even using 3D printing for small-batch production of physical goods.

Using Levitt's terminology, being *global* means standardized products, economies of scale, greater efficiency, and the ability to access resources and value chains globally—for improved profitability—but offering little attention to the needs of customers in individual foreign markets. On the other hand, being *local* means that a firm can cater to the specific needs and desires of customers in each individual market, but at a much higher cost and lower profitability. To be both global and local is a key challenge for competing globally for businesses selling physical goods, digital goods, or smart machines. As discussed in the Netflix (Chapter 4), Spotify, and Peloton case studies, even companies selling digital goods and smart machines need to localize their offerings for different national markets.

Global Strategy for Digital Businesses

The Spotify and Peloton case studies illustrated that digital businesses compete worldwide—often as they do at home—with essentially the same strategies, namely, leveraging network effects, technology, and innovation. But competing in foreign markets requires a few additional strategies, including a first-mover or a fast-second strategy, localization, licensing and partnering, and intellectual property (IP) protection. It is not that such strategies are not needed in domestic markets; they assume much greater significance in foreign markets.

Network Effects

Network effects provide the foundation for strategy-making for digital products and smart machines and for both domestic and foreign markets. As the number of users of a product increases, its value to the users (and the business that makes the product or offers the service) increases exponentially. With zero marginal cost and network effects, a digital product's business can lead to a winner-take-all or winner-take-most market. Both Spotify and Peloton benefit from network effects.

Network effects are of two kinds—direct and indirect. A business (network) benefits from *direct* network effects when users of its products benefit from the existence of other users (of the network), as in the case of fax machines. A fax machine has no value if only one or two individuals own it; however, as the number of fax machine users increases, its value to them (and to fax machine manufacturers and telecommunications service providers) rises exponentially. The same is true for social media networks, such as Facebook. All such networks exhibit positive network externalities, meaning the larger the network, the greater the benefit to its users.

Indirect network effects arise in multisided markets whereby users in one side of the market (e.g., listeners in Spotify) benefit from the existence of users in another side of the market (e.g., artists). In the case of Google search, one set of users (the advertisers) benefits from the existence of another set of users (the searchers), and vice versa. This is true for many other two-sided platforms, such as Uber and Airbnb.

Network effects arise when products and users are connected to a network, for example, users of fax machines are connected to a telecommunications network. Network effects can be strengthened with the availability of complementary products and services. For example, the iPhone comes preinstalled with a number of products and services such as Apple Maps and weather, and thousands of third-party apps are available to iPhone users—all of which help strengthen the network effect in iPhones.

A business has weak network effects when its users can access other competitors easily, that is, has low switching costs. For example, a listener of music at Spotify can easily sign up for a competing music streaming service like Apple Music for about the same price. Both music services are undifferentiated, except for their music catalogs. Marketplaces with differentiated products (and higher switching costs) tend to have stronger and longer lasting network effects.

Technology and Innovation

Over the last two to three decades, technology has advanced at an increasing rate of change in multiple fields—IT, manufacturing and automation, life sciences, genetic engineering, renewable energy, materials, automotive, services, processes, and more. In particular, IT has seen the greatest advances in recent decades. There are many more advancements yet to come, most of which cannot even be visualized at this time. This is partly because information technologies are *general purpose* technologies that can be used in multiple industries in multiple ways. As suggested by Eric Brynjolfsson and Andrew McAfee in *The Second Machine Age*, today's IT is quantitatively and qualitatively different from its earlier heyday in that it is digital, exponential, and recombinant.[23] The progress of digital technologies has been exponential, as suggested by Moore's law and Metcalfe's law of network effects and by the declining cost of digital equipment and services. Digital innovation is recombinant in the sense that each innovation becomes a building block of future innovations. Innovations from multiple sources get connected and enhanced through networks and open innovation to create entirely new products and services which may or may not bear any semblance to the products/services from which they evolved. (For more on innovation and strategies to exploit innovation, such as the Build|Buy|Ally model, refer to Chapter 9.)

First Movers, Fast Seconds, and Imitators

The success or failure in a foreign market often depends on the timing of launching a product in the market—as a first mover, a late mover, a fast second, and even as an imitator. A first mover in a new market has many advantages, such as the opportunity to:

- ride down the learning curve ahead of late movers;
- educate customers about its new product;
- pre-empt the market and valuable resources (such as specialized talent) from being accessed by late movers;
- build reputation and brand equity;
- leverage network effects; and
- build buyer switching costs.

If multiple early movers are trying to get their versions of a given product become industry standard, a *first* mover has the potential to get a head start over others. The case of Apple's iPhone, a first mover in the smartphone category, comes to mind. Even though other smartphones (such as Blackberry) existed before the iPhone was introduced in 2007, it indeed created a new category of smartphones which led to a number of followers—fast seconds, late movers, and imitators—Samsung Galaxy, Huawei, Xiomi, and others. Samsung, in fact, has a larger sales volume than iPhone; the latter continues to be the most profitable product among all competing smartphone brands. Accounting for almost 52% of Apple's total revenue in 2021, the iPhone remains an aspirational brand for many smartphone owners.

First movers also face many disadvantages. The first mover must incur pioneering costs, such as the cost of ongoing R&D, educating customers, and building a distribution system for entirely new products. The first movers also face greater risk of failure since they may be unaware of the *rules of the game* in a new foreign market, risk piracy of their IP, and risk the latecomers taking a free ride on their pioneering investments. If the market does not develop as expected or if the first mover is not able to successfully leverage the opportunity, it may also suffer from a "lock in-lock out" effect. Foreign market investments are often major investments, which can be difficult, if not impossible, to reverse without much cost. As a result, the first mover may be locked into a market and thus locked out of other potential opportunities that arise later.

The disadvantages of the first mover are advantages for fast seconds, late movers, and imitators. Since the highest rate of product failures occurs during the product's introductory stage in a market, a prospective late mover can avoid investing in markets with little potential. It is also almost always cheaper to imitate than to innovate, due to the lower cost of R&D and educating customers and the opportunity to leverage an existing distribution system. If the technology is changing rapidly, an imitator or late mover has an advantage over the first mover because it can improve upon the first mover's technology. Finally, if the first mover is a small, entrepreneurial firm, an imitator or a late entrant with market power can sometimes control the market even if it lacked enough R&D expertise at the time of entering the market.

A fast-second strategy, distinct from a first-mover or a second-mover strategy, involves waiting for the market to start developing and then moving in to help develop it further. Like late movers, fast followers also benefit from the failures of the first movers and from the opportunities not explored by them. For example, Samsung and Huawei introduced their Android smartphones about 2 years after iPhone's launch at a much lower price point.

Imitating the products, capabilities, and strategies of successful first movers and innovators has, in fact, long been the rule, rather than an exception. According to Theodore Levitt,

> ...imitation is not only more abundant than innovation, but actually a much more prevalent road to business growth and profits... Imitation is not just something which even the biggest, best managed, most resourceful company will, by force of competitive circumstances, have to be involved in; it is something it will have to practice as a carefully developed strategy.[24]

The fact that Microsoft copied the early versions of its personal computer operating system, Windows, and its application software, Word, from other companies that had also been working on the same technologies is legendary. According to a 1991 *New York Times* article, competitors "have long complained that the rest of the industry has served as Microsoft's R&D lab."[25]

Steven Schnaars has documented the case studies of 28 innovative products, where the imitators surpassed the innovators and first movers over time.[26] Table 5.1 lists some of the examples he identified.

Localization

Localization involves making a product linguistically and culturally appropriate for the target market where it is to be sold and used—to meet the specific needs, tastes, and preferences of the customers there and to meet local regulatory requirements, if any. But a company that plans for localization should look beyond simply making a product linguistically and culturally appropriate for its target markets. It is actually a three-stage process: software localization (for digital products), localization of marketing strategy, and localization of the company's overall business strategy, that is, its business model.

Software localization. A previous section (*The Globalization-Localization Dilemma*) suggested that digital businesses can be both global and local relatively more easily than nondigital businesses as far as product formulation is concerned. Localizing a product for digital businesses typically involves changing some lines of software code. Well, it is not quite as simple as that and can indeed be rather complex. Software localization begins with *software internationalization*, defined as "the process of designing a software application so that it can be adapted to various languages and regions without engineering changes." This involves such things as alternative calendars, time zones, telephone number formats, systems of measurement, voltage, handling of personal names, and forms of address. *Software localization* "is the process of adapting internationalized software for a specific region or language by translating text and adding locale-specific

Table 5.1   A List of Products for Which the Imitators Surpassed the Pioneers

Product	Pioneers/First Movers	Imitator/Later Entrants
CAT scanners (computed axial tomography)	EMI (1972)	Pfizer (1974) Technicare (1975) General Electric (1976) Johnson & Johnson (1978)
Computerized ticketing service	Ticketron (1968)	Ticketmaster (1982)
Credit/charge cards	Diners Club (1950)	American Express (1958) Visa/MasterCard (1966)
Mainframe computers	Atanasoff's ABC Computer (1939) Eckert-Mauchly's ENIAC/UNIVAC (1946)	IBM (1953)
Operating system for personal computers	CP/M (1974)	MS-DOS by Microsoft (1981) Microsoft Windows (1985)
Personal computers	Apple II (1971) MITS Altair 8800 (1975) Radio Shack (1977)	IBM PC (1981) Compaq (1982) Dell (1984)
Spreadsheet software	VisiCalc (1979)	Lotus 1-2-3 (1983) Microsoft Excel (1985)
Word processing software	Wordstar (1979)	WordPerfect (1982) Microsoft Word (1983)

Source: Adapted from Steven P. Schnaars, *Managing Imitation Strategies: How Late Entrants Seize Markets from Pioneers*, New York: Free Press, 1994.

components."[27] Localization typically requires modification of user-visible components such as websites, promotional literature, interfaces, images, and documentation, among others.

In localizing for international markets, the software development process must address and incorporate these aspects in the initial stages. Awkward add-ons can cause problems later. For example, Cisco Systems experienced production stoppages, re-engineering, and increased cost to incorporate such changes after new applications and features had been released in Japan.[28]

Localization of marketing strategy. A company's *marketing strategy* or *marketing mix* refers to the famous 4 Ps of marketing: **P**roduct, **P**rice, **P**romotion, and **P**lace—the factors within a firm's control (as against factors outside its control such as demographics, government regulations, and weather).

The **P**roduct a company sells is the first element of its marketing strategy for any market, and a company selling abroad must decide whether to sell the same products overseas that it sells at home or to customize it for each foreign market. Spotify localizes its product (music) for different markets. Besides, as observed earlier, localizing a digital product for specific markets also requires software internationalization and software localization.

Price generally depends on the cost of production and delivery of the product, the level of economic development in a country, what the market will bear, and customers' willingness to pay, among other factors. For digital products, however, where the marginal cost of production and delivery is negligible, one cannot use the traditional pricing strategy. Pricing for digital products should ideally be based on the value customers place on the product. And, of course, different customers value a product differently based on its potential usefulness to them. For such products (including services), it is a viable strategy to use many versions of the product (*versioning*) and let customers choose the price they are willing to pay by selecting the version that best meets their needs. For example, Nuance Communications offers three versions of their speech recognition software—Dragon Home priced at $150, Dragon Professional Individual at $500, and Dragon Legal Individual at $500. They also offer Dragon Anywhere for use on mobile devices priced at $15 per month or $150 per year. However, to set the prices initially ($200/$500/$500), Nuance must have had to figure out the amount customers will be willing to pay for specific versions—based on the factors such as prices being charged by direct competitors and what the market will bear.

Promotion involves both paid advertising and publicity, the latter being promotion (such as a press release or sports sponsorship) that is presented by media free of cost because they think it is newsworthy. While many companies do both, research has shown that publicity often has a greater impact on consumers' buying choices than paid advertising. What is of special interest for us is the localization and contextualization of marketing and promotional materials: product labels, user manuals, warranty information, point-of-sale (P-O-S) materials, advertising, websites, apps, and so on.

Place refers to the distribution channels used by a company—the place where customers can get access to its products. Pure digital products are often sold on the internet, or bundled with other products (e.g., telecom services bundled with music), direct to customers. Smart machines can be sold direct to customers on the internet, as well as through regular retail channels and *partners*. For example, in the US, one can buy a smartphone directly from the manufacturer, retailers such as BestBuy, and telecom companies such as AT&T while subscribing to their bundle of services.

Localization of the business model. A company's business model is the essence of its strategy—how it creates and captures value. Business models for digital products range from freemium to subscription to platform business models, discussed in the next chapter.

Licensing and Partnering

Licensing and partnering (such as strategic alliances) were introduced in Chapter 4 as entry strategies for foreign markets. It was also suggested that licensing their technology to other companies is not advisable for companies for which IP is their core competence. This is true also for digital businesses selling their products directly to final customers because the IP owner can sell its products worldwide on its own without having to go through licensees or other intermediaries. However, companies do license their technologies to other companies for use as inputs into their own manufacturing processes, a key approach for competing in foreign markets. For example, Imagination Technologies, a British technology company, licenses its software to companies making smartphones and billions of other IoT devices worldwide. Imagination Technologies Group plc, headquartered in the UK, was acquired in 2017 by Canyon Bridge Capital Partners, a private equity firm based in Beijing and beneficially owned[29] by the Chinese government—a fact that creates other potential issues, though for licensees and not for licensors.

Strategic alliances and joint ventures (JVs)[30] are popular approaches for competing in foreign markets, often preferred by multinationals even more than mergers & acquisitions (M&As). Businesses enter into strategic alliances with other businesses to gain complementary assets, enter new markets, develop new technologies, or reduce risk of foreign market entry. International strategic alliances can be with competitors, companies from related industries, and even from

Table 5.2   Importance of Alliances within Your Corporate Strategy

	Importance of Alliances in Our Corporate Strategy (%)
Extremely important	56
Important	36
Somewhat important	6
Not important	2

Source: KPMG's 2016 CEO Outlook Survey, https://assets.kpmg/content/dam/kpmg/tr/pdf/2019/
01/strategic-alliances-toolkit.pdf

different industries. According to KPMG's 2016 CEO Outlook survey of 1,300 CEOs of major companies worldwide, over 90% of the respondents said that strategic alliances are an important or extremely important part of their overall strategy (Table 5.2).[31]

Such findings are not surprising in view of the speed of industry disruption and the challenges of developing technology in-house. In the autonomous automotive industry, licensing, strategic alliances, and JVs have become the norm over the last few years. Most large automotive manufacturers have opted to enter into partnerships with technology firms or acquire technology firms and startups, rather than develop technology in-house. Some examples follow.

Some acquisitions in the autonomous vehicle industry:

■ GM invested $3.45 billion in Cruise autonomous vehicle.
■ Ford invested 1 billion dollars in Argo AI, an AI company, as well as in Journey Holding Corporation, an intelligent transportation system software provider;
■ Daimler acquired majority stake in Torc Robotics to accelerate its autonomous truck development.

Volkswagen (VW) has entered into over a dozen partnerships with a diverse set of partners. These include alliances and JVs with competitors (e.g., Audi, Daimler, Ford, and Toyota), technology companies (Qualcomm, Microsoft, and Huawei), ride-hailing companies (DiDi), as well as companies from many other industries (such as Bosch). Ford has also licensed VW's MEB modular electric toolkit technology to design a new battery-electric vehicle for Europe. Initially, Ford planned to make over 600,000 MEB-based vehicles in Europe over a 6-year period starting in 2023, under license from VW. In March 2022, Ford announced that it will make two new battery-electric SUVs, not one, that will sit on VW's MEB platform. (For details of these and other acquisitions, licenses, and JVs, see several charts at https://medium.com/@firstmilevc/avlandscape-8a21491f1f54.)

IP Protection

If a company's IP is its core competence, protecting it in foreign markets where rules, regulations, and practices regarding IP protection are often different from one's home market becomes crucial. This is especially true for digital and many other businesses whose IP—patents, copyrights, trademarks, trade secrets, or simply employee knowledge—may be more valuable than any tangible assets. Risks to a company's IP include counterfeit products, theft of technology, data, and IP through cyber intrusion in a company's computer system, reverse engineering by competitors, and misuse of IP by licensees and JV partners. Some countries may require rights to technology, data, and IP of foreign companies in order for them to do business there. Here are some examples suggested by the US Securities and Exchange Commission about possible risks to its IP a company might face in foreign markets[32]:

- Patent license agreements pursuant to which a foreign licensee retains rights to improvements on the relevant technology, including the ability to sever such improvements and receive a separate patent, and the right to continued use of technology or IP after the patent or license term of use expires.
- Foreign ownership restrictions, such as JV requirements and foreign investment restrictions, that potentially compromise control over a company's technology and proprietary information.
- The use of unusual or idiosyncratic terms favoring foreign persons, including those associated with a foreign government, in technology license agreements, such as access and license provisions, as direct or indirect conditions to conducting business in the foreign jurisdiction.
- Regulatory requirements that restrict the ability of companies to conduct business, unless they agree to store data locally, use local services or technology in connection with their international operations, or comply with local licensing or administrative approvals that involve the sharing of IP.

The risks to a company's technology, data, and IP in both domestic and foreign markets are in fact limited only by the perpetrators' ingenuity. Protecting a company's technology, data, and IP in foreign markets is a complex and legal matter, beyond the scope of this book. The stopfakes. gov website of the US Department of Commerce offers much helpful information for American companies to protect and enforce their IP abroad.

Notes

1 See, for instance, "Every business is a digital business," August 8, 2017, https://knowledge.wharton.upenn.edu/article/every-business-digital-business/; https://www.forbes.com/sites/techonomy/2011/11/30/now-every-company-is-a-software-company/#1cb108aaf3b1.
2 Accenture Strategy, https://www.accenture.com/us-en/about/strategy-index.
3 Gartner, "Digital business is everyone's business," May 7, 2014. https://www.forbes.com/sites/gartnergroup/2014/05/07/digital-business-is-everyones-business/#585977df7f82.
4 Karel Dörner and David Edelman, "What digital really means," July 1, 2015. https://www.mckinsey.com/industries/technology-media-and-telecommunications/our-insights/what-digital-really-means.
5 I use the term "product" for both goods and services.
6 Salesforce, "What is digital transformation?" https://www.salesforce.com/products/platform/what-is-digital-transformation/.
7 Much of the statistics quoted in this case study was taken from Daniel Ruby, "Spotify stats 2022," September 16, 2022. https://www.demandsage.com/spotify-stats/#:~:text=Spotify%20has%2082%20Million%20songs%20on%20its%20platform%20as%20of%202022.
8 Mansoor Iqbal, "Spotify revenue and usage statistics (2022)," September 6, 2022. https://www.businessofapps.com/data/spotify-statistics/#3.
9 Spotify playlist, "Hazed and confused." https://open.spotify.com/playlist/0zmrPgFwsZYL4QEeHnWl0i.
10 Hugh McIntyre, "Spotify has acquired machine-learning startup Niland," May 18, 2018. https://www.forbes.com/sites/hughmcintyre/2017/05/18/spotify-has-acquired-machine-learning-startup-niland/#4f5c4f337929.

11 Murray Stassen, "Spotify has spent $1.2+ bn on companies to scale its non-music business over the past three years," August 11, 2022. https://www.musicbusinessworldwide.com/spotify-has-spent-1–2bn-on-companies-to-scale-its-non-music-business-over-the-past-3-years/.

12 Nicole Laporte, "The 10 most innovative media companies of 2022," March 8, 2022, *Fast Company*. https://www.fastcompany.com/90724442/most-innovative-companies-media-2022.

13 Fast Company, "The world's 50 most innovative companies in 2020." https://www.fastcompany.com/most-innovative-companies/2020.

14 See a photo of Spotify's billboard ad in *Wired* magazine's November 28, 2018 article, "Spotify's year-end ads highlight the weird and the wonderful." https://www.wired.com/story/spotify-2018-wrapped-ads-highlight-weird-wonderful/.

15 A fast-second strategy, distinct from a first-mover or a second-mover strategy, involves waiting for the market to start developing and then moving in quickly to help it further develop.

16 Spotify, "From Bollywood to Bhangra: Spotify launches in India," February 26, 2019. https://newsroom.spotify.com/2019-02-26/spotify-launches-in-india/.

17 Sovrn Blog, "How can publishers accelerate subscription growth through telco licensing," 2019. https://whatsnewinpublishing.com/opinion-how-can-publishers-accelerate-subscription-growth-through-telco-licensing/.

18 Peloton Investor and Analyst Day Presentation, September 15, 2020 (p66): https://investor.onepeloton.com/static-files/5155a9dc-1da8-4d6a-b232–3c231b8983b6.

19 Marco Iansiti and Karim R. Lakhani, *Competing in the Age of AI: Strategy and Leadership When Algorithms and Networks Run the World* (Boston, Harvard Business Review Press, 2020).

20 Fast Company, "The 10 most innovative wellness companies in the world," March 3, 2021. https://www.fastcompany.com/90600352/wellness-most-innovative-companies-2021.

21 Jingwen Zhang, Devon Brackbill, Sijia Yang, Joshua Becker, Natalie Herbert, and Damon Centola, "Support or competition? How online social networks increase physical activity: A randomized controlled trial," December 2016. https://www.sciencedirect.com/science/article/pii/S2211335516300936?via%3Dihub.

22 Theodore Levitt, "The Globalization of Markets," *Harvard Business Review*, May-June 1983, pp. 92–102.

23 Eric Brynjolfsson and Andrew McAfee, *The Second Machine Age* (New York: W.W. Norton & Co., 2014).

24 Theodore Levitt, "Innovative Imitation," *Harvard Business Review*, September 1966.

25 Andrew Pollack, "One Day, Junior Got Too Big," *The New York Times*, August 4, 1991.

26 Steven P. Schnaars, *Managing Imitation Strategies: How Late Entrants Seize Markets from Pioneers*. New York: Free Press, 1994. See also Oded Shenkar, *Copycats: How Smart Companies Use Imitation to Gain a Strategic Edge* (Boston, MA: Harvard Business School Publishing, 2010).

27 Wikipedia, "Internationalization and localization." https://en.wikipedia.org/wiki/Internationalization_and_localization.

28 Padmaja Ravikumar, "Localization: 6 tips for success," January 7, 2019. https://blogs.cisco.com/ciscoit/localization-6-tips-for-success.

29 According to Wikipedia, "beneficial ownership is a term in domestic and international commercial law which refers to the natural person or persons 'who ultimately own or control a legal entity or arrangement, such as a company, a trust, or a foundation'."

30 A joint venture, as discussed in Chapter 4, involves two or more companies investing resources to set up a new legal entity in the home or host market. A strategic alliance, on the other hand, does not lead to the formation of a new legal entity, with the alliance partners remaining independent enterprises. They may share some corporate resources in the pursuit of a common goal, like developing new technology or strengthening a specific skill.

31 KPMG, "Strategic alliances: A real alternative to M&A?" https://assets.kpmg/content/dam/kpmg/tr/pdf/2019/01/strategic-alliances-toolkit.pdf.

32 SEC, "Intellectual property and technology risks associated with international business operations," December 19, 2019. https://www.sec.gov/corpfin/risks-technology-intellectual-property-international-business-operations.

Chapter 6

Digital Business Models

Data is the new oil.

Clive Humby, 2006

A *business model* describes how a company expects to create and capture value through its strategy. It's a core strategic choice every company must make: decide the specific customer problem it is attempting to solve (value creation) for which customers are willing to pay a price (value capture). Like businesses, business models have existed practically for ever. A company (or an individual) would use certain inputs to produce an output which it would then sell to customers for a profit; that's its business model. What makes a business model *digital* is the use of digital technologies to create and capture value. Business models that used to be based on human effort and human ingenuity now also require computers, networks, the internet, data and analytics, and artificial intelligence to help make decisions in real time, 24×7.

A company's *operating model*, on the other hand, describes the specific activities that enable the creation and delivery of its goods and services to customers. Marco Iansiti and Karim Lakhani, in their eminently readable book, *Competing in the Age of AI*, suggest that

> Operating models can be very complex, frequently including the activities of thousands of people, sophisticated technology, important capital investments, and millions of lines of code that make up the operational systems and processes that enable a company to achieve its goals.[1]

One could think of a company's business model as *theory* and its operating model as *practice*. Both are needed for strategy to achieve the company's goals.

There are perhaps as many business models as there are businesses (which sometimes tweak existing business models to serve their specific needs). Many digital business models originated in the physical world. In their book, *The Business Model Navigator*, authors Oliver Gassmann, Karolin Frankenberger, and Michaela Choudury have identified some 60 business models. These include models in both physical and digital worlds, and some are slightly altered versions of each other.[2] The following sections discuss some of the more prominent digital business models in use today by both traditional and digital businesses.

DOI: 10.4324/9781003037446-8

Direct Selling

Many businesses, both physical and digital, sell their products and services directly to consumers—through their website or company retail store (rather than through intermediaries, a different business model). One can buy, for example, the Apple iPhone 13 directly from Apple.com or from one of Apple's physical stores. (Buying an iPhone from independent retailers like BestBuy and wireless service providers like Verizon involves an intermediary and is not direct selling). Similarly, Warby Parker, the maker of prescription eyeglasses, sells its products directly to consumers—online and through its own stores. This is the meaning of direct selling implied here, not selling methods such as party plan, person-to-person selling, or multi-level marketing.

Direct selling also includes selling approaches like licensing, renting (leasing) instead of buying, digital add-on, and the like. Many companies offer customers the use of products on an annual license basis. For instance, one can license Microsoft Office 365 software directly from Microsoft.com, and EverWebinar software from the webinar marketing-software company, Genesis Digital, on an annual license. This is quite similar to the **subscription** business model, discussed later in this section, which is also a form of direct selling.

Rent (or lease) instead of buy. Many manufacturers offer rental and lease plans for their equipment directly to customers. These plans enable customers to use costly equipment without tying up capital. The Rexroth subsidiary of Germany's Bosch Group (Boschrexroth.com), for instance, offers some of its equipment, such as hydraulic power devices, integrated with Industrial Internet of Things (IIoT) features and services on rent, lease, and direct sale. Sensors integrated into the IIoT devices provide continuous information regarding the filter, oil, and drive status. Such information, including operating statuses and forthcoming maintenance work to predictive maintenance analyses, is available to users via Rexroth's Online Diagnostics Network (ODiN). Many of these features are offered by Rexroth as **add-ons** to their standard equipment or on a **pay-per-use** basis.[3] (See Box 6.1 for distinction between Internet of Things [IoT] and IIoT.)

BOX 6.1   IIoT VS. IoT

What is the difference between Industrial Internet of Things (IIoT) and Internet of Things (IoT)? The IIoT typically refers to connected devices and machines in high-stakes industries like oil and gas, power generation, building and construction, and healthcare where unplanned downtime can be very costly or even life-threatening. In the IIoT world, machines and systems are designed to operate semi-independently with minimal human intervention—intelligently responding in real time to changes based on information received—thus reducing the cost and risk of human error. The IIoT enables remote monitoring of equipment, predictive analysis and maintenance, and automation of a machine's performance. The *Internet of Things* (IoT), on the other hand, tends to apply to consumer industries such as smart home appliances, smartphones, and heart-monitoring fitness bands. The IoT devices have similar characteristics but do not generally create emergency situations if downtime occurs. The IoT are typically employed in business to consumer (B2C) situations, whereas the IIoT devices operate in the business-to-business (B2B) world. The worldwide market for IIoT devices is estimated to grow from $89.3 billion in 2022 to $110.6 billion by 2025.[4] And the worldwide market for IoT devices (including IIoT) is projected to grow from $441 billion in 2021 to $677.4 billion by 2025.[5] (One can think of IIoT as a subset of IoT).

Digital add-on. We are all familiar with automobile purchases, where the dealer offers several add-ons such as a technology package, an infotainment package, or navigation. Digital add-ons are enhancements to standard software suites offered by digital-product companies, made popular by video game companies offering avatars and advanced gaming levels, generally for a fee. The enterprise management software company, SAP, offers its standard software suite at a moderate price, as well as digital add-on features like CRM (customer relationship management), plug-ins, customer-specific development projects, and even third-party add-ons certified by SAP at an additional fee. Some of the add-on features, such as for accounting, sales, and purchasing, tend to be industry specific and help improve the management of these functions in client organizations. With hundreds of possible add-ons, this is a major revenue-earning source for SAP, gaming, and other digital-product companies. Refer to Wikipedia for a complete list of SAP's add-ons; industry software and infrastructure add-ons are additional.[6] Here is a short list of SAP's software add-ons.

- SAP Advanced Planner and Optimizer
- SAP Analytics Cloud
- SAP Advanced Business Application Programming (ABAP)
- SAP Business One
- SAP Business Partner Screening
- SAP Portal (EP)
- SAP Extended Warehouse Management (EWM)

Subscription

Companies in both physical and digital worlds have been *selling* their products and services for a long time on a monthly or annual subscription. In addition to *The New York Times*, Netflix, Spotify, and HelloFresh, one can subscribe to an astonishing array of products and services. Some of the more unusual examples of the use of subscription model include: Panera Bread Unlimited Sip Club (with a subscription price of $11.99 per month, a customer can get unlimited drinks, coffee, tea, soda, etc.), Rent the Runway (rents up to eight designer clothes monthly at a subscription price of $144 per month), Magic Stream (offers unlimited access to its video library of magic tricks and skills to budding and experienced magicians at $9.99 per month), Surf Air of California (offers members unlimited flights on scheduled flights for $2,999 per month; other subscription plans start at $199 per month), and the Tony Robbins Platinum Program (first year membership subscription is $85,000). With the low-cost availability of the cloud, almost any product or service can be offered on subscription in a virtual manner (through the internet).

Companies offering their products or services on subscription are assured of recurring, predictable revenue for the duration of the subscription, while customers benefit from not having to tie up capital for products they need and be assured of automatic supplies replenishment, and product updates, generally without any additional cost. The subscription model also helps create deeper customer engagement, compared to direct selling, and provides the company with data on customer behavior and purchase patterns that it can use to improve its offerings or monetize in some other manner (see *data monetization* business model later in this chapter).

The key idea here is customers' increasing preference for *access* over *ownership*, a situation we have met before—with Netflix offering customers access to thousands of movies and Spotify offering access to tens of millions of songs to listeners without expecting them to buy even a single DVD or song. While technology has enabled such changes in business thinking and consumer behavior, it's the economics and psychology of buying goods and services that have been the true torchbearers of this trend. The trend coincides with the growing role of intangibles and services in the economies of most countries. Services, for example, now account for up to 80% of many developed countries' annual gross domestic product (GDP).

Some of the more common applications of the subscription business model, especially for industrial products, are Product-as-a-Service (PaaS), Software-as-a-Service (SaaS), and Infrastructure-as-a-Service (IaaS), though its potential applications are limited only by the ingenuity of the business looking for new ways to monetize its products and services.

Product-as-a-Service (PaaS): Companies that sell physical and IoT products are increasingly adding services to their products and moving away from one-time sale to *servitizing* their products (selling outcome-based services). The practice is also called *product servitization*. Under PaaS, the product is expected to perform without any quality problems since the manufacturer is paid for the service the product offers, not the product per se. This is essentially a ***payment-by-results*** (or ***outcome-based***) business model. Besides, under PaaS, companies typically add updates to their products over time without an increase in cost to the customer. If it were a sale, the customer would need to purchase a new product every time the company issued an update or pay for the update, not so with the PaaS model. Sensors, data analytics, and cloud computing have turned products into IoT devices, thus enabling a broad adoption of the PaaS subscription model by industrial product manufacturers.

The term PaaS also refers to *platform-as-a-service* (PaaS) business model. For instance, Amazon Web Services (AWS), in addition to offering infrastructure services, is effectively a platform with tens of thousands of partners (independent software vendors and systems integrators) who adapt their technologies to work on AWS for their own customers. Thus, AWS uses the PaaS business model.

From the customers' perspective, no capital investment is necessary and yet they benefit from error-free equipment performance. The risk inherent in any major capital investment passes from customer to the supplier. Equipment manufacturers used to view after-sales service of their equipment as a revenue opportunity, but under PaaS, they forego the additional revenue they could earn from servicing. They must offer guaranteed error-free service of the equipment to customers. But by absorbing the risk, they also expand their customer base.

Rolls-Royce, the storied manufacturer of jet engines, sells the hours an engine is actually flying the airplane rather than selling the jet engine itself. This allows the customer (the airline) to transfer the risk of a costly purchase to Rolls-Royce. Under its *TotalCare®* offering, Rolls-Royce charges its customers for the hours of defect-free use of the jet engines that Rolls-Royce owns, maintains, and repairs. Rolls-Royce is able to do so through sensors embedded in the engines that allow the company to continuously monitor engine performance, predict any failures, and make adjustments or repairs as needed.

Under its *Care by Volvo* program, Volvo offers most car models on subscription, an alternative to buying or leasing a new car—without the hassle of buying or leasing the car at a dealership, down payment, long-term lease contract, cost of factory scheduled maintenance, roadside assistance, tire and wheel protection, and insurance. All these are included; the customer just pays a monthly subscription fee for use of the car. The subscription is cancelable by the customer after 5 months in most US states. Several luxury car makers offer subscription programs, including Audi Select, Porsche Drive, Lexus One, and Jaguar Land Rover Pivotal. Many other companies along the automotive supply chain now play in this space (Table 6.1).

Software-as-a-Service (SaaS): For software companies, the SaaS subscription model is the most common means of doing business. Adobe and Microsoft used to sell their software, but

Table 6.1 Players in the Automotive Subscription Market

Category	Types	Examples		
OEMs	OEMs	Audi on Demand Lexus One	Care by Volvo Lynk & Co	Hyundai Porsche Drive
Traditional Downstream Entities	Dealerships	Small independent shops and large dealership networks		
	Rental	HertzMyCar	Sixt+	Subscribe with Enterprise
	Leasing	ALD Automotive	Athlon	LeasePlan
Mobility Platforms & Startups	Platforms	AutoScout2	MeinAuto.de	
	Startups	Bipi	Cluno[a]	Drover[a], Fair, Finn.auto

[a] Acquired by Cazoo in February 2021 (Cluno) and December 2020 (Drover).
Source: Adapted from https://www.bcg.com/publications/2021/how-car-subscriptions-impact-auto-sales?utm_medium=Email&utm_source=esp&utm_campaign=&utm_description=&utm_topic=&utm_geo=&utm_content=&utm_usertoken=07e3f3533a28feda5485c70bcdbaf33bf8602419.

now require users to subscribe to the software on a monthly subscription. Dropbox, MailChimp, Slack, Salesforce, HubSpot, Google Workspace, and hundreds of other software companies offer their software on subscription. They host their software applications in the cloud and make them accessible to users through an internet-enabled device such as a smartphone, a laptop, or a desktop. According to Gartner, more than 90% of software companies will have adopted the subscription business model by 2022.[7]

Infrastructure-as-a-Service (IaaS): Infrastructure-as-a-service is an instant cloud computing resource available to companies that need computing, network, and storage resources without requiring them to invest in the infrastructure. With each resource offered as a separate service component, the client of the IaaS provider pays only for what it needs when it needs, a *pay-as-you-go* model. The IaaS provider manages the underlying cloud infrastructure located in a private or public data center. Several companies (including Amazon AWS, IBM Cloud, Microsoft Azure, and VMWare) offer IaaS services to thousands of their clients.

Free offering. Companies like Google and Baidu offer their search services free of cost to users; they make money through advertising by selling access to users to advertisers. The real innovation here is innovation in pricing—changing the payer from users to service providers. (Refer to "pricing innovation," Chapter 7.)

Freemium

The word Freemium is a blend of two words, *free* and *premium*, just like smog is the blend of *smoke* and *fog*. It's a business model whereby the seller offers a basic version of its product to customers for free but charges a price for enhanced (premium) product features. Thousands of companies have used the freemium business model to build initial demand for their offering. It makes sense especially for digital-product companies because the marginal cost of production and distribution of digital products is effectively zero. It also makes sense for makers of *experience goods* where a customer cannot determine the quality and value of a product without first trying it out. Besides, the word *free* helps remove any mental reservation a customer may have before purchasing a product. The key issue with using the freemium model is that it might be difficult to convert freemium customers into paying customers later on.

Dropbox, a cloud file storage and sharing business launched in 2008, currently has over 700 million users, of which 15.48 million were paid subscribers as of 2020. Anyone can sign up for free storage of up to 2 GB, but if they need larger storage, they need to sign up for the premium Pro Plan for 2 TB of storage space at $9.99 per month for a single user. Dropbox is a great example of an experience good. In the words of Dropbox CEO Drew Houston, "The fact was that Dropbox was offering a product that people didn't know they needed until they tried."[8]

Note that the freemium model is not the same as the *free trial* plan that some businesses offer to prospective customers. The free trial plan typically offers prospective customers access to the full product range, but for a limited period of time, after which the free trial ends and they can subscribe to or purchase the product to continue using it. The Hulu video streaming service is a good example of a company that offers a free plan to prospective subscribers. Under its free plan, Hulu allows anyone to watch movies and other shows from the current and past seasons free for 1 month, after which Hulu subscription costs $14.99 per month for ad-free viewing. (Netflix also used to offer free trial but stopped doing so in October 2020).

Outcome Based

A previous section mentioned the outcome-based business model in the case of Rolls-Royce jet engines, where the customer pays only for the results (hours of defect-free use of the jet engines) achieved, not for the product. The growth of Internet of Things, cloud computing, and data analytics is driving the move toward outcome-based business models, leading to gains for both the manufacturers of IoT devices and customers. In fact, many B2B companies now use the outcome-based pricing model, for their IoT (IIoT) devices, to improve customer outcomes and enhance revenue opportunities. Even IT services firms, such as Wipro, which typically bill clients based on time and materials (T&M) needed for an assignment, are increasingly moving toward outcome-based business models.[9]

Xerox, the print and digital equipment and services company, now offers its customers a *Xerox® All In Plan* that includes the printer, with a 36-month lease, a fully inclusive maintenance agreement, and automatic supplies replenishment. The customer pays a monthly invoice (starting at $59 for small businesses), fixed for the duration of the contract, irrespective of what they print (print volume limited by the printer model selected).

Kaeser Kompressoren of Germany is a 100-year-old, leading manufacturer of compressed air products used in dozens of industries to transfer energy in industrial processes, for example, to operate power tools and propel vehicles. In addition to selling its equipment, Kaeser now also offers it on subscription. With its *SIGMA AIR UTILITY* (outcome-based) contracting model, Kaeser offers customers guaranteed and uninterrupted compressed air as and when needed—with the customers paying only for the compressed air actually used. Kaeser owns, installs, and maintains the equipment at customer premises, thus assuming the risk that typically accompanies equipment ownership. Through sensors embedded in its equipment, Kaeser monitors its compressed air stations around the clock and services them before a fault can occur. The sensors provide data and insights on customers' usage patterns, thus allowing Kaeser to plan preventive maintenance of its equipment and offer enhanced customer service. Servicing its equipment used to generate additional revenues for Kaeser, but under the *SIGMA AIR UTILITY* subscription model, it has become a cost for the company—an interesting swap that benefits the customer.[10]

The outcome-based business model is not really a new business model. India's largest telecom operator in the early 2000s, Bharti-Airtel, entered into a $2 billion, 10-year agreement with IBM Global Business Services to supply, install, and manage Bharti's end-to-end IT infrastructure as well as a wide range of customer-facing and back-office processes. In addition, Bharti negotiated deals with Ericsson, Nokia, and Siemens to obtain network capacity and a full range of managed services, including network design, optimization, operation, and field maintenance. Payment for network capacity to the vendors was to be made only when the capacity was actually used by Bharti's customers.[11] (Bharti, now the second largest telecom operator in India and the second largest in the world, operates across Asia and Africa in 18 countries with 491 million subscribers, of which 326 million are in India, as of FY 2022).

Google's ***pay-per-click*** and the ***pay-per-use*** models are effectively outcome-based business models. In a pay-per-use situation, the advertiser pays for the product or service used, billed based on the number of times or duration of use. In the case of Google's pay-per-click model, the advertiser is billed based on the number of clicks an internet ad generates. The pay-per-use model is used in both B2C and B2B situations. For IoT (IIoT) devices, the sensors embedded in the products monitor usage such that the company can bill its customers based on the actual use of the devices. For instance, AWS bills clients for the service (such as data storage, computer power, and content delivery) used and the duration of its use; this is somewhat similar to what we pay for utilities like electricity and water. Similarly, Michelin Tires charges truck owners for the miles driven by installing GPS devices on trucks.

Razor and Blade

The Razor and Blade is an age-old business model traditionally used by consumer product companies, including Gillette razors and blades and Keurig coffee machines and K-Cup Pods. The idea is to sell the basic product (the razor or the coffee machine) at a low price, even below-cost, and then charge a high price for accessories and replenishment supplies (shaving blades or coffee pods). With the addition of sensors and software, IoT device companies now offer automatic replenishment of supplies. Hewlett-Packard has followed this model for their inkjet printers for a long time, pricing the printers relatively low, and then charging a high price for replacement ink cartridges. Their newer model (such as the HP OfficeJet 9020 All-in-One Wireless Printer), a connected printer priced at about $350, comes with an offer of automatic ink-cartridge replacement through its subsidiary instantink.com. Automatic ink-cartridge replacement costs $11.99 per month (for 300 pages printed per month) and $24.99 per month (for 700 pages printed per month).

The SAP example discussed above also fits the Razor and Blade framework. The enterprise management software company, SAP, sells its standard software suite at a moderate price and offers hundreds of digital add-ons—an important revenue-earning opportunity for the company.

An advantage of using the Razor and Blade model is that customers can purchase the product at low upfront cost and then decide whether it fits their needs. Also, low cost can encourage customers to try the product without much risk. The company that successfully uses the model is assured of recurring revenues, which, in some cases, can even exceed the original price of the product manyfold, such as for SAP. However, there is always a risk of competing firms selling replenishment parts and consumables at a lower price than the original company; it's always a possibility if customers cannot be locked-in to the original product they purchased. For instance, HP printers now have a *cartridge protection* chip that does not allow customers to use refilled ink or non-HP cartridges on their HP printers.

Data Monetization

The chapter began with the quote, "data is the new oil." Like crude oil, raw data is not quite usable in and of itself; it must be refined and analyzed before it becomes valuable to a user. However, oil causes environmental pollution, while data also has a dark side as recently highlighted by the actions of social media companies like Facebook (new name, Meta) and must be managed. That's where the analogy ends. In fact, data is much more valuable than oil. Unlike oil, data is a *renewable resource*.[12] And, data has all the characteristics of digital goods, as discussed earlier (Chapter 3)— zero marginal cost, non-rivalry, network effects, no need for inventory, and customizability. While it may be costly to produce a first set of data about a certain phenomenon, it costs little or nothing to make and deliver digital copies of the same. The same set of data can be used by as many people and organizations as desired, generally at no additional cost to the customer. Data also exhibits network effects, meaning the value of data (to the users and to the owner) increases as the number of users increases. Data cannot be used up and does not degrade over time as more copies of the same are produced (though it can become obsolete) and, unlike oil, does not need to be stocked in a firm's inventory. Finally, it is possible to customize a set of data for different applications relatively easily.

A most valuable characteristic of data, deriving from the principles shown above, is that it can be monetized by its owners. Data monetization helps companies derive monetary value from data and data-driven process improvements. Most companies collect data from their customers— some much more than others—which can potentially be used to cut costs, improve performance, increase revenue, and even create new service offerings. Some companies, such as major retail chains, social media platforms, and IoT (IIoT) device manufacturers collect massive amounts of data (Big Data) from customers in the normal course of their business operations, which they use in multiple ways. Many retailers have loyalty cards which are scanned at checkout, thus helping them track customer purchases. They can then send appropriate coupons or other promotional offers to the customers. Retailers like Target and Walmart, which do not have loyalty cards, track individual customer purchases through the credit cards they use by assigning a unique code to each card. At Target, these are called *Guest ID* numbers. According to Andrew Pole, Target's Director of Guest Data, in *The New York Times* of February 19, 2012:

> If you use a credit card or a coupon, or fill out a survey, or mail in a refund, or call the customer help line, or open an email we have sent you or visit our Website, we will record it and link it to your Guest ID.[13]

Platforms like Spotify and Netflix make personalized recommendations to their users—recommendations based on the data they collect continually from them. Spotify's *Daily Mix* playlists are personalized for individual listeners, even for Free listeners, globally, and the playlists evolve over time as individual listening tastes evolve. Spotify's algorithms create the playlists based on each listener's listening habits, preferred artists and genres, and the decades they listen to most, even excluding songs from a listener's playlist that the listener fast-forwarded within the first 30 seconds. All of these help retain listeners to the Spotify platform. Netflix also uses personalization to make recommendations to viewers based on their viewing history. Netflix claims that its recommendation engine saves it a billion dollars each year by helping keep subscribers on the platform (getting new subscribers is very expensive).[14]

Google, LinkedIn, Facebook, and other social media platforms are essentially tools for collecting data that they leverage in the conduct of their business and *sell* to advertisers. Google Search, for instance, is Google's search engine that responds to over 8.5 billion searches per day.[15] Anyone can search for information on google.com without paying a penny to the company. Google then lets advertisers target specific groups of people by bidding on individual ads. Along with Search and other Google services like Gmail and Google Maps, Google builds profiles of people based on what they are searching and their demographic data (such as name, location, language, email address, telephone number, services used, search queries, AdWords clicked, device used, and even credit card information if entered by the user). When Google claims that they are not selling your data, it will perhaps be more accurate to say that they are selling *you*.[16] Online advertising at google.com and other Google websites contributed almost 82% of Google's $256.73 billion revenues in 2021.[17]

A key advantage of IoT (IIoT) devices is that, through the sensors embedded in them, they generate massive amounts of data the company can use in many ways (including data monetization). Rolls-Royce, for instance, uses data on engine performance that it gathers continually to plan maintenance and repair activities proactively to minimize disruption, thus adding to its bottom line and providing error-free service to its customers.

In 2017, Telefónica, the multinational telecom company headquartered in Madrid, Spain, acquired Statiq, a British geolocation data startup. Statiq collects and processes large amounts of data to identify the places people visit and builds consumer profiles. With access to such consumer profiles, Telefónica can better target its promotional messages to specific users.

Sometimes, companies with massive amounts of data sell anonymized and aggregated data to third parties, called ***data-as-a-service*** or ***data syndication***, who then mine it for business insights for their own decision making. A telecom company, for instance, could sell customer geolocation data to local governments for, say, better traffic management.

A 2017 McKinsey & Co. global survey[18] of 530 C-level executives and senior managers representing the full range of regions, industries, and company sizes, *Fueling Growth Through Data Monetization*, found that data monetization was relatively new in most industries at the time of the survey. The survey also found that more than half of the respondents in basic materials, energy, financial services, and high tech said that their companies already had data monetization programs within their companies. High-performing companies are already monetizing their data and doing so in many ways, such as adding new services to existing offerings and developing entirely new business models. High-performing companies are also three times more likely (17%) than others (5%) to say that their monetization efforts contributed over 20% to company revenues. (High performers had annual growth rate of over 10% over the past 3 years).

Platform

Platforms are intermediaries that connect and facilitate interactions between two or more sets of users, such as sellers and buyers or producers and consumers. Some prominent examples are Amazon, Facebook, Google, and Uber. Platforms have almost always existed. For example, marketplaces such as *bazaars* and *suqs* have been around for thousands of years. It's just that the term *platform* in its current usage refers to a digital intermediary—a digital marketplace—that facilitates not only interactions between different sets of users but also business transactions between them, such as accepting payment for products or services bought and sold on the platform. While the (physical) marketplaces have many inbuilt inefficiencies, platforms help resolve such inefficiencies with digital technologies.

For example, writing about inefficiencies in the bazaar in a small town in Morocco in the 1970s, anthropologist Clifford Geertz says,

> ... in the bazaar information is poor, scarce. maldistributed. inefficiently communicated. and intensely valued... The level of ignorance about everything from product quality and going prices to market possibilities and production costs is very high. and much of the way in which the bazaar functions can be interpreted as an attempt to reduce such ignorance for someone, increase it for someone, or defend someone against it.[19]

This is a decent description of the bazaar in the pre-digital era, even though for a small town in a less developed country. What successful platforms do is to help remove such inefficiencies in everyday business transactions with the help of digital technologies. For instance, information about goods and prices is instantly available to all market participants in a platform such as Amazon.

One of the earliest examples of a (digital) platform for industrial products was FreeMarkets, Inc., founded in Pittsburgh, PA, in 1995. The company created online B2B (reverse) auctions for industrial raw materials, parts, and services. Companies needing certain supplies or services would post their requirements at freemarkets.com and suppliers of such products and services from anywhere in the world could bid to supply them. For example, let's say a company wanted to purchase a certain quantity and quality of steel, and their requirement was posted at freemarkets.com at 8:00 a.m. on a certain day. Sellers of steel could bid for this requirement from almost anywhere in the world. Hypothetically, the first bid comes in at ten million dollars. By the time the auction closed at, say, 1:30 p.m. the same day, the accepted bid might be for six or seven million dollars. By year 2000, FreeMarkets had hosted over 5,000 auctions, in which 5,600 suppliers from 50 countries had participated. During its heyday, some 30 languages were spoken at FreeMarkets. The company was acquired by Ariba of the US in June 2004 for $493 million, which itself was acquired by SAP SE of Germany in 2012 for $4.3 billion. Today, the SAP Business Network (formerly known as the Ariba Network) is the world's largest internet-based trading platform serving millions of companies from 190 countries that did more than 699 million B2B transactions worth $4.1 trillion in a recent 12-month period.[20] It's a broad-based platform for most business-to-business transactions, including e-procurement, e-invoicing, and working capital management, among many other functions.

Most of the world's most valuable companies (such as Apple, Microsoft, Alphabet, Facebook, and Alibaba) run on the platform business model. They create value by enabling interactions between one set of users with another set of users, capturing value by charging them fees for making the connections and providing them services. This is different from how product (non-platform) businesses create and capture value; they do so by offering a product or service that customers need and charging a price for that. Product businesses own their inventory that gets included on their balance sheets. Platform businesses do not own the inventory of goods and services being sold on the platform. Many platform businesses started out as product businesses that later transitioned to the platform model. Apple, for instance, started out making computers, software, and games and became a platform only after it launched iTunes in 2001. On iTunes, one can purchase music, movies, apps, games, and many other third-party products and services.

A platform is a digital business, even though its participants could be buying or selling physical products and services. As such, the platform model benefits from all five characteristics of digital products (Chapter 3): network effects, zero marginal cost of production and distribution, non-rivalry, no need for inventory, and customizability. Platforms generate huge amounts of data (Big Data) about participants, their choices, prices charged, payments, and more, which is also a source for capturing value. These are the key reasons why platform businesses tend to have powerful competitive advantage, can scale up significantly, and show excellent financial results. Despite the substantial benefits digital businesses enjoy inherently, a platform business model is very difficult to implement and scale, which is why so many platforms languish. Three key challenges that all platforms face are critical mass, disintermediation, and multi-homing.

Critical mass. Network effects are a most important benefit of the platform business model; the larger the network, the greater the network effect and hence greater its benefit to the owners and users of the network. A larger network attracts new users more easily than a smaller network does. It's obvious that a two-sided platform must have a *critical mass* of users on both sides to kick in network effects. A B2C sales platform, for instance, must have a large number of buyers looking to buy things in order to attract a sufficient number of sellers, and vice-versa; this is the age-old chicken-or-egg problem. Inability to resolve the problem is why many platforms fail to take off.

Direct and indirect network effects in platform businesses: *Direct network effect* applies when an increase in one side of the user base leads to an increase in the other side of the user base. For instance, when Spotify adds a new artist to its network, it encourages more listeners to sign up for Spotify, which, in turn, encourages more artists to sign up on Spotify (a direct network effect). But adding a new artist to the Spotify network does not benefit other artists on the network. In fact, it might decrease opportunities for existing artists. The addition of a new artist on Spotify, however, does benefit the other artists—although *indirectly*—by making Spotify more attractive overall to both artists and listeners (an indirect network effect).

Disintermediation. Disintermediation occurs when users of a platform, on either side, bypass it to connect directly with the other side—after making the first connection through the platform. Angi.com (formerly Angie's List), for instance, is an American internet service that connects local businesses and contractors to customers needing such services. However, once a customer has a good experience with a contractor, they may go directly to the contractor for future jobs, bypassing angi.com.

Multi-homing. Multi-homing occurs when users on either side participate in multiple platforms offering similar services. For instance, in the US, riders on Uber often sign up also with Lyft, and many drivers drive for both Uber and Lyft. When this happens, it will be difficult for the platform to become profitable. Companies using the platform business model use a variety of approaches to resolve these challenges.

For more on platforms, refer to the excellent 2016 book, *Matchmakers: The New Economics of Multisided Platforms*, by David Evans and Richard Schmalensee (Harvard Business School Press).

Although platforms are typically two-sided marketplaces, they can also be multi-sided with several distinct sets of users. A two-sided marketplace has two sets of users—supply side users and demand-side users—providing value to each other through the marketplace. Some examples: eCommerce (Amazon, Alibaba, and eBay); media (Facebook, Google, and Wikipedia); matchmaking (Craigslist, OpenTable, and Indeed); and payment (American Express, Visa, and PayPal). A multi-sided platform has more than two sets of users. For example, *Fortune* magazine has at least three sets of users—content providers, readers, and advertisers—and is thus a multi-sided

Table 6.2 Differences Between B2B and B2C eCommerce Platforms

Parameter	*Business to Business (B2B)*	*Business to Consumer (B2C)*
1. Target audience	Other businesses	End users or consumers
2. People involved in decision making	Researchers, managers, sales representatives, brokers	End users
3. Purchase quantity	Bulk orders	Small orders
4. Pricing	Dynamic (changes with increase or decrease in quantity)	Consistent
5. Customer service assistance	Throughout all stages of the customer journey	After-sales or pre-sales assistance; usually one time.
6. Product detailing	Case studies, product videos, explainer videos, buying guides	Product videos, features, discounts available
7. Call to action	Business-centric (how the product will benefit the business on the whole)	User-centric (how the product will benefit the individual)

Source: Adapted from https://www.netsolutions.com/insights/difference-between-b2b-b2c-web-sites/.

marketplace. Two-sided markets can sometimes become multi-sided markets when other distinct sets of users participate in the market.

In the last decade or so, digital platforms have disrupted industry after industry. They enhance competition in industries by reducing barriers to entry, resulting in entry of new sellers into the industry. Different sellers on amazon.com, for example, compete for customers' business and must offer low prices in addition to products of acceptable quality. And, for many products and services, there typically are many other prospective sellers ready to join the Amazon platform.

While the B2C platforms currently dominate the business world, B2B platforms (such as Salesforce and SAP Business Network) continue to grow in importance and reach. Table 6.2 offers a comparison between B2B and B2C eCommerce platforms.

Ecosystem

An ecosystem is a group of companies from different industries offering bundles of products and services to meet specific customer needs. This concept is based on the idea that customers aren't just looking for a specific product or service but typically a solution to their needs. The solution often involves a joint offering by many companies, including companies from different industries. The Microsoft Windows ecosystem, for instance, includes computer manufacturers, software developers, manufacturers of computer accessories like mouse pads, keyboards, surge protectors, and a whole host of related service providers. Many of the fastest growing companies (such as Apple, Amazon, and Google) are ecosystems where they themselves act as a hub for networks of customers, suppliers, and providers of complementary goods and services, often integrated with each other. Such ecosystems can improve customer experience, even lead to reduced prices.

Like marketplaces, ecosystems, known by various names, have existed for a long time. For instance, several Japanese manufacturing and trading companies had had their own *keiretsus* for decades, which operated effectively as ecosystems. Keiretsus were huge networks of partners, including suppliers, distributors, bankers, and others. With the dawn of the digital era, automotive manufacturers like Toyota have added software, semiconductor, and other high-technology companies to their keiretsus—driven by the entry of autonomous, electric, and shared vehicles into everyday use.

Most businesses, however, are neither platforms, nor ecosystems; they are *linear* businesses in the sense that they take in certain inputs and create certain outputs or finished products, which are then sold to customers.[21] Platforms and ecosystems have no inventories of their own; they create value through relationships and networks—linking one group of users with another group of users. They make money through membership fees, advertising, commissions on transactions, providing services to users, revenue sharing with third parties, and (with access to data on the entire platform or ecosystem) through data monetization as well as through other possible revenue streams. The SAP Business Network is both a trading platform (a B2B marketplace) and an ecosystem of interconnected partners—buyers, suppliers, logistics companies, and providers of other complementary products and services. Walmart is a discount store, thus a linear business. Amazon is a linear business (has its own products and services, such as Alexa), a platform (a B2C marketplace, where third-party sellers sell their products), and an ecosystem (Prime video streaming, self-publishing, Amazon Web Services (AWS), and much more). By contrast, eBay and Airbnb are global platforms (Peer-to-Peer or P2P marketplaces)—connecting one set of users with another set of users—but not ecosystems.

Google (Alphabet) started out as a search engine (a linear business), became a two-sided platform (serving searchers and advertisers), and then added many other products and services over time (such as Gmail, Google Maps, Google Calendar, advice for small businesses, and so on) to become an ecosystem. Combining many services within an ecosystem, even complementary services, helps attract new users on both sides. In fact, Google is a hub for many ecosystems, such as an innovation ecosystem, the Android ecosystem, and a devices ecosystem.

Google's Innovation Ecosystem, for Example, Consists of At Least Four Different Groups of Individuals and Companies

- Consumers: Over 271 million unique visitors to google.com as of January 2022—searching for information, thus revealing their interests, for example, for targeted advertising;
- Advertisers: Over seven million companies and individuals advertise at google search—delivering ads to search-identified users;
- Content providers: Media companies and individuals who create information, stimulate customer interest, foster community, and provide delivery mechanisms for targeted ads;
- Mashup creators, independent software developers and vendors, Google engineers, and open-source community.

Table 6.3 Competing Ecosystems (Selected Components)

Product/Service	Google	Apple	Amazon	Microsoft	Samsung
Operating system	Android OS; Chrome OS	iOS	Fire OS	Windows	Android, Tizen
Web browser	Google Chrome	Apple Safari		Internet Explorer, Edge	Samsung Internet Browser
Cloud infrastructure	Google Cloud	iCloud (also uses AWS)	AWS	Azure	Samsung Cloud
Search	Google Search			Bing	
Tablet	Google Chromebook	iPad	Fire Tablet	Surface Pro	Galaxy
Laptop	Pixelbook	MacBook		Surface Laptop; Surface Book	Samsung Galaxy Book
Smartphone	Pixel	iPhone		Surface Duo	Galaxy
Smart TV	Google TV	Apple TV	Fire TV		Samsung TV
Selected IoT devices	Nest Thermostat; FitBit	Apple Watch; HomeKit			Galaxy Watch
Smart speaker	Google Home; Google Nest Audio	HomePod	Amazon Echo	Intelligent Speaker	Bixby Home
Voice assistant	Google Assistant	Siri	Alexa (works with Echo)	Cortana	Bixby

Source: Updated from https://ausdroid.net/2020/07/06/just-where-is-googles-ecosystem-up-to/.

Google's innovation ecosystem is an innovation hub where third parties can share access and create new applications that incorporate elements of Google functionality. These outsiders can easily test and launch applications and have them hosted in the Google world, where there is an enormous, targeted audience—132 million customers globally—and a practically unlimited capacity for customer interactions.[22]

Google and other major IT companies can themselves be visualized as ecosystems in their own right, offering complementary and integrated products and services. Table 6.3 presents ecosystems inside Google, Apple, Microsoft, and Samsung that compete with each other in different product domains.

Business Models for Professional Services Firms

Businesses offering professional services (such as IT services, management consulting, public relations, and legal services) create value for their clients by providing services efficiently and cost-effectively. How they capture value for their company depends on many factors, such as the type of service provided, duration, billing method, and so on. A common approach service businesses use for billing their clients is time and materials (T&M) and the hourly billing rate. If no materials are needed for a service project, billing is largely based on time and the billing rate. There are also many other billing approaches service businesses use, including fixed price, retainership, subscription, and, for some law firms, even contingency-based pricing—an outcome-based business model.

How Law Firms Bill Their Clients

Like most other service businesses, law firms also have no standard billing structure for their work; every firm has its own fee structure for each type of service it offers. *Time and billing rate* is a common approach law firms use for billing clients for legal services rendered. A second common approach is charging a *fixed fee* or flat rate for specific, well-defined legal tasks such as mortgage foreclosure or drafting a simple contract. A law firm or an individual attorney may also work on a *retainer* for clients needing certain legal services for an indefinite period. The client pays a retainer fee (effectively a deposit) in advance to *retain* the firm, which then bills the client for work done against the retainer based on its hourly billing rate. Every time the firm bills its client, the amount of retainer gets depleted. When a retainer account is nearly or fully depleted, the client may either refill the account for future work or cancel the retainer relationship with the law firm. Law firms sometimes also offer their services to clients on *subscription* whereby the firm bills the client a fixed amount of money monthly for specified ongoing legal services, rather than billing the client by the hour every time. Under the subscription model, clients can reach out to the law firm any time they need legal help. The subscription arrangement is used by businesses that have a continuing need for certain legal services.

Under a *contingency*-fee arrangement, the law firm (or attorney) receives a percentage of the monetary damages a client receives as a result of their lawsuit after settlement. Effectively an outcome-based, or payment-by-results, business model, this billing approach is used in personal-injury cases, class-action suits, and some commercial litigation cases—where the client can't afford the cost of protracted litigation and potential damages award is large. Win or lose, a client is typically obligated to pay other costs, like court filing fees. If the client wins the case and an award is made, the contingency-fee law firm takes a share of the judgment amount, often between one-third and 40% of the award. If the client loses the case, the law firm gets nothing.

Litigation for complex, contingency-fee cases can sometimes be very expensive and prolonged. In such situations, a law firm may not be able to afford or want to take on the expense involved—because case outcomes are typically uncertain. Enter *litigation funders*—finance companies that finance such contingency-fee legal cases. This is a very new, perhaps only 5- or 6-year-old, practice created specifically for law firms (attorneys) who accept large contingency-fee cases. The litigation funder advances money to the law firm to cover the cost of litigation against anticipated damages recovery. If the case is successful, they get a share of the damages award. If it is unsuccessful, there's no award and the litigation funder (and the law firm) receives nothing. The litigation funders are like venture capitalists, who make money if the company they fund becomes hugely successful and exits (for example, is acquired by another company or goes public with an IPO). And, like VCs, litigation funders might fund several cases hoping that at least some of them will have large damages awards.

Productization of Services

We discussed servitization of products earlier in the chapter; its counterpart for services is *productization of services*. As indicated above, service businesses often bill their clients based on the T&M model, which implies that to double their revenue (for instance), they must nearly double their professional manpower. A law firm, as an example, must add new attorneys on its payroll if it wants to increase its revenue by taking on new clients or new work for existing clients. Not so for product businesses, especially businesses selling digital or IoT products. For a product firm, there's no such direct association between number of employees and revenue. This is true even for physical-goods businesses. Recall the scalability and repeatability characteristics of digital products discussed earlier. They don't need to double their manpower and investment in plant and machinery to double output. Products are scalable, services are not. (This also explains why revenue per employee is generally substantially higher for product businesses than for service businesses—for the same number of employees.) The productization of services makes a business scalable, repeatable, more efficient, and thus more profitable.

Productization at professional services firms can involve developing products that operate on their own or automatically, without necessarily needing services of a human being. For example, H&R Block, with over 10,000 retail locations, offers income tax preparation services for individuals and organizations in the US, Canada, and Australia. Over the years, H&R Block developed tax-preparation software that individuals and businesses can use on their own to prepare their annual tax returns. H&R Block now has several tax-preparation software products, ranging from a free version for individuals to paid versions for both individuals and businesses. Their most expensive product is for businesses and costs $89.95, a tiny fraction of what a business might pay H&R Block to prepare its tax returns. The software also allows the users to e-file their tax returns and request refund of any extra taxes paid.

Electronic discovery (eDiscovery or e-Discovery) in law firms is a critical need in case law involving disputes to be resolved by courts based on unique facts of a case. It involves collecting, preserving, reviewing, and exchanging information—electronically—to be used as evidence in a court case. With data and information sources exploding over the years, eDiscovery involves searching for information in emails, instant messages, social media, smartphones, audio/video files, and physical and electronic files held by a company, among other sources. Technologies used in eDiscovery include AI, machine learning, and data analytics for litigation applications. With machine learning, eDiscovery software *learns* from every document it processes—becoming better at identifying and extracting critical information needed by the law firm. Some law firms outsource eDiscovery to specialist firms with expertise in this kind of work, while others do it themselves, in-house. Law firms that bring the eDiscovery function in-house know that the skills needed for legal practice are very different from those needed for eDiscovery, especially with constantly changing technologies. Therefore, large law firms sometimes create a separate practice group or subsidiary to handle eDiscovery for their own cases, and even as a profit center offering such services to other law firms.

Similarly, many other professional services firms create products to supplement their services or as additional revenue streams. Deloitte, an audit, accounting, and consulting firm, for instance, developed Argus, their *first cognitive audit* product, that learns from every human interaction to identify and extract key accounting information from different kinds of electronic documents. In 2015, Deloitte received the Audit Innovation of the Year award from the *International Accounting Bulletin* based on its successes with Argus. Indian IT services firms like TCS and Infosys have similarly developed products to serve their clients. Infosys Finacle, for instance, is a digital banking solution used by financial institutions in over a hundred countries. Finacle, developed by EdgeVerve Systems, a subsidiary of Infosys, helps banking institutions achieve digital transformation of their operations for improved customer experience through automation and insights-driven interactions.

Notes

1 Marco Iansiti and Karim R. Lakhani, *Competing in the Age of AI: Strategy and Leadership When Algorithms and Networks Run the World* (Boston, Harvard Business School Press, 2020), p. 30.
2 Oliver Gassman, Karolin Frankenberger, Michaela Choudury, *The Business Model Navigator: The Strategies Behind the Most Successful Companies* (Harlow, UK: Pearson Education Limited, 2nd Edition, 2020).
3 Rexroth Press Release, October 23, 2018. https://dc-corp.resource.bosch.com/media/xc/company_1/press/product_information/product_information_2018/october_2018/PI_027_18__CytroBox_en~1.pdf.
4 Statista, "Regional industrial internet of things market size 2017–2025 by region," March 18, 2022. https://www.statista.com/statistics/1102164/global-industrial-internet-of-things-market-size/.
5 Statista, "Internet of things (IoT) global total revenue 2019–2030, by use case," August 12, 2022. https://www.statista.com/statistics/1194719/iot-revenue-worldwide-use-case/.
6 Wikipedia, "List of SAP products: Revision history," June 11, 2022. https://en.wikipedia.org/w/index.php?title=List_of_SAP_products&action=history.
7 News9.com, "Subscription management software," April 15, 2020. https://www.news9.com/story/5e98764ecc9ea5695635cd68/subscription-management-software.
8 Liz Gannes, "Case studies in fremium: Pandora, Dropbox, Evernote, automatic, and MailChimp," March 26, 2010. https://old.gigaom.com/2010/03/26/case-studies-in-freemium-pandora-dropbox-evernote-automattic-and-mailchimp/.
9 Jasvinder Singh and Pranjali Bhatia, "Outcome-based pricing model – a win-win approach for the service provider and the buyer," October 2020. https://www.wipro.com/travel-and-transportation/outcome-based-pricing-model-a-win-win-approach-for-the-service-provider-and-the-buyer/.
10 Kaiser Kompressoren, "Operator models: Smart, safe, and secure." https://www.kaeser.com/int-en/solutions/operator-models/.
11 Vinod K. Jain, *Global Strategy: Competing in the Connected Economy* (Routledge, 2017).
12 Kiran Bhageshpur, "Data is the new oil – and that's a good think," *Forbes*, November 15, 2019. https://www.forbes.com/sites/forbestechcouncil/2019/11/15/data-is-the-new-oil-and-thats-a-good-thing/?sh=74dff5e73045.
13 Neel Mehta, Parth Detroja, and Aditya Agashe, *Swipe to Unlock: The Primer on Technology and Business Strategy* (Bell Applications, Inc., 3rd Edition, 2020), pp. 119–120.
14 John Lincoln, "8 companies using cutting-edge personalization strategies to maximize profits." *Inc.* magazine. https://www.inc.com/john-lincoln/how-coca-cola-amp-netflix-and-more-are-using-per.html.
15 Maryam Mohsin, "10 Google search statistics you need to know in 2022," January 2, 2022. https://www.oberlo.com/blog/google-search-statistics#:~:text=Google%20processes%20over%208.5%20billion,traffic%20originated%20from%20mobile%20devices.
16 Mark Hachman, "The price of free: How Apple, Facebook, Microsoft and Google sell you to advertisers," October 1, 2015. *PCWorld*. https://www.pcworld.com/article/423747/the-price-of-free-how-apple-facebook-microsoft-and-google-sell-you-to-advertisers.html.
17 Statista, "Advertising revenue of Google from 2000 to 2021," July 27, 2022. https://www.statista.com/statistics/266249/advertising-revenue-of-google/.
18 Josh Gottlieb and Khaled Rifai, "Fueling growth through data monetization," December 1, 2017. McKinsey & Company. https://www.mckinsey.com/capabilities/quantumblack/our-insights/fueling-growth-through-data-monetization.

19 Clifford Geertz, "The Bazaar Economy," *The American Economic Review,* Vol. 68, No. 2 (Suppl.: Papers and Proceedings of the Ninetieth Annual Meeting of the American Economic Association) (May, 1978), pp. 28–32.

20 SAP, "Explore SAP Business Network." https://www.sap.com/products/business-network/solutions.html.

21 The term "product" includes both products and services.

22 Bala Iyer and Thomas H. Davenport, "Reverse engineering Google's innovation machine," *Harvard Business Review,* April 2008. (The 132 million number is as of 2008 when this article was published).

Chapter 7

Digital Strategy for Global B2C Businesses

You have no choice but to operate in a world shaped by globalization and the information revolution. There are two options: adapt or die.

Andrew S. Grove, former COO, CEO, and Chairman, Intel Corporation

Chapter 5 was about global strategy for digital businesses; Chapter 7 is about digital strategy for global B2C businesses. This approach raises two questions: (1) What is a global business? (2) What is digital strategy?

Let us explore these two questions before proceeding with the subject matter of the chapter.

What Is a Global Business?

A global business is a company with presence in many countries around the world. From our perspective, a global business is a company that competes with companies from around the world—at home or in foreign markets. Today, virtually any company competes with (or has the potential to compete with) companies from around the world and can therefore justifiably be called a global business.

For this chapter, I select a subset of global businesses that are brick-and-mortar, traditional businesses involved in physical goods and services. Why? Since this chapter is about *digital strategy* for global businesses, and since businesses are of three kinds—physical, digital, and physical-and-digital or Internet of Things (IoT) (Box 7.1); physical businesses, not being digital, need digital strategy.

The chapter is, therefore, concerned with traditional or legacy businesses belonging to what is generally known as the *old economy*. A legacy business can be a small business or a large business that has existed for many years and operates from one or more physical locations, producing physical goods, providing services—or both—to their customers. Many such businesses are already on path to digitalizing their operations and are within the purview of this chapter. Chapter 7 is about B2C legacy businesses and Chapter 8 is about B2B legacy businesses.

DOI: 10.4324/9781003037446-9

BOX 7.1 THREE KINDS OF BUSINESSES

Businesses are of three kinds (Figure 7.1): physical, digital, and physical-and-digital and connected to the internet (Internet of Things, or IoT).

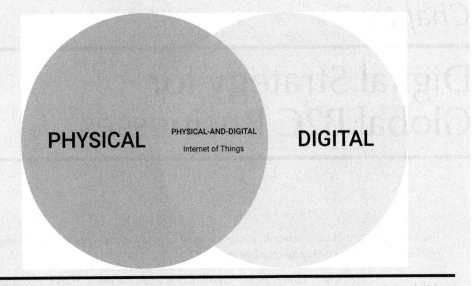

PHYSICAL   PHYSICAL-AND-DIGITAL
Internet of Things   **DIGITAL**

Figure 7.1   The intersection of the physical and digital worlds creates Internet of Things (IoT). (Same as Figure 5.1 Chapter 5 [this book].)

Even though the digital world has existed for a very long time, the domain of Internet of Things (IoT) is a relatively recent phenomenon. The term, *Internet of Things*, itself was first coined by Kevin Ashton in 1999, though IoT existed before that. The world of IoT grew slowly at first but exploded in the 2010s and 2020s.

The IoT are products (*things* or devices) that are physical and digital and connected to the internet—created at the intersection of the physical and digital world. Being digital means these products have sensors, software, and digital technologies embedded into them, which enable them to communicate with other connected products over the internet. Today, the most common IoT products are the digital voice assistants such as Siri on iPhone, digital home assistants like Alexa, digital doorbells, autonomous cars, drones, health and fitness trackers, and an increasing number of industrial IoT (IIoT) products (Chapter 8).

A Key Characteristic of the IoT. Smartphones are both physical and digital (they have dozens of sensors, software, and technologies embedded into them), and connected to the internet, yet they are not considered IoT devices. An important characteristic of IoT devices is that they can communicate with their network and **act** on commands *independently of human action*. A smartphone cannot act on its own; it's the apps on the smartphone that do what the owner wants done, though the apps themselves, being software, are not IoT device. For instance, Siri is an advanced, voice-controlled digital personal assistant on the iPhone (and iPad, Apple Watch, and many other Apple products); it can play music, order food, send an email, and so on, as directed by the iPhone owner. Siri has access to all the in-built applications on the iPhone, such as Mail, Messaging, Maps, etc., and can independently use them as directed by the iPhone owner. However, smartphones do have a major role in the IoT world because they, through apps, control IoT devices and instruct them to do what they are supposed to do. Some would argue that smartphones, with apps integrated into them, are effectively IoT devices.

Today, there are literally billions of IoT devices in the world—ranging from smart home devices (smart thermostats, doorbells, security cameras, digital assistants, connected appliances, and so on), wearables (smart watch, fitness trackers, smart glasses, even smart clothing), and autonomous vehicles to parking meters, industrial machinery, and more. Adding sensors to such products make them *smart* (or intelligent); they can communicate information and take actions in real time without the involvement of human beings.

Some other products that are physical and digital and connected to the Internet but are not IoT are PCs, laptops, tablets, and gaming consoles.

This chapter is essentially about legacy businesses and how they adopt digital strategy and digital business models to create and capture value and build competitive advantage. We will learn from a few legacy businesses that plunged into the digital world—how they went about it, the digital strategies and digital business models they employed, and the outcomes they achieved. This chapter covers legacy businesses in the B2C (business-to-consumer) category, such as Nestlé, which has by now made significant progress toward digitalization of its operations and external relationships. Chapter 8 covers B2B (business-to-business), legacy businesses, typically industrial companies, such as Germany's Bosch Group, a 138-year-old manufacturer of industrial equipment that had been a traditional business in the old economy for decades. The Bosch Group is now a prominent manufacturer of industrial IoT (IIoT) equipment such as parking meters and power tools and offers related services—clearly a *new economy* business.

What Is Digital Strategy?

Digital strategy is *strategy*, first and foremost, and is concerned with (1) how companies create and capture value and (2) how they establish and sustain competitive advantage. Strategy helps companies create value for the customer. In other words, through their products and services, they solve customers' problems for which the customers pay a price—allowing the company to capture at least some of the value for itself (Figure 7.2). And strategy is concerned with how to compete, establish, and sustain competitive advantage.

Digital strategy is also intended to help companies achieve the same two objectives—create and capture value and establish and sustain competitive advantage—but with the adoption of digital technologies and digital business models. Digital strategy is often confused with *digital transformation*, the latter being intended to move a business to the digital world, essentially reinventing the company as a digital business. The two terms are related to each other—in the sense that digital strategy shapes digital transformation, and digital transformation shapes digital strategy. Companies need digital transformation to *play*, and strategy to *win*.[1] (It's like the classic duality in Strategic Management—what comes first... strategy or structure? In most organizations, they happen concurrently.)

Economics of Digital Markets

The typical assumptions used in economics of traditional businesses such as resource scarcity, decreasing returns to scale, and non-zero marginal costs do not hold for digital goods. Digital goods exhibit

Table 7.1 The Economics of Physical vs. Digital Goods

Physical Goods	*Digital Goods*
Positive marginal cost of production and distribution	Zero (almost zero) marginal cost of production and distribution
Rivalry (a product can be used by only one person at the same time)	Non-rivalry (a digital product can be used by any number of people at the same time)
Diminishing returns to scale	Increasing returns to scale (due to network effects)
Scarcity of resources; limited supply of most resources	Inexhaustible supply; quality does not deteriorate as more units are produced
Customizability is expensive and time-consuming	Customizability is generally low cost and quick

network effects which implies increasing returns to scale. Besides, the marginal cost of production (and distribution) of digital goods is practically zero, which implies a digital-product company can have inexhaustible supply of its products and have no inventory issues. Digital goods also have scale and scope advantage, and their quality does not deteriorate as more units are produced (Table 7.1).

The economic principles underpinning digital strategy include, among others, non-rivalry network effects, zero marginal cost, and increasing returns to scale. Each product type shown in Figure 7.1 represents a different economic and strategic profile. This is so because several core economics concepts, such as diminishing returns to scale and resource scarcity, do not apply to digital products (Table 7.1).

Rivalry, in economics, means that a product can be used by only one individual at the same time. This is true for all physical products. On the other hand, *non-rivalry* means that a (digital) product can be used by any number of people at the same time. For instance, Microsoft can sell Microsoft 365 to any number of people and organizations, who can use the product anytime irrespective of who else is using it at the same time; this is because of the zero marginal cost principle of digital goods.

A product has *network effects* if its value to users grows exponentially as more and more individuals begin using the product. As the number of users of a product grows, its value to its users (and to the owners of the network) grows exponentially. It's also known as the Metcalfe's Law applicable to products connected to a network, such as the telecommunications network or the internet. Strictly speaking, the Metcalfe's Law states that "the value of a telecommunications network is proportional to the square of the number of connected users of the system."[2] (More on network effects later in the chapter). Table 7.2 distinguishes between the core properties of the three kinds of products.

Value Creation and Value Capture

The concept of value (and value creation) is fraught with much misconception. What value is, how it is created, for whom it is created, and who captures it are often misunderstood, even by successful companies and prominent consulting firms. The prestigious Boston Consulting Group (BCG), for example, equates *value creation* with *shareholder value creation* in their otherwise excellent 2018 Value Creation Report.[3] As suggested earlier, a company creates value when it provides a

Table 7.2   Core Characteristics of Physical Products, Digital Products, and Internet of Things

Characteristics	Physical Products	Digital Products	Internet of Things
Zero marginal cost		✓	
Non-rivalry		✓	
Network effects		✓	✓
Inexhaustible supply		✓	
Customizability		✓	✓

problem solution the customer is willing to pay for. Value is in fact what the company's customers, shareholders, and multiple stakeholders receive, with customers first in line to receive value. The word *customer* appears exactly five times in the BCG report and that too in the context of treating investors as customers (Lesson No. 10). As I show later, unless a customer receives value, no purchase takes place and there will be no question of value creation.

Many companies are beginning to appreciate that any value they create must be shared with multiple stakeholders, not just the shareholders. In August 2019, the Business Roundtable (BRT), an association of the CEOs of leading US corporations, completely redefined the purpose of the corporation. In a 300-word statement, signed by 184 CEOs, BRT declared that a corporation had a fundamental responsibility toward all stakeholders and specified commitments to customers, employees, suppliers, communities, and shareholders.[4] The statement superseded its 1997 statement that "the paramount duty of management and of boards of directors is to the corporation's stockholders."

That the customer comes first in sharing the value captured by a company is fundamental to the product-as-a-service (PaaS) business model, as discussed in Chapter 6. Companies, especially B2B companies, that previously sold physical products are increasingly adding services to their products and moving away from a one-time sale to *servitizing* their products (selling outcome-based services). Under the PaaS model, the company changes the manner in which value is created and shared. Under PaaS, the product is expected to perform without any quality problems because the manufacturer is paid for the guaranteed service the product offers, not the product per se, essentially a *payment-by-results* (or *outcome-based*) business model.

Value creation and value capture are why firms exist; they are a critical aspect of strategy for any firm. Firms create value so customer purchases can take place, and they are able to capture some of that value for themselves to remain in business. Business transactions are intended to create certain benefits for customers, with the cost of creating such benefits accruing to the firm. Value is created when benefits (B) exceed the cost (C) of providing the benefits (Figure 7.2). From a customer's perspective, *willingness to pay* (WTP) is the monetary value of the perceived benefit of the product or service being purchased, or the highest price a customer is willing to pay for the product. In economics, the difference between WTP and price (P) is called *consumer surplus*. For a purchase to occur, WTP must be positive. What about the firm bringing its products to the market? The difference between its price and its cost is the *producer surplus* (the firm's profit). Value created is the difference between benefits (B) and cost (C), or the sum of consumer surplus and producer surplus.

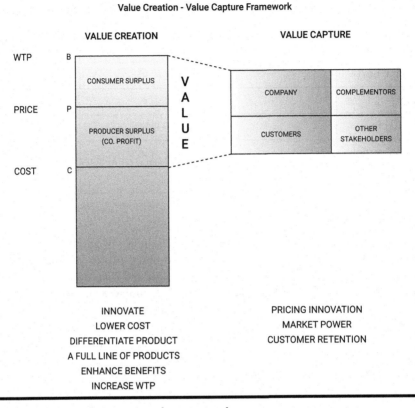

Figure 7.2 presents a generic representation of the individual components of value creation and value capture. The areas within value creation and value capture as shown in the figure depend on several factors such as innovation, market power, and pricing strategy.

Figure 7.2 How companies create and capture value.

Who captures the value thus created? Well, value is shared among the customer, the firm, complementors, and any other stakeholders. *Complementors* are firms that sell a product or service that complements the product or service of another company by adding value to their mutual customers. For instance, Microsoft is a complementor to Dell Computers; Microsoft operating system is used in Dell computers. The other stakeholders can be any other firms or organizations that expect some financial gain from the transaction, such as government (taxation authorities), lenders, ecosystem partners, and so on. (Suppliers to the company are not included among those who capture value; they are included as cost in value creation).

Figure 7.2 presents a generic representation of the individual components of value creation and value capture. The areas within value creation and value capture as shown in the figure depend on several factors such as innovation, market power, and pricing strategy.

How Value Is Created

To create value, find ways to serve customers better than competition, keeping company operations efficient and effective. This may involve approaches such as innovation, lowering cost, offering a differentiated product so that it meets the specific needs of the customers being targeted, offering a full line of products, and providing enhanced benefits to increase their willingness to pay. Some of these approaches may indeed imply a higher cost, but if the increase in value is greater than the increase in cost, more value is created. Besides, such approaches can also help with customer retention.

This is exactly what Nike, the world's largest seller of athletic footwear and apparel, has been doing over the last decade or so. Nike started its digitalization journey with digital transformation—investing aggressively in digital technologies such as AI, machine learning, computer vision, and data analytics. For instance, Nike acquired Zodiac, a predictive analytics company in 2018. Using each customer's prior interactions with the company, Zodiac helps predict individual customers' likely future purchases—thus improving customer acquisition and retention. Also in 2018, Nike acquired Invertex Ltd. to enable 3D foot scanning with computer vision technology. Combined with AI, machine learning, computer vision, and recommendation algorithms, Nike is able to recommend *perfect fit* for each customer and each shoe style. Using the *Nike Fit* app, customers take photographs of their feet and get recommendation of their perfect shoe size. In 2021, Nike acquired Datalogue that helps automate the preparation and integration of data from multiple sources, such as Nike apps, supply chain, e-commerce, and retail in a standardized format.

Nike had traditionally followed the retail-first model, with most of its revenue coming from wholesale operations. While wholesale still represents a greater share of Nike's total worldwide revenue, its direct-to-consumer (D2C) model has been growing faster than wholesale. Direct-to-consumer revenue in 2022 was 42 percent of Nike's worldwide sales.

Not just D2C, Nike has adopted several approaches to serve customers better—with customization, vast product selection and availability at over one thousand stores in some 120 countries, and Nike apps that track workout and training data—thus offering better customer experience and deepening company relationship with customers.

Nike used to segment its market in terms of products (footwear, equipment, apparel, and so on) but changed its segmentation approach in 2008 from products to sports (global football, basketball, women's training, running), an approach it termed *Category Offense*. This was clearly a customer-oriented strategy focusing on athletes' needs in different sports. The strategy not only served customers better, but it also helped increase revenue by 70% by 2015. "The initial focus of Nike's Category Offense is not to create better shoes or apparel; it's to identify what athletes are trying to accomplish and where they currently struggle."[5] Having seen the impact of customer focus on growth, Nike in 2017 introduced *Consumer Direct Offense* (CDO)—to better serve the customer—personally and at scale. In the latest phase of CDO, Nike launched *Consumer Direct Acceleration* in 2020 designed to create a connected digital marketplace of the future and accelerate the company's digital transformation.

All such initiatives have helped Nike create more value by serving its customers better—with a full line of products, vast availability, technology, and innovation to personalize its offerings—and providing them enhanced benefits. As a result, Nike's total worldwide revenues increased five-and-a-half times from FY 2010 ($8.324 billion) to FY 2022 ($46.71 billion).[6] And Nike's direct-to-consumer revenues grew even faster over the same period: from $2.48 billion in FY 2010 to $18.73 billion in FY 2022.

For digital goods and IoT companies, the most important factor in value creation is network effects, whereby the value created by a product or service increases, exponentially, as the number of users of the product or service increases. In the Spotify case study (Chapter 5), the company employs technology and network effects to create value for both listeners and artists. Spotify helped increase customers' willingness to pay by offering them a convenient and legal means of listening to music, thus shifting consumer behavior from ownership (purchasing music CDs) or theft (illegal copying of music) to access (listening to music anytime, anywhere without owning it). It offered listeners enhanced benefits through the premium subscription plan. Spotify increased its market size through globalization and by offering podcasting and videocasting, again creating more value for customers (and the company).

How Value Is Captured

Companies spend a good deal of time and effort creating value for customers, but sometimes not enough to capture some of it for themselves and their stakeholders. When a company creates value, it captures some of it for itself. So, all the value-creation approaches listed above also help companies capture some of the value so created. Companies capture value from the prices they charge for their products and by keeping their costs low.

Nike, for instance, captures value from its multiple product offerings, personalized offerings, improved customer acquisition and retention, and a larger market share than any other competitor. Spotify, as previously discussed, makes money from premium subscriptions, advertising, and through price discrimination (different price levels for individuals, families, students). A larger customer base and high customer retention (e.g., by allowing them to create their own playlists) help Spotify lower its costs—thereby helping it to capture more value.

Product servitization. In product servitization, companies receive revenue through their subscription model and by monetizing the massive amounts of data they collect through connected IoT devices. Customers capture value through guaranteed service and by avoiding major capital expenditure as in a one-time sale. Service businesses in both B2C and B2B environments can create and capture value through *productization* of their services.[7]

Pricing innovation is a common approach many businesses use to capture more value. Stefan Michel of IMD Lausanne, Switzerland, offers an interesting framework for pricing innovation to help capture value in business transactions.[8] His framework offers several approaches for pricing innovation, some of which are discussed here.

Change the price-setting mechanism. Prices are often set based on cost or what the market can bear. Instead, charge different customers different prices based on their willingness to pay or based on the benefit they expect to derive from the purchase. There are several possible ways of achieving this, including auctioning and demand-driven pricing. Auctioning works well for Google AdWords, sellers on eBay, and for many other businesses. Auctions help bring to surface the highest acceptable price customers are willing to pay. Under demand-driven pricing, companies set prices based on demand fluctuations, a common practice in airline and hotel bookings for example.

Change the payer. In referral-service businesses, the actual payer for a service being provided to final customers is generally the company advertising their services, not the final customers. For instance, a job board like indeed.com provides information on available jobs to jobseekers without cost; the cost is paid for by the companies advertising their jobs at indeed.com. Dozens of two-sided platforms have a similar pricing mechanism; they sell access to their network to companies interested in reaching the network. A company with a two-sided platform can charge a different price for each side, depending on each side's willingness to pay. Most magazines and newspapers are sold at prices that wouldn't cover the cost of producing them; advertisers in those publications cover the bulk of the cost.

Change the price carrier. Changing the price carrier involves changing the part of a product or service on which a price is attached; it can be an individual item or a bundle of items. Airlines used to offer seats at an all-inclusive price for different classes of travel. Now, most airlines, not just the discount airlines, charge a separate price for each product or service they offer. United Airlines, for instance, offers different classes of service at different price points. Economy seating is available in four categories—Basic Economy, Economy, Economy Fully Refundable, and Premium Economy—each with a different set of cabin experiences and price level. The choices a traveler has include seat selection, accompanied baggage, unaccompanied baggage, type of seat, possibility of upgrading the seat, and fees for changing the flight itself—each with a separate price. Each of these unbundled services is priced separately for Basic Economy, but all included in the Premium Economy package. For instance, someone purchasing a Basic Economy seat can pay for seat selection in advance, for an accompanied bag, and so on.

The bundling concept is used by many firms that use all-inclusive pricing, such as cruise ships and many resorts. Customers end up paying for all services included in the all-inclusive offering whether they want to use each service or not. I subscribe to the Microsoft 365 Family plan at $99.99 per year; this includes Word, Excel, PowerPoint, OneNote, cloud storage, and some other services for up to six computers. Not everyone who subscribes to Microsoft 365 uses all of the software and apps included in the plan or has six computers for maximum benefit. B2B companies servitizing their products typically offer an all-inclusive monthly subscription price, inclusive of the equipment, maintenance, any upgrades, and with guaranteed performance. They changed the price carrier to a monthly subscription price, an operating expense; in the past, they would charge separately for the equipment (a capital expense), after-sale service, maintenance, and so on. These used to be revenue-generation offerings, but now, they are a cost to the company; revenue comes only from the monthly subscription.

Change the timing. The subscription business model involves changing timing of payment for products or services *sold* to a client. As discussed in Chapter 6, most of the digital-product companies now use the subscription model. The company receives payment for its products or services at regular intervals in the future, rather than through a one-time sale.

As these examples show, capturing value from business transactions is limited only by the creativity and innovation on the part of the seller.

Competition and Competitive Advantage in Digital Markets

The second aspect of (digital) strategy is how to compete and establish and sustain competitive advantage. It was highlighted in Chapter 1 that, with *new technologies* (e.g., AI and 3D printing), *new players* (digital natives), *new products* (IoT devices), *new playing fields* (digital markets), *new challenges* (digital disruption), *new rules of the game* (network effects), and *new market dynamics* (winner-take-all or winner-take-most), competition today is an entirely new ballgame. The old rules of competition no longer work for an increasing number of products and services. Competitive advantage in traditional industries with physical products and well-defined industry boundaries used to be based on generic strategies developed in the 1980s[9]—*differentiation* and *cost leadership*—when there were no smart phones, no internet, and no social media. And competition used to take place within industries—automakers competing with other automakers—not anymore.

As global meets digital, competition in literally every industry, traditional or digital, is impacted by digitalization. Digitalization (or, more generally, information technology) is changing business in profound ways—especially how to operate and how to compete. Companies like Spotify, Google, and Uber have shown how digital operating models make a business more scalable, more scopable (greater product variety), enable network effects, and create opportunities for learning and improvement. All of these have great implications for how businesses create and capture value, establish competitive advantage, and may even reach a winner-take-all (or winner-take-most) status.[10]

Research by McKinsey & Company[11] shows that digitalization impacts industry competition and legacy incumbents' profits negatively. First, new digital entrants into an industry have a major impact on incumbents' fortunes. For instance, the introduction of the Google Maps navigation app in 2009 for smartphones depressed the market capitalization of incumbent GPS device makers by up to 85%. Second, incumbents themselves create more intense industry rivalry as they respond to digital entrants. Oftentimes, they aggressively imitate each other's digital moves leading to greater competition for everyone.[12] The competition between UPS and FedEx for overnight package delivery service has been becoming more and more intense as they imitate each other's digital moves, such as introduction of handheld devices for delivery confirmation and online package tracking. Such tit-for-tat competitive responses are, of course, not new. The Cola Wars (competition between Coca-Cola and PepsiCo over decades) are legendary.

Establishing Competitive Advantage in Digital Markets

Legacy businesses, when they digitalize their internal systems and external relationships, enter digital markets, where, as we saw earlier, the sources of competitive advantage are quite different from what they were used to as non-digital businesses. In today's context, practically all markets are digital markets. The sources of competitive advantage in digital markets include:

1. *Technological innovation.* Starting with digitalization of the operating system and creation of digital and IoT products and services, legacy companies have many opportunities to take advantage of technological innovation.
   - Software and logarithms: Technical experts design a company's operating system, but it is the software and algorithms that operate the business in real time—functions that used to be performed by humans in the past.
   - Digital products: Digital products have all five characteristics specified in Table 7.1. By adding digital products to their offerings, legacy companies have the potential to become hugely profitable (recall their *zero* marginal cost characteristic).
   - Internet of Things: Internet of Things (IoT) products are both physical and digital, and connected to the internet (Figure 7.1), and operate without human intervention. They offer companies several potential benefits, including remote diagnostics, asset tracking, and automatic fulfillment—all without need for human intervention. For B2B companies, IoT (or IIoT) products offer even more benefits, such as compliance monitoring and preventive maintenance, again without need for human intervention (discussed in Chapter 8). Besides, they generate masses of data which can help operations and can be monetized.
   - Data: Data, being a true digital product, helps companies that use it strategically to stay ahead of competition. They can use data to acquire a deep understanding of customers and customer behavior, to make content recommendations based on their interests which helps in customer retention, to forecast demand, and to monetize it in many ways (see Data Monetization, Chapter 6).
2. *Network effects.* Both digital and IoT products benefit from network effects. For example, the value (to users) of Facebook increases as more individuals join Facebook. Joining Facebook helps individual users increase their network of friends and thus derive more value from the platform. This is *direct network effects.* Subscribing to Spotify, a two-sided platform with both artists and users, benefits also from *indirect network effects.* As more users subscribe to Spotify, more artists benefit from joining the streaming service, and vice versa.
   Industries with strong network effects tend to be highly concentrated. They have high buyer switching costs, implying customer lock-in. This, along with exponential properties of digital and IoT goods, can lead to *winner-take-all* (or winner-take-most) market dynamics.
3. *Complementary products and services.* In the late 1800s and early 1900s, industrial companies like Standard Oil in the US and German chemical companies like Bayer and Hoechst

became huge and very successful through economies of scale and economies of scope.[13] A company achieves *economies of scale* when an increase in the size of a single manufacturing unit decreases the per unit cost of production (or distribution). And a company has *economies of scope* when it uses the same production (distribution) facilities for producing (distributing) more than one product. Digital companies increase their competitive advantage by adding complementary products and services to their portfolio of products and services.

4. *Scale and scope.* As we saw above, in the 1800s and 1900s, many companies became hugely successful through economies of scale and scope. Digital businesses are eminently scalable and scopable; they benefit from such economies by orders of magnitude compared to physical businesses. Just look at Apple, Amazon, Google, and Alibaba; they all grew exponentially through economies of scale, benefiting from technological innovation, network effects, and offering complementary products and services using economies of scope. Apple, for instance, makes personal computers (Mac), music players (iPod, being discontinued in 2022), smart phones (iPhone), tablets (iPad), wearables (Apple Watch), and accessories. Apple's services include Apple Music, Apple TV+, Apple Fitness+, Apple News+, Apple Card, and Apple Arcade. The addition of complementary products and services not only increased Apple's customer base but also locked-in customers to its platform. With the addition of several products and services, Apple has become a conglomerate, achieving winner-take-most market dynamics in several of its markets.

Uber is fast developing into a mobility *Super App*, "a mobile application that provides multiple services … effectively becoming an all-encompassing self-contained commerce and communication online platform."[14] Uber currently offers services such as mobility (formerly rides), delivery (formerly Uber Eats; and packages), and Uber freight. As a purely digital business, it could potentially add other complementary services relatively easily as shown in Figure 7.3.

Figure 7.3   Uber's Super App opportunities.

Source: Lokesh Kumar, "Uber Super App Opportunities", January 15, 2022. Reprinted with permission. https://www.linkedin.com/pulse/uber-super-app-opportunities-lokesh-kumar/?trk=eml-email_series_follow_newsletter_01-hero-1-title_link&midToken=AQG9tgG8Yx2MMg&fromEmail=fromEmail&ut=2WOq9-uViD1W81

5. *Business model.* Digital businesses (and legacy businesses) use digital business models to create competitive advantage... business models like razor and blade, Product-as-a-Service (PaaS), and platforms and ecosystems, discussed in Chapter 6. Unlike products, which can sometimes be reverse-engineered, business models are much harder for competitors to replicate. This is because a business model can involve the activities of hundreds and thousands of people and key aspects of organization design, including organizational culture, which cannot be easily replicated and thus act as sources of competitive advantage.

Digital Strategy for Global B2C Businesses

Developing digital strategy for a legacy business begins with *digital transformation* that involves digitalization of its internal systems, processes, and external relationships—the process of moving from an analog to a digital business. Digital transformation also involves the use of digital technologies, like AI, cloud computing, robotics, 3D printing, and data analytics. Obviously, for digital transformation to be successful, the company must have the right kinds of talent and a culture that supports innovation. The company can buy any amount of technology, but if it does not have the kinds of skills among its workforce needed to successfully adapt the technology to its needs, digital transformation will be a failure. Digital transformation is a journey, not a destination.

Legacy businesses often have elements of digitalization already embedded in their organizations; the use of electronic data interchange (EDI) in supply chain management, for example, goes back decades to the 1960s. All of this would facilitate the process of digital transformation. Several erstwhile legacy businesses, such as John Deere, New York Times, Disney, and Bosch, having gone through digital transformation, are now effectively digital businesses or *digital incumbents*[15]. You will find examples of both B2C and B2B companies having gone through digital transformation in the mini case studies included in this and next chapter.

Beyond digital transformation, implementing digital strategy in a legacy business involves at least four steps.

1. As part of digital transformation, make sure to leverage the full power of digitalization—from internal operations to external relationships.
2. Add digital or IoT products (or both) to the company's product portfolio. If a company's existing physical product can be converted into an IoT product by embedding it with sensors and connecting it to the internet, so much the better. If not, consider developing digital or IoT products in-house or acquiring a company that has such products. (Today, there are even connected shoes. Apple had taken a patent for smart shoes, with embedded sensors as early as 2013. Now, Nike, Under Armour, and a few startups offer smart shoes with embedded sensors, with Bluetooth connection).
3. Leverage the economic principles that underpin digital strategy such as network effects, zero marginal cost, and non-rivalry (Table 7.1).
4. Use digital business models (Chapter 6) to create and capture value and establish competitive advantage.

We next explore how certain traditional, legacy businesses reinvented themselves as digital businesses in the B2C world. (Examples of legacy B2B companies that went through similar transformation and reinvention are contained in Chapter 8).

Hewlett-Packard's HP OfficeJet 9020 All-in-One Wireless Printer is an IoT device for home offices and small businesses. Through sensors and software embedded in the printer, it monitors ink consumption and offers owners automatic ink-cartridge replenishment through its subsidiary instantink.com on monthly subscription. The subscription is priced at $11.99 per month (for 300 pages printed per month) and $24.99 per month (for 700 pages printed per month).

Nestlé

Nestlé S.A., a 155-year-old Swiss company, is the world's largest manufacturer of foods and beverages. It has factories in 86 countries (including 11 in Switzerland), sells its products in more than 186 countries, had group sales of CHF 87.1 billion (US$ 95.7 billion), and 276,000 employees as of 2021. Currently, the company's vast product portfolio has more than 2,000 global and local brands of infant and toddler foods, nutrition, confectionary, snacks, ice cream, beverages like coffee and water, and pet foods. The United States is Nestlé's largest market by sales volume, followed by Greater China accounting for less than a fourth of US sales; Switzerland accounts for about 1.4 percent of the company's total global sales. Several Nestlé brands, like Nescafé, KitKat, and Maggi, have achieved iconic status globally.[16]

Nestlé's value-creation strategy has an overarching focus on consumers first and then on shareholders and other stakeholders.[17]

Digital Transformation at Nestlé

Digitalization at Nestlé covers practically all aspects of the company's business—to help new growth, enhance agility, and generate efficiencies. Currently, Nestlé's digital footprint involves:

- Four online orders for *Nespresso* per second.
- 47 percent of total media spend on digital media.
- 185 million visits to its Latin American platform, *Recetas Nestlé*.
- 11.9 million conversations on *Workspace*, Nestlé's internal social networking platform.

Nestlé has been involved in e-commerce for over a decade, with increasing share of e-commerce sales in total group sales. E-commerce sales contributed 14.3% of Nestlé's total group sales in 2021—almost three times the share of e-commerce sales in total group sales in 2016—with plans to increase e-commerce sales to 25% of total group sales by 2025. Nestlé expects to achieve this by continuing to offer online and offline choices to consumers wherever and whenever they decide to shop, growing first-party consumer data records, and increasing investment in digital marketing from 51% of total media spend in 2021 to 70% by 2025.

Started in 2018, digital transformation at Nestlé is a huge, complex, and continuing effort, given:

- Nestlé's 850 Facebook (now Meta) pages with 210 million fans, plus Google and Twitter pages.
- 2,000 company websites.
- 1,300 pieces of unique content posted each day.
- 5,000 IT professionals and hundreds of partners.
- More than six million IT support interactions each year.

Digital transformation at Nestlé involved virtual rebuilding of the company, using latest technologies, and covering practically all business and management functions, including financial planning, HR, supply chain, customer service, and others. It involved several steps, including digitalization of operations, digital innovation, raising the digital expertise of employees, using analytics to reshape the company's marketing practices backed by powerful data models and algorithms, personalizing consumer engagement and experience, and accelerating learning through experimentation. All such initiatives are ongoing at the company. Digital transformation—remember—is a journey, not a destination.

Digitalization of operations. It includes multi-year initiatives throughout the company's operating network, applying technologies such as AI, predictive analytics, collaborative robots supporting factory automation, and blockchain. It has also helped strengthen Nestlé's capacity to capture and share data across the value chain.

Digital innovation. A program to continuously learn from consumers, customers, and technology partners to develop new business opportunities such as offering personalized nutrition advice and deploying AI chatbots, like cooking assistants, to boost consumer engagement.

Employing analytics. By partnering with leading digital innovators, Nestlé is using its technologies to, for instance, understand the return on marketing spend, the effectiveness of each brand interaction, and maximize the value of strategic direct-to-consumer investments.

Raising employees' digital expertise. To build employees' digital competence, Nestlé has established e-business academies that offer employees relevant, easy-to-consume learning materials. These academies are built on a gaming format so that employees have fun while learning. Building a data culture within the company meant overhauling the company's internal culture with data placed at the center of decision making. A social media platform was established within the company to encourage a culture of social networking among employees.

Nestlé's Digital Strategy

Digital transformation of practically all company processes paved the way for digital strategy implementation. It also gives an indication of how the company is attempting to create and capture value and stay a step ahead of competition.

Value creation and value capture. Nestlé creates value by offering products that meet customer needs, even customizing and personalizing them for specific customer groups, such as personalized nutrition for consumers and customization of dog food in terms of activity and dog's physical characteristics, like weight.

Nestlé helps drive consumer experience and engagement through innovative technologies—such as AI, machine learning, blockchain, and advanced data analytics. Artificial intelligence is used to offer consumers personalized health and wellness advice, custom recipes, answer their queries, and so on—which help improve consumer retention and willingness to pay. With technologies like voice assistants and intelligent chatbots, Nestlé maintains a one-on-one relationship with consumers. Advanced data analytics helps Nestlé identify consumer needs, behaviors, and preferences, which aid in product design and decision making. As the world's largest maker of food and beverage products—some 2,000 local and global brands—Nestlé's scale of operations gives it economies of scale and scope. All such initiatives help create value shared with consumers, Nestlé itself, and with other stakeholders.

IoT products. In 2016, Nestlé introduced their first Bluetooth-connected Nespresso coffeemaker, the *Prodigio*. Its functions include remote and scheduled brewing (with a smartphone, you can order Prodigio through its app to make coffee at a pre-scheduled time), coffee capsule stock management, and maintenance alerts. Now, Nestlé has their second connected coffeemaker, the NESCAFÉ Dolce Gusto Esparta® 2, a professional grade coffeemaker. One can make lattes, cappuccinos, espressos, and over a dozen other coffee varieties using the NESCAFÉ® Dolce Gusto® app. As IoT devices, both machines have the potential to leverage network effects.

Creating competitive advantage. Nestlé creates competitive gaps through data, digital marketing, AI, predictive analysis, and other technologies. In addition, Nestlé enjoys competitive advantage through its high-quality products, established brands, high investment in R&D and innovation, strong market position, partnerships with strong companies (such as Starbucks, whereby Nestlé sells Starbucks-branded coffee), product availability at multiple offline and online sales channels, and of course strong marketing and advertising.

Using business models. Nestlé uses a variety of business models to reach consumers, adapting the model to wherever and whenever consumers shop. These include direct-to-consumer channels as part of Nestlé's e-commerce initiatives, retail channels such as convenience, club, value, natural, and specialty stores, as well as out-of-home channels like billboard advertising. The subscription model is used for direct-to-consumer marketing, especially for pet care and other personalized offerings.

Notes

1 Borrowing the language from *Playing to Win* by A.G. Lafley and Roger Martin (Harvard Business Review Press, 2013).

2 Metcalfe's Law: https://en.wikipedia.org/wiki/Metcalfe%27s_law.

3 BCG, "Ten lessons from 20 years of value creation insights," November 27, 2018. https://www.bcg.com/publications/2018/value-creation-insights-ten-lessons-20-years.

4 Business Roundtable, "Statement of the Purpose of a Corporation," https://opportunity.businessroundtable.org/ourcommitment/.

5 Urquhart (Urko) Wood, "Take a lesson from Nike's strategy playbook." https://revealgrowth.com/take-a-lesson-from-nikes-customer-diagnosis-approach/.

6 Statista, "Nike's global revenue, 2005–2033," August 15, 2022. https://www.statista.com/statistics/241683/nikes-sales-worldwide-since-2004/.

7 Refer to Chapter 6 for servitization of products and productization of services business models.

8 Stefan Michel, "Capture more value." *Harvard Business Review*, October 2014.

9 Michael E. Porter, *Competitive Advantage: Creating and Sustaining Superior Performance* (New York: Free Press, 1985).

10 Winner-take-all or winner-take-most markets have existed for a long time in sports, politics, entertainment, and other sectors of the economy. In technology businesses, this phenomenon often occurs as a result of Moore's Law, Metcalfe's Law (principle of network effects), and other factors.

11 Jacques Bughin and Nicolas van Zeebroeck, "The best response to digital disruption." *Sloan Management Review*, April 6, 2017.

12 When a legacy company responds aggressively to digital entrants or to other legacy companies that were ahead of the curve in digitalization, it can lead to "Red Queen competition," as suggested by Jacques Bughin and Nicolas van Zeebroek, "The best response to digital disruption," *Sloan Management Review*, May 9, 2017. ("This kind of competition is named for the Red Queen, a character in Lewis Carroll's *Through the Looking-Glass*, who engages in a foot race in which competitors run hard just to stay in the same place.")

13 Alfred D. Chandler, Jr. *Scale and Scope: The Dynamics of Industrial Capitalism.* (Cambridge, MA: The Belknap Press, 1994.)

14 Super-app, https://en.wikipedia.org/wiki/Super-app.
15 The Boston Consulting Group calls them *digital incumbents*, new players in the digital world—formerly legacy businesses that have gone through the process of digital transformation. https://www.bcg.com/en-us/publications/2022/rise-of-digital-incumbents-building-digital-capabilities.
16 Much of the information in this case study was obtained from the company website, www.nestle.com, annual report, https://www.nestle.com/investors/annual-report, and www.statista.com. Any other sources utilized are shown separately.
17 Much of the information in this case study was taken from various company websites, such as https://www.nestle.com/investors/annual-report.

Chapter 8

Digital Strategy for Global B2B Businesses

> *Digital technology is both a global trend and an opportunity for China. The industrial internet, like the construction machinery industry, is not a 'fast food restaurant'. It is a lifelong business that needs to withstand loneliness and withstand competitive pressures. There is no end to digital transformation.*
>
> Wang Min, Chairman, Xuzhou Construction Machinery Group Co. Ltd., China

Chapter 7 was about digital strategy for global B2C businesses; this chapter is about digital strategy for global B2B businesses. Why make the distinction?

The final consumers for B2C (business-to-consumer) businesses tend to be individuals and households, even though their direct customers are generally companies like major retail chains; much of their advertising is directed at consumer media. The customers of B2B (business-to-business) businesses are other businesses that use their industrial purchases to make goods for other businesses. The buyers of B2B goods are generally much more knowledgeable than individual buyers of consumer goods; they buy in much larger quantities and the purchase process for B2B goods and services tends to be much more involved, with the buyers requiring a lot more information about what they are buying.

In terms of the technologies used by B2B vs. B2C businesses, many of the technologies are essentially the same, such as AI, sensors, connectivity, cloud, and data analytics. The difference is how they are used. As shown later in the chapter, technologies used in B2C businesses are often aimed at improving the lives of individual consumers. Technologies used in B2B businesses are often intended for more sophisticated and complex equipment used for improving production processes and supply chains.

The Four Industrial Revolutions

The world has gone through three industrial revolutions since the late 1700s, and we are currently in the early phases of the fourth industrial revolution, also known as *Industry 4.0* or *smart*

DOI: 10.4324/9781003037446-10

Table 8.1   The Four Industrial Revolutions

1st *Late 1700s*	2nd *Early 1900s*	3rd *1970s*	4th *Today*

Mechanization
Water and steam
  power
1784: First
  mechanical loom
	Electrification
	Mass production
	  (assembly lines)
	1901: First patented
	  production line,
	  Ransom Olds
	  (Oldsmobile)
		Automation
		Electronics and
		  computers replace
		  manual work
		1969: First
		  programmable
		  logic controller
			Tech Revolution
			Industry 4.0
			AI, robotics, data
			  analytics, and IoT
			Convergence of
			  physical, digital,
			  and virtual worlds

manufacturing. Each of the industrial revolutions was led by new technologies and new ways of working—water and steam power replacing manual labor, mass production through assembly lines powered by electricity, and computers and electronics replacing manual labor. New technologies in each industrial revolution disrupted industries of the time and transformed how people lived and worked. The current fourth industrial revolution is led by digital technologies where the physical truly meets digital. Table 8.1 briefly describes the four industrial revolutions.

Industry 4.0

Popularized by Klaus Schwab, the Founder and Executive Chairman of the World Economic Forum, in 2015, the term *Industry 4.0* refers to the use of digital technologies to transform how industrial companies operate. Technology and Industry 4.0 are revolutionizing manufacturing and supply chains end-to-end, led by automation, industrial internet of things (IIoT), AI, data analytics, 3D printing, and other digital technologies. Smart autonomous systems use computer-based algorithms to monitor and control physical things like machines, robots, and vehicles.

> Industry 4.0 makes everything in your supply chain 'smart' – from smart manufacturing and factories to smart warehousing and logistics… gives companies unprecedented level of visibility and control [of operations]. Ultimately, Industry 4.0 is a major part of any company's digital transformation… These innovations bridge the physical and digital worlds and make smart, autonomous systems possible.[1]

Some of the technologies that form the backbone of Industry 4.0 are AI, data analytics, cloud computing, augmented reality, 3D printing (additive manufacturing), robotics, digital twins (simulation), cybersecurity, and, of course, IIoT. Industry 4.0 is where the physical, digital, and virtual worlds merge. The emphasis in Industry 4.0 is creation of smart (intelligent) products, smart factories, and smart assets (assets embedded with sensors, software, and technologies).[2] It makes decision making in real time possible, improves productivity and quality, and replaces manual work with IIoT equipment. The term *Industry 4.0* is applicable to both B2C and B2B industries.

Industrial Internet of Things (IIoT) or *Industrial Internet*, terms coined by General Electric (GE) in 2012, refer to physical devices such as industrial equipment and vehicles, embedded with sensors, software, and connectivity that enable them to connect and exchange data with other connected devices over the internet.[3] Major industrial companies like GE and Bosch have made industrial internet a core foundation of their business through subsidiaries like GE Digital and

Bosch.IO, respectively. General Electric, as a part of its digital transformation, invested over a billion dollars to restructure the company almost completely as an industrial internet business. Now, GE Digital offers digital solutions for dozens of industries, including automotive, aviation, power generation, utilities, and pharmaceuticals. The Bosch Group offers connected products and services for both consumer and industrial markets (more on the Bosch Group later in the chapter).

How IoT (IIoT) Changes Manufacturing

In 2022, there were an estimated 14.76 billion IoT devices worldwide, expected to grow to 25.44 billion by 2030. They are used in all types of industries, both B2C and B2B, with B2C industries accounting for about 60% of all IoT-connected devices as of 2020. The largest numbers of IoT devices are in industry verticals like electricity, gas, steam and air-conditioning, water supply, waste management, transportation, retail and wholesale trade, and government.[4]

As the population of IoT devices reaches critical mass, manufacturing is already going through a major transformation—how products are made, delivered, and used by customers. Internet of Things (IoT), combined with AI, is improving operational efficiencies through better visibility and better control of operations. For instance, if a machine breaks down, inbuilt sensors alert operators about the problem, even triggering a service request—without human intervention. Beyond making manufacturing operations more efficient, IoT-enabled robots can work in dangerous conditions, keeping workers safe. Besides, the IoT has enabled newer, business models, such as product servitization, digital add-ons, and outcome-based business models (Chapter 6).

Some Specific Advantages of the IIoT

Although many of the following advantages are applicable in B2C businesses, they are especially valuable in B2B businesses. Sensors embedded in IIoT equipment monitor operations continuously, send data to an AI platform which analyzes the data for multiple applications in real time, and even triggers action if needed.

Preventive maintenance. Preventive maintenance (or preventative maintenance) means scheduled, regular maintenance of machines and equipment to reduce the possibility of unexpected breakdowns, expensive repairs, and loss of production. This used to require human intervention and a visit to wherever the faulty equipment was located. In the age of IIoT, however, it's the sensors embedded in the equipment that monitor equipment performance continuously, remotely, and act autonomously if a problem is detected—correcting the problem or triggering a service request. Even more important, monitoring of plants and equipment with subsequent data analytics can be used for *predictive* maintenance to detect potential issues before they arise.

Remote monitoring and diagnostics. The sensors in IIoT equipment offer continuous updates of its operating status and can remotely diagnose a system, change settings, and halt a process or activate equipment as needed. All of these diagnostic steps and actions occur remotely and autonomously through an IIoT gateway. The use of IIoT improves machine uptime, reduces cost, and enables predictive maintenance.

Remote software updates. Given the growth of IoT devices in both B2C and B2B worlds, it has become imperative for IoT manufacturers to keep the embedded software updated. With billions of IoT devices worldwide, updating their software manually is a literally impossible task. Hence the need for automatic, remote software updates—needed to fix bugs, add new features, or improve device functionality. The luxury carmaker BMW makes remote software upgrades to improve the functionality in its vehicles from time to time. For example, in October 2021, the company remotely upgraded the vehicle operating system to the BMW Operating System 7 (Ver. 21-07) on some two million cars worldwide, its third software upgrade for the year. Simultaneously, Spotify also upgraded owners' entertainment experience through *BMW Connected Music* by adding podcasts to its streaming.

Asset tracking. IIoT-based asset tracking systems include identifying the location of an asset and its status, thus removing the time and cost involved in manual tracking of the asset and safeguarding against human error. It's a fast-growing application of IIoT technologies. For instance, sensors installed in vehicles, shipping crates, or construction equipment permit the organization to continuously track the physical location of assets—whether at a job site or on the move. In fleet management, sensors provide much more valuable information than GPS could—information like vehicle status, fuel consumption, route optimization, compliance with safety requirements, and so on.

Automatic fulfillment. Asset tracking throughout the supply chain permits automation of fulfillment centers and reordering processes. Sensors help monitor stock levels in real time and trigger a reorder, without human intervention, when inventory levels become low or reach a certain level. From the customer perspective, automatic fulfillment reduces the time and cost of reordering, detects theft or other stock issues such as delays due to weather or traffic conditions, and reduces the risk of running out of supplies when needed.

Compliance monitoring. Sensors in IIoT equipment not only help monitor equipment conditions (such as temperature and power consumption), but they can also be used for complying with regulations, such as occupational safety and health regulations, as well as any required guidelines. During the COVID-19 pandemic, the ability to track employees through wearable trackers or smartphones proved to be especially valuable to ensure compliance with, for instance, social-distancing requirements.

CAPEX to OPEX. With an appropriate business model (such as the product-as-a-service business model), an industrial company can use the IIoT to replace capital expenditure (CAPEX) with operating expenditure (OPEX). This not only reduces the company's financial risk (by transferring the risk of big capital expenditure to the equipment manufacturer), it also benefits from guaranteed equipment performance as part of the Product-as-a-Service (PaaS), outcome-based business model.

How XCMG Benefits from the IIoT[5]

The Xuzhou Construction Machinery Group Co. Ltd. (XCMG) is a state-owned heavy machinery company founded in 1943 and headquartered in Xuzhou, China. By now, it has 14 overseas manufacturing and KD (assembling equipment from *knocked-down* parts and components) plants and exports its industrial equipment (such as heavy-duty trucks and heavyweight cranes) to over 180 countries and regions, serving them from 40 overseas offices and 300+ distributors. It is the fifth largest construction machinery company in the world.

The company started its digitalization in 2009 with an SAP resource planning project, which over the next ten years had made significant progress toward XCMG's digital transformation. The digital transformation was carried out in six phases (Table 8.2).

In 2016, in partnership with Alibaba Cloud, XCMG developed its own industrial internet cloud platform, Xrea. By 2019, the cloud platform was serving more than 1,000 industrial enterprises in 20 countries, covering 63 industries. Once a piece of equipment from anywhere in the world is connected to the Xrea platform, it can be remotely diagnosed and maintained—without need for human intervention. By 2019, more than 760,000 pieces of equipment worldwide had

Table 8.2   The Six Phases of XCMG's Digitalization Process (2009–2019)

Phase	Description
1	Digitalization of a single function
2	Digital integration of front- and backend systems
3	Improved offerings through connected services
4	Adoption of new business models, including a multi-sided platform
5	Evolution of a business ecosystem
6	Extending business scope through technology to serve an almost *unlimited* number of connected devices

been connected to the Xrea cloud, which monitored their locations, tracked operations and equipment statuses, predicted timing of potential equipment failure, and more.

XCMG uses data at the Xrea platform received from multiple sources (such as sensors in equipment connected to the platform, IoT terminals, and enterprise information systems), collected and processed in real time. Data thus generated is analyzed at the platform for various decision-making applications—for example, predictive maintenance and energy management—via mobile apps; accessible to XCMG itself, customers, and third-party developers. Data is also reported to the relevant Chinese authorities for compliance purposes and used by the State Council Office as an indicator of macroeconomic trends in the country.

Value Creation-Value-Capture Framework for IoT (IIoT) Businesses

This section is about how industrial companies create and capture value in the IoT world. Although industrial companies can indeed create and capture value without going the IoT route, the IoT (including IIoT) business models are of special interest because they can be applied in situations where non-IoT business models cannot. In addition, they offer significant value-creation opportunities. While B2C firms create and capture value through IoT business models, the B2B businesses have much greater opportunity to create and capture value through the IoT.

Sometimes, companies that make equipment for other companies don't make much money from equipment sales, though they do make money by selling parts, consumables, and after-sale service. However, given cut-throat competition in most industries, competitors can often make near copies of the original equipment and parts and sell them at lower prices. Instead of selling the equipment, parts, consumables, and after-sale service, original equipment manufacturers benefit from IIoT in another way. They offer the equipment on *subscription*, with guaranteed performance—retaining equipment ownership. They convert one-time sale of the equipment into a stream of regular revenues through subscription. We came across an example of this business model in Chapter 6 as product-as-a-service (PaaS) or product servitization or the outcome-based business model. Recall Michelin Tires which had adopted the PaaS model for some customers. These customers make no capital investment, pass the risk of ownership to the manufacturer, and still receive guaranteed equipment performance.

This approach helps in customer retention and is much harder, though not impossible, for competitors to copy. With connected products, a manufacturer can remotely monitor equipment performance, take corrective action as needed, and offer guaranteed, error-free service as a result—exactly what the customer needs. Besides, connected products generate huge amounts of data, which can be monetized in many ways. See Box 8.1 how Rolls-Royce does it.

BOX 8.1 ROLLS-ROYCE

Rolls-Royce of UK manufactures and services aircraft engines it sells to aircraft manufacturers like Boeing. Airlines and other customers then purchase the aircraft, which need ongoing servicing throughout the engines' lifespan. Rolls-Royce is one of several companies (including the other engine manufacturers, GE and Pratt & Whitney) that offer MRO (maintenance, repair, and overhaul) services for aircraft.

As reported in 2015 by StackExchange.com, a network of Q&A websites, some 80% of Rolls-Royce engines are sold at a loss, with the company making money from its MRO (maintenance, repair, and overhaul) services for airlines and other customers—an example of the *razor and blade* business model.[6] Rolls-Royce's TotalCare® program, offering "Power by the Hour"®, is a Rolls-Royce innovation under which airlines pay Rolls-Royce for the number of hours an engine is actually in the air. This program entails fixed, predictable costs to airlines for engine repair and maintenance. In return for these regular revenues, Rolls-Royce assumes the risk of keeping the engines in full working order. Nowadays, more and more airline customers are moving away from traditional maintenance servicing contracts to a power-by-the-hour arrangement. Both GE and Pratt & Whitney also have similar programs for aircraft fitted with their engines.

With hundreds of sensors embedded in its engines and other equipment, Rolls-Royce continuously monitors thousands of aircraft in air at any time from its Derby, UK, operations center (or from one of its three other operations centers). The wealth of data provided by the sensors helps Rolls-Royce continuously assess the performance of its engines, spot problems before they occur, and schedule maintenance as needed, well in time. The data are also valuable to client airlines that have fewer breakdowns and fewer unhappy flyers.

According to *The Economist*, "gross margins from rebuilding engines are thought to be about 35%; analysts at Credit Suisse, an investment bank, estimate that some makers of jet engines get about seven times as much revenue from servicing and selling spare parts [throughout their lifespan] as they do from selling engines."[7]

From the perspective of this chapter, a useful value-creation/value-capture framework for IoT/IIoT businesses was suggested by Elgar Fleisch, Felix Wortmann, and Markus Weinberger in their September 2014 Technical Report, "Business Models and the Internet of Things" (Figure 8.1). The framework has five value-creation/value-capture layers, starting with the physical *thing* itself, the device or machine embedded with sensors, software, and technologies, and leading up to digital services offered through the physical, connected device. A company employing IoT has opportunities to create and capture value at each of the five stages. How and to what extent the company derives value from each stage depends on the creativity of the people involved. Notice that the arrows in Figure 8.1 are bidirectional, highlighting the integrative nature of the IoT value-creation

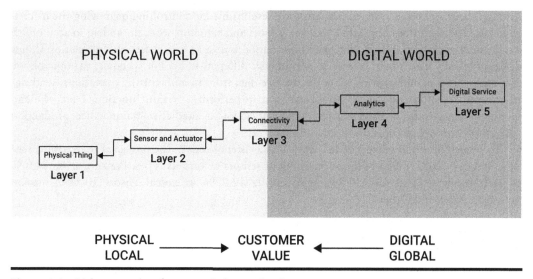

Figure 8.1   Value-creation framework for IoT businesses.

Source: Adapted from Elgar Fleisch, Felix Wortmann, and Markus Weinberger, "Business Models and the Internet of Things" September 2014. Bosch IoT Lab, ETH Zurich. Used with permission.

framework. In an IoT world, none of the layers can adequately create value on its own, if at all. In order for an IoT product to effectively create value, all five layers are needed.

Value-Creation Layer 1: Physical Thing

Companies can indeed create value through outright sale (or leasing or rental) of its physical product without going through the other layers; this is how businesses always operated in the pre-IoT world, and most still do. They have many ways to create value for the company by selling their equipment, for example, though direct sale, e-commerce, on a platform, and in many other ways. As for platforms for B2B transactions, the SAP Business Network (formerly known as the Ariba Network) is the world's largest internet-based trading platform serving millions of companies from 190 countries that did more than 699 million B2B transactions worth $4.1 trillion in a recent 12-month period.[8] It's a broad-based platform for business-to-business transactions, including e-procurement, e-invoicing, and working capital management, among many other functions (more on the SAP Business Network in Chapter 6).[9]

In the IoT world, however, a physical product creates value by using all five layers in an integrated manner (Figure 8.1). In the Rolls-Royce example mentioned earlier, the company makes money by selling engines to aircraft manufacturers (Layer 1) as well as by providing MRO services to airline customers (Layers 2–5).

Value-Creation Layer 2: Sensors and Actuators

Sensors and actuators are key components in IoT machines of all kinds. Network sensors detect information (such as change in temperature, vibration, or an open valve), which they transmit through their connected system. Actuators are responsible for controlling or moving the mechanism based on the information they receive. Sensors and actuators work in tandem to accomplish a task, such as closing a valve, when the information indicates it is necessary. Internet of Things devices typically have many sensors to accomplish different tasks. For instance, various robotic arm sensors in a manufacturing plant can receive data from manufacturing operations, send signals to the actuator, and cause one robotic arm to perform a certain function. Data, the end product of sensors, can be used to accomplish such actions as predictive maintenance, production scheduling, throughput optimization, and more.

There are billions of sensors in IoT devices in existence today. The projected IoT-enabled sensors market in 2022 is $56 billion, consisting of sensors of various types: Pressure sensors (36% of total), temperature sensors (26.2%), light sensors (12.27%), chemical sensors (10.21%), motion sensors (8.35%), and Others (1.97%).[10]

Value-Creation Layer 3: Connectivity

Much of what IoT devices can achieve depends on the strength of their connectivity to the internet. Connectivity allows them to connect and share live data with other connected devices, customers, employees, and operations centers worldwide—for improved business processes and better, faster decision making. The examples used in this section (such as Rolls-Royce and Philips Lighting) showcase how connectivity makes IoTs functional.

Value-Creation Layer 4: Analytics

Irrespective of what IoT (IIoT) devices are designed to do, they create huge amounts of data that offer the organization instant, live visibility into operations. They can also enable better, faster decision making and offer opportunities for data monetization. Data coming from sensors in IoT devices are combined with data from many other sources, such as transactions, RFID tags, audio, video, images, and social media, and autonomously analyzed for decision making. The Michelin Group, for instance, now embeds sensors in certain tires to continuously measure tire pressure and temperature, transmit the readings through radio signals—eventually reaching a smartphone through Bluetooth. Data is processed by an app previously installed on the smartphone.

Michelin® Tire Care system for fleet management, for example, helps with tire maintenance by offering "access to a customizable tire maintenance and reporting service that helps reduce road service calls, improve CSA [Compliance, Safety, Accountability] scores, and optimizes safety and performance."[11] Michelin® Tire Care currently services over 260 fleets and 36,000 commercial vehicles throughout the US.

Value-Creation Layer 5: Digital Service

Digital services are the end product of this value-creation model for IoT businesses. The PaaS business model (from Chapter 6) is an ideal example of how a physical products company can offer digital services in the IoT world. With the addition of sensors, connectivity, and data analytics, the IoT company derives value from the services the product offers rather than (or in addition to) the product itself.

Bosch[12]

Bosch (Robert Bosch GmbH) is a pre-eminent, global engineering and technology company founded by Robert Bosch in Stuttgart, Germany, in 1886 as the "Workshop for Precision Mechanics and Electrical Engineering." Starting with literally any kind of electrical work that came his way, such as production and installation of telephone systems and electric bells, Bosch became a world-leading supplier of automotive products like ignition systems by 1902. During the next few decades, Bosch diversified into many areas, including automotive electric lighting, power tools, radios for cars and homes, cinema projectors, equipment for television studios, diesel engines, and household appliances, among others.

Bosch's entry into electronics in 1959 paved the way for the development of an electronically controlled gasoline injection system in 1967, electronic diesel controls in 1986, and other major innovations, especially in automotive technology. Bosch also adopted the divisional organization structure throughout the company by creating independent divisions, each responsible for achieving its sales and profit targets. These included the Power Tools division, the Packaging Technology division, and the Automotive Technology division. Much of the innovation and growth at the Bosch Group resulted from inhouse research and development as well as from acquisitions and partnerships.

Robert Bosch believed in globalization almost from the company's very founding. He established a sales office in the UK in 1898, in France a year later, and in most European countries shortly thereafter. Bosch entered the US and South Africa in 1906, Australia in 1907, Argentina in 1908, China in 1909, and Japan in 1911. In 1906 itself, Bosch received orders worth over a million dollars for its magneto ignition systems from the US, and double that amount the following year. Not just sales operations, Bosch launched production facilities in many countries, starting with France in 1905 and the US in 1912. By 1913, Bosch was generating over 88% of its sales from outside Germany.[13]

Bosch today. The Bosch Group today is a leading supplier of consumer, industrial, and technology goods and services with almost 403,000 employees worldwide as of December 31, 2021. With global sales of €78.75 billion ($89.40 billion) in 2021, the company operates in four business sectors: Mobility Solutions (2021 sales of €45.3 billion), Consumer Goods (€21.4 billion), Industrial Technology (€6.1 billion), and Energy and Building Technology (€5.9 billion). Table 8.3 lists some representative products sold by each of the four business sectors.

The Robert Bosch Foundation (Robert Bosch Stiftung GmbH) currently holds 92% of the company's share capital, much of the balance being held by the Bosch family. The Foundation

Table 8.3 Bosch Group's Four Business Sectors—Selected Products

Mobility Solutions	Consumer Goods	Industrial Technology	Energy & Building Technology
Powertrain solutions Electrical drives Automotive electronics Automotive steering Car multimedia Two-wheeler and powersports Bosch eBike systems	Power Tools BSH Hausgeräte GmbH	Drive and Control Technology (Bosch Rexroth)	Building Technologies Thermotechnology Bosch Global Service Solutions

supports numerous social projects in the areas of education, health, international relations, society, culture, and science. To ensure that the company remained under family ownership, Robert Bosch changed the company's structure from an AG (a public limited company) to a GmbH (a private limited company) in 1937, a move made possible by a change in German company law that year.

Bosch.IO. In the mid-2000s, the Bosch Group, like some other large industrial companies (such as GE and Schneider Electric), decided to make industrial internet the core of its business foundation and created the Bosch.IO subsidiary in 2008. Headquartered in Berlin, Germany, Bosch.io has offices in Bulgaria, China, Japan, Singapore, Spain, and the US. Its wide range of IoT products and services includes consulting to implementation and operation. Project teams typically have interdisciplinary experts—hardware and software developers, project managers, cloud specialists, solution architects, UX (user experience) designers, business model innovators, and trainers.

Speaking at the ThingMont event in London, UK in September 2016, Stefan Farber, vice president of engineering at Bosch (now CEO of Bosch.IO) said,

> Bosch started to engage with the Internet of Things in 2008. At that time we saw that the internet was taking over communications channels everywhere…. We decided we didn't want to be a tier 2/tier 3 supplier of dumb devices. We wanted to build intelligent devices. And up to today still, intelligence meaning that we put electronics and software in the device. Our CEO made a plan that every device in the Bosch group needs internet connectivity.[14]

As a vertically integrated business, Bosch.IO has expertise in sensor technology, manufacturing, systems integration, AI research, and software and services. It has over 900 professionals worldwide focused on digitalization and IoT, collaborating with over 38,000 software developers and AI experts throughout the company. Bosch manufactures over four million sensors every day for internal use and third-party applications. Bosch and its customers have connected over ten million devices and machines to the *Bosch IoT Suite*, its technical platform for IoT applications. These include gateways in buildings, sensors in urban infrastructure and digital agriculture, and connected vehicles. Recently, Bosch also set up a one-billion-euro semiconductor plant in Dresden, Germany, to manufacture sensors and chips. With years of experience, Bosch.IO had worked on over 250 digital and IoT projects for international customers by 2020.

The Bosch Group has a long history of making household appliances for the mass consumer market. These are now being turned into connected devices with the idea of engaging customers throughout the product lifecycle (as against one-off sale of appliances). With data being generated continuously by the connected devices, triggering action by Bosch, the company continues to make money (*value capture*) during the device's lifetime from services offered to customers and even monetizes the data collected through its IoT devices. And the customer captures value from the device through regular upkeep, upgrades, and guaranteed service by Bosch. Bosch's medium-term objective is to follow every hardware sale with service—gradually expanding the services offerings in all its business sectors—with more value being created by software, data, and services than by *things* (physical products).

Digital Transformation at Bosch

Digital transformation at a legacy, established company requires not just changes in technology but also changes in organizational structure, organizational processes, investment priorities, new capabilities, and—more than anything else—changes in organizational culture. Bosch faced many challenges during its digital transformation from an industrial company to an industrial-internet company:

- Managing tension between traditional business and the IoT way of doing things, and balancing investment priorities between traditional businesses (still very substantial) and IoT businesses.
- Tying products with services to derive revenue from not just product sales but also by providing ongoing services to customers; this involved increasing the value of hardware sold through the company's *3S Strategy*—sensors, software, and services—in everything the company made.
- Changing approach to product development—balancing user experience, for example, ease of use of a device with device data security.
- Changing approach to sales and customer relationship management—from one-time sale to continuing customer relationships with the company (and recurring revenues).
- Updating organizational culture, a major driver of digital transformation (e.g., staff to *rip off* ties, celebrate *error culture*, and adopt a *just do it* way of doing things).
- Building capabilities for the new digital environment:
  - sourcing tech talent from universities,
  - a comprehensive AI training program to make almost 30,000 associates AI-savvy,
  - acquiring smaller companies with the technologies and skills Bosch needed, and
  - developing pockets of excellence within the company.

All of the above needed continuing focus on innovation, being achieved through:

- inhouse AI research centers (in Bangalore, Palo Alto, and Deiningen),
- *grow platform*, an internal incubation platform at Bosch for startups and intrapreneurs originating from within the company,
- a €420 million venture fund created in 2017, and
- partnerships (e.g., with Tesla for autonomous vehicles and with Amazon for Alexa to be used in smart-home systems).

Bosch Group's Digital Strategy

As indicated earlier, Bosch.IO followed a *3S Strategy*—sensors, software, and services—for practically everything the company made, with most hardware sold by the company being transformed as IoT devices. In addition to digital transformation, the key elements of Bosch.IO's digital strategy included the familiar concepts of value creation, value capture, and establishing competitive advantage.

Creating and capturing value at Bosch.IO. Bosch.IO approaches value creation almost by the book, incorporating technology, innovation, IoT, network effects, digital business models, and extending the company's scale and scope.

Bosch.IO is at the forefront of using latest information technologies, including AI, its own cloud for the IoT, 3D printing, robotics in manufacturing, and data analytics, among others. For instance, at the new semiconductor plant in Dresden, Bosch Group's single largest investment so far, natural and artificial intelligence work together with the IoT. Internet connectivity and IoT, combined with AI, are used to continuously improve products, processes, and services. Using the company's own IoT cloud, Bosch.IO offers customers connected, cross-domain solutions from a single source. As more and more products are converted into IoT devices, the cloud-based Bosch IoT Suite connects different devices to relevant IT infrastructure (backend) and collects data transmitted by these devices. The IoT products help Bosch benefit from network effects. The IoT cloud is the company's universal platform to securely store and process data. For example, Bosch's Manufacturing Analytics Solutions is a system for the continuous collection, visualization, monitoring, and analysis of manufacturing data. Staff at Bosch plants then analyze manufacturing processes, detect any problems with the help of AI, and identify and eliminate causes of any problems at an early stage.

The Bosch Center for Artificial Intelligence is a center of competence that operates in seven locations—in Germany, the US, China, India, and Israel. It has successfully obtained over 1,000 patent families in multiple countries in the field of AI. Bosch's *grow platform GmbH*, based in Ludwigsburg, is a platform within the company for developing and implementing new business models. A part of Bosch's global innovation network, it helps develop and evaluate new business models to be pursued in startup teams.

Bosch.IO uses different digital business models for different applications. Internet of Things (IoT) is Bosch.IO's key business model, much else follows from the IoT. Some of other business models used by the company include direct selling (including leasing and rental), product servitization (PaaS), subscription, platform and ecosystem, and data monetization. With over 2.5 quintillion bytes of data generated by IoT devices each day, Bosch.IO has numerous opportunities to use data for its operations and to monetize it.

Creating competitive advantage. Table 8.3 showed the different business sectors in which Bosch competes. As expected, the competitive environment faced by Bosch varies considerably from sector to sector as well as Bosch's relative competitive strength in each. In some sectors, like Mobility Solutions, Bosch operates in a consolidated industry, competing with a few major players, while in some others, such as the Drive and Control division, Bosch operates in a fragmented industry with many competitors.[15] No single competitive strategy can, therefore, work for all business sectors. It's enough here to review the sources of competitive advantage (from Chapter 7) for legacy businesses as they enter digital markets and explore how and to what extent Bosch uses such sources. The sources of competitive advantage for digitalizing legacy businesses include technological innovation, network effects, digital or IoT products, complementary products, scale and scope, and business models.

Technological innovation was the very basis for the formation of Bosch.IO. In addition, Bosch has a number of initiatives to encourage internal innovation, including the *grow incubation platform* and AI research centers. Bosch also benefits from innovation approaches leveraging non-Bosch resources, such as the €420 million venture fund that invests in promising startups around the world, and partnerships with companies like IBM, Tesla, and others. Practically, all physical products manufactured by Bosch are now IoT devices that help create powerful *network effects*. Bosch has entered into partnerships with many automotive and technology companies for *complementary products and services*. Some recent examples are:

- A Networking Autonomous Vehicle (NAV) alliance with Volkswagen and the US semiconductor company Nvidia. The alliance offers a collaboration framework around technologies, specifications, interoperability, and product development for multi-gigabit in-vehicle networking.
- Bosch joined with Intel to monitor air pollution with an air quality measuring kit; measurement of air quality is a key component of smart city infrastructure.

- Bosch and Nvidia are developing an AI-powered autonomous vehicle system, used for *training* vehicles remotely, operated autonomously, and updated via the cloud.
- Bosch is partnering with Software AG to develop a range of new IoT products, services, and solutions—adding to their existing offerings. The idea is to integrate the Bosch IoT cloud with Software AG's Digital Business Platform to offer real-time data analytics services for improved business processes and better decision making.

As the world's largest supplier of many kinds of automotive products, and a leading global supplier of technology and services, Bosch benefits from *economies of scale and scope* in many of its business divisions. For instance, the Bosch IoT Suite has already connected over ten million devices in all kinds of products, such as vehicles and sensors in urban and agricultural applications.

Bosch uses *digital business models* in its business divisions as needed. The *Internet of Things* (and IIoT) is the principal business model used for all business activities at Bosch.IO. Bosch uses *direct selling* (including leasing and rental) for some industrial equipment, such as Bosch Rexroth's products (discussed below). For its electric scooter-sharing business in Berlin and Paris, Bosch uses the *direct-to-consumer* business model; with no hardware of its own for the sharing business, Bosch only provides the platform for scooter sharing. Some of the other digital business models being used by Bosch are *product servitization (PaaS)*, *subscription*, and *data monetization*.

Bosch Rexroth, a subsidiary of the Bosch Group, offers solutions for factory automation, hydraulics, and mobile machines throughout the world. More specifically, Bosch Rexroth's product and services portfolio includes components and complete solutions for hydraulics, electric drives and controls, and linear motion and assembly technologies with intelligent, plug-and-produce solutions. With 31,000 employees, Rexroth has operations in 80 countries with revenues of €6.2 billion in 2021.

As an example, Rexroth's *CytroBox* is an intelligent, all-in-one connected hydraulic power unit for industrial applications needing power in the range 7.5–30 kW. It offers cost savings up to 80% over conventional hydraulic power units. It comes integrated with *CytroConnect* IIoT services to help avoid unplanned downtimes. Bosch Rexroth creates value through its CytroBox product in many ways (refer to value-creation/value-capture framework, Figure 8.1). Rexroth offers CytroBox in direct sale (value-creation Layer 1). Integrated and wired sensors in CytroBox provide continuing information regarding the filter, oil, and drive status (Layers 2 and 3). As a connected device, it monitors equipment status and plans maintenance in a cost-effective manner (Layers 3, 4, and 5). Such information, including operating statuses and forthcoming maintenance work to predictive maintenance analyses, is available to users via Rexroth's Online Diagnostics Network, ODiN (Layers 3 and 4).[16]

Bosch Rexroth, in addition to planning and installing the ODiN condition monitoring system at client premises, offers many other services, such as cloud data storage and analysis, continuous reporting of machine status and variations that could lead to failure, and recommendations and advice regarding needed maintenance.

Notes

1 SAP, "What is Industry 4.0?" https://www.sap.com/insights/what-is-industry-4-0.html.
2 SAP, *op. cit.*
3 GE, "Everything you need to know about the Industrial Internet of Things." https://www.ge.com/digital/blog/what-industrial-internet-things-iiot.

4 Statista, "Number of IoT connected devices worldwide, 2019–2030," August 22, 2022. https://www.statista.com/statistics/1183457/iot-connected-devices-worldwide/.

5 Mark Greeven and Yunfei Feng, Summary of the case study "XCMG: Digital transformation of a manufacturing giant," IMD-7-2142, copyright © 2020 by IMD—International Institute for Management Development, Lausanne, Switzerland (www.imd.ch). <u>No part of this publication may be reproduced, stored in a retrieval system, or transmitted in any form or by any means without the permission of IMD</u>. (Used with permission from the copyright owner, IMD.)

6 Stackexchange, "Jet engines: Are they owned by airlines or just rented," October 9, 2017. https://aviation.stackexchange.com/questions/12528/jet-engines-are-they-owned-by-the-airline-or-just-rented.

7 Economist, "Britain's lonely high-flyer," January 8, 2009. https://www.economist.com/briefing/2009/01/08/britains-lonely-high-flier.

8 SAP, "Explore SAP business network." https://www.sap.com/products/business-network/solutions.html.

9 SAP News Release, June 21, 2021, "SAP expanding world's largest business network." https://www.prnewswire.com/news-releases/sap-expanding-worlds-largest-business-network-301304127.html.

10 Statista, "Projected global Internet of Things enabled sensors market in 2022, by segment," July 12, 2022. https://www.statista.com/statistics/480114/global-internet-of-things-enabled-sensors-market-size-by-segment/.

11 Michelin, "Get the most out of your tires with Michelin tire care." https://business.michelinman.com/tirecare.

12 Information in this mini case study is based largely on various Bosch websites, including the 2021 annual report, https://assets.bosch.com/media/global/bosch_group/our_figures/pdf/bosch-annual-report-2021.pdf. Any other sources are identified separately.

13 Bosch Company History, https://assets.bosch.com/media/global/bosch_group/our_history/publications_ordering/pdf_2/Bosch_History_at_a_Glance.pdf.

14 Derek du Preez, "How Bosch is becoming an Internet of Things business," September 13, 2016. https://diginomica.com/interview-how-bosch-is-becoming-an-internet-of-things-business.

15 For more on the competitive environment faced by Bosch's different divisions, refer to Bosch Group 2021 annual report, section on Organization and Competitive Environment. https://assets.bosch.com/media/global/bosch_group/our_figures/pdf/bosch-annual-report-2021.pdf.

16 Rexroth Press Release, October 23, 2018. https://dc-corp.resource.bosch.com/media/xc/company_1/press/product_information/product_information_2018/october_2018/PI_027_18__CytroBox_en-1.pdf.

Chapter 9

Reinventing Innovation

Innovation comes ultimately from a diversity of perspectives. So when you combine ideas from different industries or different cultures, that's when you have the best sense of developing groundbreaking ideas.

Frans Johansson, *The Medici Effect*, 2004

In 1999, Eli Lilly, a US-Based, R&D-focused pharmaceutical company, had about 6,050 researchers, including physicians, scientists, and other highly skilled technical personnel, and an R&D budget of $1.78 billion. Most of the products the company sold were discovered or developed by its own scientists. Yet, despite the large R&D staff and many successful products, there was a feeling that they were not being as effective in developing and bringing products to market as they could be.

In a brainstorming session at Lilly in 1998, Dr. Alpheus Bingham and Aaron Schacht came to the realization that no matter how smart the people are in a company, there are always smarter people outside the company than those inside the company. They also realized that a diversity of fresh perspectives was key to effective problem solving and asking the right questions was key to getting the right answers. The idea they came up with was to set up an incubator within Lilly to attract outside talent to contribute to their in-house R&D.

This led to the formation of the InnoCentive incubator within the company in 2001. To crowdsource solutions to their technology-related problems, they offered a cash prize to the individual or company that came up with a successful solution to a problem. The practice of offering a financial incentive for a solution to a problem is an age-old idea, but the word *crowdsourcing*[1] was coined by Jeff Howe of *Wired* magazine only in 2006. And InnoCentive was the first company to develop a systematic approach and a platform to connect organizations seeking answers to their questions with potential solvers from outside the company. Initially, the InnoCentive incubator worked on company problems, but as the InnoCentive platform became well known, other companies wanted to use it.

InnoCentive connects organizations (seekers) with specific problems (challenges) to people all over the world (solvers), who can win a prize by solving the problem. InnoCentive makes money by charging fees to its clients using the platform. InnoCentive ensures IP confidentiality for both the seeker and the solver and helps transfer IP rights from the solver to the seeker.

DOI: 10.4324/9781003037446-11

One of the early successes InnoCentive had was a challenge posted at innocentive.com by the Oil Recovery Institute of Cordova, Alaska, to enable the pumping of highly viscous crude oil at sub-freezing temperatures, with a prize of $20,000 for a solution acceptable to the Institute. A chemist from the construction industry, John Davis, won the prize by suggesting that they could maintain flow at high viscosities by using a device like the one used in the construction industry to keep viscous concrete flowing by use of ultrasonic agitators on tanks and dispensing channels, without solidifying in the process. This was a simple solution that took John Davis just a few minutes to figure out, and he was not even from the oil industry. This is a key rationale for opening innovation to anyone and everyone.

In 2007, SunNight Solar wanted to develop a dual-purpose, solar-powered lamp/flashlight for use in African villages and other areas without access to electricity. The company had already spent $250,000 in R&D, without success. Mark Bent, SunNight CEO, approached InnoCentive to create a challenge for developing the solar-powered lamp/flashlight. The challenge ran for 2 months and attracted almost a thousand solvers; SunNight received 78 solutions within the challenge duration. A product design submitted by Russell McMahon, an engineer from New Zealand, was accepted, which had the additional benefit of a 20-year lifespan, and for which he received a $20,000 prize.

This approach, along with other innovation strategies reaching outside of a company's closed R&D organization, came to be known as *Open Innovation* after the publication of Henry Chesbrough's groundbreaking 2003 book, *Open Innovation: The New Imperative for Creating and Benefiting from Technology* (Harvard Business Review Press).

In 2020, InnoCentive was acquired by Wazoku, an idea management and software company of the UK, creating the world's most successful open-innovation platform. As of mid-2022, almost 500,000 people from 195 countries were registered as solvers at innocentive.com, which had a reach of millions more potential solvers through its strategic partners (e.g., Scientific American). Its solver community includes engineers, scientists, doctoral students, entrepreneurs, CEOs, retired technologists, business leaders, and others. So far, InnoCentive has awarded over $60 million in prizes to thousands of solvers for some 2,500 challenges, leading to 200,000 innovations. The average prize money is $20–30,000, though awards worth $100,000 or more are not uncommon. Successful solvers come from all kinds of industries, not just from the industry whose problem is being solved, and they are not necessarily the most educated or people with the most expertise in the specific fields under consideration, as correctly predicted by Thomas Kuhn in *The Structure of Scientific Revolutions* (University of Chicago Press, 1962, 1986).

InnoCentive's client base includes AstraZeneca, VW, Enel, National Aeronautics and Space Administration (NASA), among many other private and public sector organizations. Some of the challenges InnoCentive has worked on include facilitating access to clean water at household level, passive solar devices designed to attract and kill malaria-carrying mosquitos, wildfire detection at powerplants, and methods of identifying illegal seafood. Currently, open challenges (as of October 2022) include new uses for nanoporous Nickel Aluminum powders (prize money, $15,000), innovative process for high organic content sludge treatment ($20,000), and improving patient experience and adherence for diabetes medicines ($25,000).[2]

Similar prize-based challenges are now announced by hundreds of organizations each year on intermediary platforms, like innocentive.com, as well as on their own corporate open-innovation platforms. Governments and non-profits have also decided to get into the action. (More on open innovation later in the chapter.)

InnoCentive reinvented innovation!

****

Innovation involves creating something significantly new, better, and of value.[3] The *something significantly new* can be a product, service, process, design, business concept, business model, code, or even a new feature in an existing product or service. Innovation is often incremental but can also be disruptive, breakthrough, or transformational. It can arise from anywhere inside an organization, from its ecosystem that extends to individuals and entities outside the organization, and, increasingly, from sources beyond its ecosystem.

In the early 2000s, InnoCentive *reinvented* innovation as the world knew it. Now, over two decades later, there is an urgent need to explore even newer approaches to innovation, though not forgetting the innovation approaches that brought us here.

Inflation, the war in Ukraine, COVID-19 pandemic, nationalist urges in many parts of the world, including in highly developed nations (such as Italy and BREXIT in the UK), closing of open borders through trade barriers, supply-chain tangles, and oil shocks have all destabilized life and the business world. All these events and trends call for us to rethink and reimagine how innovation takes place, how business is conducted, and how businesses create and capture value. Irrespective of how companies pursued innovation in the past, it is time now to reassess innovation successes and failures and explore how it can be reinvented for improved performance. (See also the next chapter on reimagining business.)

Why innovation matters. Innovation helps create new industries, new products, and better-paying jobs in nations. According to Michael Porter, innovation leads to productivity growth, firms' and nations' international competitiveness, GDP growth, and prosperity for a nation's citizens.[4] Innovation provides the foundation for organizations' superior performance. Innovation has also helped solve some of the most critical challenges facing humanity.

How Innovation Happens

To reinvent innovation, it will be helpful to see what approaches have been successful in the past, though not all innovation resulted from conscious human effort. So, let us first explore how innovation happens and then how to innovate.

With multiple potential sources of innovation, how it happens remains an elusive question. True innovations are improbable events and they are hard to predict. Even smart people sometimes make predictions that turn out to be wrong—to their chagrin and to the amusement of others. A simple Google search will produce many predictions by important people that proved to be wrong. For instance, William Stewart, a former Surgeon General of the US, who did a great deal of important work during his lifetime, said in 1967, "The time has come to close the book on infectious diseases. We have basically wiped out infection in the United States." Nobel Laureate in economic sciences, Paul Krugman, at the start of the dot-com boom, wasn't too hopeful about the growth of the internet and penned an article in the June 10, 1998, issue of the *Red Herring* magazine, "Why Most Economists' Predictions are Wrong", claiming that:

> The growth of the Internet will slow drastically, as the flaw in 'Metcalfe's Law' – which states that the number of potential connections in a network is proportional to the square of the number of participants – becomes apparent: most people have nothing to say to each other! By 2005 or so, it will become clear that the Internet's impact on the economy will have been no greater than the fax machine's.

There is no single explanation for how innovation happens, irrespective of what some scholars and executives, promoting their own theories, often without evidence, may tell you. (I started writing this chapter during the deliberations of the US House Select Committee investigating the January 6 attack on the US Capitol. Arizona House Speaker Rusty Bowers repeated to the Committee what Rudy Giuliani had told him, "We've got lots of theories, we just don't have the evidence.")

Here are some possible explanations of how innovation happens.

Serendipity

While businesses, governments, universities, and other institutions invest to intentionally create innovations, there is also evidence that sometimes it happens serendipitously. *Serendipity* means finding something valuable just by chance, without looking for it. There are two aspects behind serendipity—chance and a beneficial outcome. For instance, the technology behind the VELCRO® brand of hook and loop fasteners evolved quite by accident when George de Mestral went hunting with his dog in Switzerland in 1941. During the walk, he found that cockleburs on the roadsides stuck to his clothes and the dog's fur. Upon examining the cockleburs under a microscope, he found that tiny hooks on the cockleburs had attached themselves to his clothes (Figure 9.1). The rest is history of how VELCRO® branded hook and loop fasteners found thousands of uses.

There are dozens of examples of innovative products and services that happened to be results of accidental discovery. Roy Plunkett of Dupont accidently created Teflon in 1938 while attempting to develop a better refrigerant. Teflon has since found numerous uses including non-stick pans and Gore-Tex clothing. In 1968, Spencer Silver of 3M in Minneapolis was looking to develop a strong and permanent glue; instead, the glue he developed was weak and temporary, and for which no one could think of a possible use. Silver, along with a colleague, Art Fry, later used the glue on paper and discovered its potential uses. Thus, Post-it note was born. A re-adherable strip of glue allowed you to temporarily attach a note on documents or other surfaces, remove it, and attach again and again.[5] In the pharmaceutical and medical field, numerous products (such as penicillin, Viagra, and the pacemaker) owe their birth to accidental discovery.

Figure 9.1   Cocklebur.

Source: https://www.backyardnature.net/ (Image in public domain).

Invisible Hand of Market

Adam Smith, in his seminal work, *The Wealth of Nations* (W. Strahan and T. Cadell, 1776), suggested that individuals in a society acting in their own self-interest can have unintended outcomes that benefit the whole society—as if there were an *invisible hand* behind their actions. Self-interest and competition are the forces behind invisible hand—the mechanisms that create social and economic benefits in free-market economies. In Adam Smith's own famous words:

> It is not from the benevolence (kindness) of the butcher, the brewer, or the baker that we expect our dinner, but from their regard to their own interest. (Vol I: 18)

Over time, the invisible hand metaphor has been used to explain many kinds of economic and social outcomes, including innovation, of the actions of individuals and organizations that were not necessarily acting in societal interest. So, individuals and organizations, acting in their own interest and responding to market forces can create innovations that benefit everyone. It's the invisible hand of the market that continually prods entrepreneurs and businesses to create innovations that end up benefiting everyone. Search engines Yahoo! and Google are just two examples of products that have proved to be of immense value to practically everyone.

Writing in 1934, Joseph Schumpeter suggested that capitalism or the free-market system is an evolutionary process of innovation, entrepreneurial activity, and *creative destruction*. Industries contain the seeds of their own destruction through incursions by both new and established firms using innovative products and strategies to destroy the incumbents' advantage.[6] Schumpeter's seminal insights are truer today than ever before. This is because the digitization of an analog object, as discussed in previous chapters, renders it infinitely scalable, replicable, and transmittable at zero—or near zero—marginal cost, thus permitting an upstart to destroy the competitive advantage of incumbents.

Visible Hand of Management

In his influential 1977 book, *The Visible Hand: The Managerial Revolution in American Business* (Belknap Press), business historian Alfred Chandler, Jr., of the Harvard Business School, practically rewrote the history of big business in the US in the nineteenth and early twentieth centuries, showcasing how the control of business and industry changed from *robber barons* and *captains of industry* to a *salaried managerial class*. Chandler suggested that it was middle management's *visible hand* that replaced Adam Smith's invisible hand as the primary force creating newer goods and services.

> The visible hand of management replaced the invisible hand of market forces where and when new technology and expanded markets permitted a historically unprecedented high volume and speed of materials through the processes of production and distribution. Modern business enterprise was thus the institutional response to the rapid pace of technological innovation and increasing consumer demand in the United States during the second half of the nineteenth century. (12)

The invisible hand and the visible hand explanations are the *yin* and *yang* of innovation—two complementary approaches—each leading to innovation.

In addition to the serendipity and invisible hand explanations, much innovation happens aided by the visible hand of organizations and management. Here are a few key examples of the role of the visible hand in innovation.

Research and Development. Research and development involves generating new knowledge and creating new technologies, new products, new processes, and new services—key inputs for creating innovation. Innovation requires activities that are novel, creative, uncertain, systematic, and transferable or reproducible.[7]

In-house research and development used to account for much of the innovation in the business world, and it still does. Crowdsourcing made available external resources to businesses to accomplish innovation as part of their R&D.

There are essentially three kinds of R&D, all involving a visible hand of an organization: basic research, applied research, and experimental development. In the business world, we are largely concerned with applied research, though basic research and experimental development, typically undertaken by governments and universities and other research organizations, have often produced outcomes that developed into commercial products. For instance, basic research led to the development of satellite-based global positioning systems (GPS), the discovery of the first human cancer gene, and the first chemical synthesis of penicillin, among hundreds of other innovative products.[8]

Who funds R&D? According to the Federal Reserve Bank of St. Louis (Figure 9.2), R&D spending by business in the US has been consistently going up since the mid-1950s, while R&D spending by government has lately been going down, especially since 2010.[9] The same trend holds for OECD (Organisation for Economic Cooperation and Development) countries. In addition,

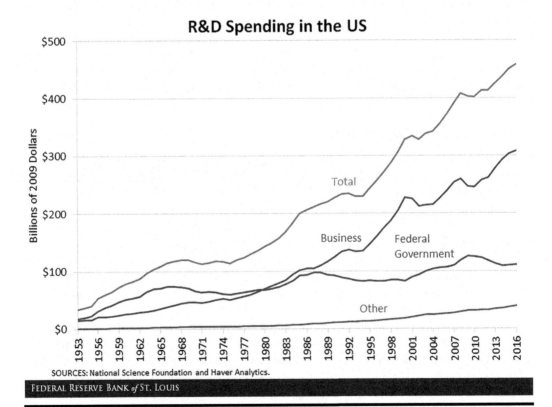

Figure 9.2   Funding of R&D by source in the United States, 1953–2016.

Source: Federal Reserve Bank of St. Louis. https://www.stlouisfed.org/on-the-economy/ 2018/may/rd-business-spending-up-government-spending-flat.

the share of global R&D investment by business was 64% in 2019, followed by government at 24%, and higher education, non-profits, and foreign sources at 12%. The OECD report also shows that the US continues to lead the world in R&D investment, though China has been fast catching up.[10]

PricewaterhouseCoopers' (PwC) strategy consulting arm, *Strategy&*, had been conducting an annual *Global Innovation 1000* study of the top 1,000 public corporations worldwide that spent the most on R&D; the last report came out in 2018. Here are some interesting findings of the Global Innovation 1000 studies:

The 2015 Global Innovation 1000 study found that more and more of the top R&D spenders were conducting some of their R&D abroad in search of talent and high-growth markets.

> An overwhelming 94 percent of the world's largest innovators now conduct elements of their R&D programs abroad... These companies are shifting their innovation investment to countries in which their sales and manufacturing are growing fastest, and where they can access the right technical talent. Not surprisingly, innovation spending has boomed in China and India since our 2008 study... Collectively, in fact, more R&D is now conducted in Asia than in North America or Europe.

Furthermore, companies that disperse their R&D globally perform as well as, or better than, companies with a focused R&D footprint.[11]

The 2015 study also identified the top ten R&D spenders (Table 9.1) and the ten most innovative companies based on the study participants' responses (Table 9.2). It is interesting to note that

Table 9.1   The Top Ten R&D Spenders, 2015

2015 Rank	2014 Rank	Company	2015 R&D Spend ($Bn)	% of Revenue	Headquarters	Industry
1	1	**Volkswagen**	$15.3 Bn	5.7%	Europe	Automotive
2	2	**Samsung**	$14.1	7.2	South Korea	Computing and Electronics
3	3	**Intel**	$11.5	20.6	US	Computing and Electronics
4	4	**Microsoft**	$11.4	13.1	US	Software and internet
5	5	**Roche**	$10.8	20.8	Europe	Healthcare
6	9	Google	$9.8	14.9	US	Software and internet
7	14	Amazon	$9.3	10.4	US	Software and internet
8	7	**Toyota**	$9.2	3.7	Japan	Automotive
9	6	**Novartis**	$9.1	17.3	Europe	Healthcare
10	8	**Johnson & Johnson**	$8.5	11.4	US	Healthcare

Source: Adapted from the 2015 Global Innovation 1000 Study, p. 6.

Note: Companies shown in **bold** have been among the top 20 R&D spenders every year since 2005.

Table 9.2 The Ten Most Innovative Companies, 2015 (Based on Study Participants' Responses)

2015 Rank	2014 Rank	Company	Geography	Industry	R&D Spend ($Bn)
1	1	**Apple**	US	Computing and Electronics	6.0
2	2	**Google**	US	Software and internet	9.8
3	5	Tesla Motors	US	Automotive	0.5
4	4	**Samsung**	South Korea	Computing and electronics	14.1
5	3	Amazon	US	Software and internet	9.3
6	6	**3M**	US	Industrials	1.8
7	7	**General Electric**	US	Industrials	4.2
8	8	**Microsoft**	US	Software and internet	11.4
9	9	**IBM**	US	Computing and electronics	5.4
10	N/A	Toyota	Japan	Automotive	9.2

Source: Adapted from the 2015 Global Innovation 1000 Study, p. 9.

Note: Companies in **bold** have been among the 10 most innovative companies every year since 2010.

the top R&D spenders are not necessarily the most innovative companies, a result PwC found consistently every year since 2008. Furthermore, the ten most innovative companies outperformed the ten biggest R&D spenders on revenue growth, in terms of EBITDA (earnings before interest, taxes, depreciation, and amortization) as a percentage of revenue, and market-cap growth.

The 2018 Global Innovation 1000 study found no statistically significant relationship between how much a company spends on its innovation efforts and its sustained financial performance.[12]

Crowd. Crowdsourcing (open innovation) involves presenting a problem to a large, diverse group of people (the crowd), generally external to the organization, some of whom decide to try and solve the problem on their own time, typically with the expectation of a financial reward. (Large organizations sometimes use their own employees for a crowdsourcing challenge.) A solution presented by someone from the crowd is selected by the organization that created the crowdsourcing challenge as being the best for their purpose, based on pre-defined criteria. This method is known as prize-based open innovation (crowdsourcing) and involves a two-sided platform or marketplace. Companies can crowdsource solutions to their technology problems through their own open-innovation platform or use an open-innovation intermediary like InnoCentive or HeroX. The InnoCentive opening case showed how more and more organizations are using the crowd to solve their critical technology and business challenges. There are literally hundreds of use cases for this approach to innovation, presented in books,[13] journals and magazines, and open-innovation seminars and conferences. And it all started with InnoCentive. (Box 9.1 makes a distinction between crowdsourcing and wisdom of the crowds.)

BOX 9.1   CROWDSOURCING VS. WISDOM OF CROWDS

James Surowiecki's bestselling book, *The Wisdom of Crowds* (Anchor Books, 2005), presented a well-reasoned argument that "under the right circumstances, groups are remarkably intelligent, and are often smarter than the smartest people in them." Essentially, Surowiecki contended that if the group consists of people with diverse, independent opinions, they are *collectively* smarter than any individual expert in decision making and problem solving. In crowdsourcing also, a problem is presented to a group of diverse, unrelated people (the crowd), but the solution presented by *one of the group members* is selected as being the best for the problem under consideration.

Visible hand of government. As discussed in the previous section, governments, universities, and research organizations are generally involved in basic research and experimental development. Their research output can often lead to innovative products and services that can be commercialized. In the US, DARPA (Defense Advanced Research Projects Agency) is one of several government agencies that are the source of major technological innovations which define how people worldwide live, do business, and work. Some such innovations that resulted from DARPA research are the internet, GPS, Siri (Apple's digital virtual assistant), and BigDog (the Boston Dynamics robot).[14] Similarly, research by NASA has led to many spinoffs, including space blankets, freeze-dried food, cochlear implants, and memory foam (originally named temper foam).[15]

The *visible hand* metaphor can indeed be applied to many different approaches to innovation.

How to Innovate

Except when it happens serendipitously, innovation always requires conscious human effort—guided by the invisible hand of the market or the visible hand of organizations. (Even in case of innovations led by *invisible hand*, an entrepreneur or a business responds to an emerging opportunity by creating innovation.) The *Build|Buy|Ally framework* (Figure 9.3) encapsulates all such approaches neatly into a single model. Innovation at organization level occurs through internal development (Build), through M&A (Buy), and/or through partnerships (Ally). Irrespective of the method used, having an effective innovation system requires an organizational structure and culture that support innovation, an absence of the NIH (*Not Invented Here*) syndrome, and an appropriate benchmarking and control system. In addition, according to a 2012 McKinsey & Company global survey, for an organization to be successful at innovation, it is vitally important that it has an innovation strategy and that it is well integrated with its overall corporate strategy.[16] The Build|Buy|Ally framework for creating innovations is discussed in the following section.

The Build|Buy|Ally Framework

Build: Innovation through Internal Development

Multinationals have employed some of the following *structural approaches* for creating innovations internally through their own efforts: R&D or a corporate innovation function, new-business development function, global innovation center, emerging-business-opportunity group, advanced-technology institute, innovation hub, and an in-house incubator or accelerator, among other approaches. Such efforts are good for innovation but, in a multinational with far-flung operations,

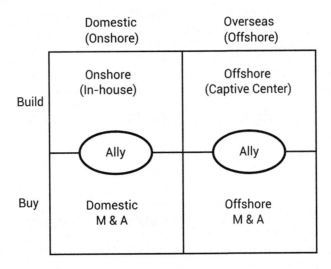

Figure 9.3 The Build|Buy|Ally framework for creating and acquiring innovations.

Source: Adapted from Vinod K. Jain, Global Strategy: Competing in the Connected Economy. New York: Routledge, 2016.

can also lead to dispersed teams of researchers, unconnected with each other—unless effective integration and control mechanisms are in place.

Hundreds of companies have corporate innovation labs and global innovation centers at home (onshore) or abroad (offshore). A global innovation center, also referred to as a global in-house innovation center or a *captive center* (when offshore), can be involved in problems facing the company, its clients or customers, its partners, its industry, or society in general. The following examples offer a look at a few such corporate innovation centers.

Accenture plc is an Irish American consulting and professional services firm specializing in information technology. It has 710,000 employees, 7,000 clients, and 185 partners in its ecosystem and operates in 200 cities worldwide. Its flagship R&D and global innovation center, the Dock, is a multi-disciplinary research and incubation hub located in Dublin's Silicon Docks. It has over 250 cross-industry specialists working on a diverse range of problems for its clients—from financial services to public services. A few sample assignments Accenture consultants have worked on in the past include creating new efficiencies in clinical trials using AI, developing new products and services using digital technologies for retail industry, and advancing machine learning and intelligent human–machine collaboration.[17]

DuPont de Nemours, Inc. (DuPont), an American company headquartered in Wilmington, Delaware, is involved in modern technologies and performance materials and offers a broad range of technology-based products and solutions for clients in the automotive, electronics, industrial, consumer, medical, photovoltaic, and telecom markets. DuPont's Wilmington Global Innovation Center (WGIC) offers scientists, engineers, business professionals, and entrepreneurs opportunities to tackle challenging problems at the Center. A few problems the WGIC has worked on in the past include *cool roofs* that reflect rather than absorb sun's solar energy, new drug delivery systems, global water issues, and resilient buildings using construction materials to help keep them safe during storms and other natural disasters.[18]

Visa Inc., the American multinational financial services corporation headquartered in Foster City, California, facilitates electronic funds transfers worldwide. Visa has five global innovation centers—San Francisco, Dubai, Singapore, Miami, London—that offer its clients opportunities to explore new technologies in areas such as authentication, digital, security, and cloud.

Wolters Kluwer, a Dutch information services company, headquartered in Alphen aan den Rijn, the Netherlands, and Philadelphia, US, offers information and software solutions and services for clinicians, accountants, lawyers, and tax, finance, audit, risk, compliance, and regulatory sectors. It runs an internal R&D program through a central technology organization and its innovation labs. Collaborating with customers across many industries, the labs use advanced technologies to extract actionable insights from data. Wolters Kluwer runs a *Global Innovation Awards* internal competition for its employees to develop innovative solutions to problems facing the company or its clients. Some 75% of the winning ideas in the global competition have been implemented, leading to new products and innovative solutions. Since 2018, Wolters Kluwer Legal & Regulatory division has run a *Global Legal Hackathon* every year—to collaboratively develop innovative solutions to the most pressing legal, regulatory, and civil society challenges facing the world. Since 2018, the Hackathon has attracted over 20,000 participants from 75 countries and is the world's largest learning laboratory for legal industry innovations.[19]

Some companies, in addition to an R&D unit, set up their own incubator or accelerator to innovate from within. An in-house incubator allows highly creative and motivated employees to work on specific projects in which they or the company might be interested. Many companies, including Microsoft and Google, have their own in-house incubators. For instance, the *Microsoft Garage* serves as an in-house incubator for employees to work on projects they are passionate about, even if the projects have no relation to their primary function at the company. More recently, the Garage has started teaming customers with employees to work on high-speed growth mindset projects. The Garage is in various Microsoft locations around the world, including Redmond, Vancouver, Atlanta, Reston/DC, San Francisco Bay Area, New England, New York City, Dublin, Israel, Hyderabad, Bengaluru, East Africa, West Africa, and Beijing.[20]

Such incubators are to be distinguished from company-owned incubators/accelerators that provide venture-capital funding to seasoned entrepreneurs and founders from outside the company. An example is Samsung NEXT, also known as Samsung Accelerator or Samsung Global Innovation Center, which invests in early-stage software and services startups. Headquartered in Mountain View, CA, Samsung NEXT works with startups from all over the world.[21] (See also discussion on *corporate venture capital* in the next section.)

Buy: Acquiring Innovation through M&A

Acquiring innovations through M&A, rather than doing innovation organically, is a common method used by MNEs. Sometimes such acquisitions are opportunistic, but often an MNE waits for someone else to innovate and build a business around the innovation and then attempts to acquire the whole company. Building innovation capabilities and acquiring innovations through M&A is undertaken by companies entering new markets, as well as by companies wanting to strengthen their existing product portfolio and innovation capabilities. For instance, Apple introduced *iTunes* in 2001, which was based on the SoftJam MP technology developed by Casady & Greene, a company Apple had acquired the previous year; SoftJam MP was an early Mac Operating System-compatible MP3 player. Apple's iTunes, and its *iPod* introduced in 2003, eventually disrupted the digital music industry. IBM made several acquisitions to support its new

Table 9.3 Origins of Selected Drugs Manufactured by Pfizer and Johnson & Johnson in 2017

Drug	Brand	2017 Revenue	N
Pneumococcal 13-valent Conjugate Vaccine	Prevnar (Pfizer)	$5.6 b	Wyeth Pharmaceuticals first introduced Prevnar in 2000; Wyeth was acquired by Pfizer in 2009
Pregabalin	Lyrica (Pfizer)	$5.1 b	Northwestern University (NWU; 1980s); NWU entered into a licensing agreement with Warner-Lambert, which was acquired by Pfizer in 2000
Apixaban	Eliquis (Pfizer)	$2.5 b	DuPont Pharmaceuticals (1995), acquired by Bristol-Myers Squibb in 2001; BMS and Pfizer entered into an agreement in 2007 to jointly develop Apixaban
Celecoxib	Celebrex (Pfizer)	$775 m	G.D. Searle (1990s), the pharmaceutical division of Monsanto; acquired by Pharmacia & Upjohn in 2000; Pharmacia acquired by Pfizer in 2003
Infliximab	Remicade (J&J)	$6.3 b	Synthesized at New York University (1980s) in collaboration with Centocor Ortho Biotech, acquired by J&J in 1999
Rivaroxaban	Xarelto (J&J)	$2.5 b	Bayer (1990s), which later entered into a collaboration with J&J to jointly develop Rivaroxaban

Source: Adapted from Emily H. Jung, Alfred Engelberg, and Aaron S. Kesselheim, "Do large pharma companies provide drug development innovation?" STAT, December 2019. https://www.statnews.com/2019/12/10/large-pharma-companies-provide-little-new-drug-development-innovation/

Information on Demand business-intelligence service launched in February 2006. As part of this initiative, IBM acquired Cognos from Canada in 2007, as well as many other companies to support this new line of business.[22]

While pharmaceutical companies are among the largest investors in R&D, they routinely also acquire or invest in other pharma companies working on or with new and novel drugs. For instance, Pfizer merged with Wyeth in 2009 in a $64 billion combination, acquiring Prevnar 13, a vaccine for pneumococcal disease. In addition to their respective strong product pipelines, the merger brought to Pfizer new scientific and manufacturing capabilities for continued innovation. Here is a listing of a few successful Pfizer and Johnson & Johnson drugs that were developed by other companies, before being acquired by Pfizer or J&J (Table 9.3).

Table 9.4 The Ten Largest Ever Pharmaceutical Industry M&As Worldwide Until Early 2022

Acquirer	Target	Year	Deal Value (Billion Dollars)
Pfizer (US)	Warner-Lambert (US)	1999	$87.30 b
Bristol-Myers Squibb (US)	Celgene (US)	2019	$74.00 b
Sanofi (France)	Aventis (France)	2004	$73.50 b
Glaxo (UK)	SmithKline Beecham (US)	2000	$72.40 b
Allergen (US)	Actavis (US)	2015	$65.00 b
Pfizer (US)	Pharmacia (Sweden)	2002	$64.30 b
Pfizer (US)	Wyeth (US)	2009	$64.20 b
AbbVie (US)	Allergen (US)	2019	$63.00 b
Takeda (Japan)	Shire (UK)	2018	$62.00 b
Roche (Switzerland)	Genentech (US)	2009	$46.80 b

Source: Updated from Statista, Largest Pharmaceutical Deals Ever as of Early 2022 https://www.statista.com/statistics/518674/largest-mergers-acquisitions-pharmaceutical/

Even emerging-market pharmaceutical firms have often acquired specific drug businesses of large Western pharmaceutical companies. In April, Dr. Reddy's Laboratories of India agreed to acquire Novartis AG's cardiovascular brand Cidmus in India for $61 million.

Table 9.4 shows the largest ever acquisitions of pharmaceutical companies by pharmaceutical companies until early 2022.

The Walt Disney Company acquired Pixar, an animated studio headed by Steve Jobs, in May 2006 to strengthen its animation-innovation capabilities. Disney had been the distributor for all of Pixar movies in the past, but its contract was slated to end by summer and there had been disagreements between the two companies on profit sharing and movie rights. The acquisition brought to Disney Pixar's blockbuster animated movies like Toy Story and The Incredibles. In 2009, Disney acquired Marvel Entertainment, which makes movies based on Marvel's comic-book characters such as Spider-Man, Iron man, and Captain America. Both acquisitions have been highly successful for Disney in terms of strengthening its entertainment-innovation capabilities and producing high levels of profits. From 2005 to 2019, during CEO Bob Iger's tenure at the company, Disney's net income increased 404%.[23]

Ally: Acquiring Innovation through Alliances

An alliance is a partnership arrangement between two or more companies sharing resources in the pursuit of a common goal, such as innovation, while remaining independent. An alliance can be formed with suppliers, customers, universities, government agencies, even with direct competitors, and is often intended to enter new markets, acquire a resource, strengthen a specific capability, share the cost and risk of a major project, develop technology, and so on. Alliances with direct competitors, especially in developed nations, often invoke antitrust issues, though not always.

(Discussion of antitrust aspects in alliances is beyond the scope of this book. For information regarding antitrust in the US, refer to the "Antitrust Guidelines for Collaborations Among Competitors" issued by the Federal Trade Commission and the US Department of Justice.[24])

Alliances also have many possible drawbacks, such as lack of control over critical decisions, risk of losing IP or core competence to the alliance partner, and the need to share profits with the partner. Shared ownership sometimes leads to conflict if the goals of the two partners do not align. An alliance is a race to learn; the partner who learns the fastest may end up controlling the alliance.

Alliances are increasingly common in industries such as life sciences, IT, automation, renewable energy, and automotive. In fact, more and more companies now seek resources, capabilities, and innovations externally, not just developing them internally. In addition to joint ventures, an alliance can take many forms, such as co-development, licensing, corporate venture capital (CVC), innovation ecosystems, outsourcing innovation, and open innovation, among others. Many innovations, especially those involving frontier science and technology, necessarily require collaboration among multiple partners having complementary capabilities, which any one of them is unable to undertake on its own. Partnering with others on an R&D project enables a firm to expand its innovation capabilities and outcomes, while sharing the cost and risk of getting into new technologies and new markets.

Joint ventures. An alliance may or may not involve equity investment by either party. If both parties in an alliance make an equity investment, or contribute some other assets such as their IP or plant and machinery, and join to form *a new legal entity*, it is a *joint venture (JV)*.

Microsoft and GE Healthcare entered into a 50:50 JV in February 2012, named Caradigm, designed to enable health systems and professionals to use real-time, systemwide intelligence for improving healthcare quality and patient experience. The two parent companies brought their respective technologies and intellectual property to the JV, designed to integrate Microsoft's Amalga enterprise healthcare data with GE Healthcare's eHealth, a health information exchange as well as other technologies. The JV ended in 2016, with Microsoft selling its 50% stake to GE Healthcare; Caradigm then became a GE company. In June 2018, cancer informatics and digital pathology services provider Insparta acquired Caradigm from GE Healthcare.

In 2016, GlaxoSmithKline of the UK entered into a 55:45 JV with Verily Life Sciences, a subsidiary of Google's parent company Alphabet. The JV, Galvani Bioelectronics, was designed to leverage GSK's life sciences knowledge and Verily's expertise in software and electronics for clinical applications. The partners agreed to contribute their respective IP to Galvani and invest £540m over 7 years. Galvani works on developing miniature electronic implants for the treatment of asthma, diabetes, and other chronic conditions.

Co-development. Co-development alliances are quite common in the life sciences industry where different collaborating partners have different capabilities. Development of the *Pfizer-BioNTech COVID-19 vaccine* is a case in point. In March 2020, Pfizer signed an agreement with Germany's BioNTech to co-develop a potential vaccine for COVID-19, which the World Health Organization had previously declared a pandemic. Over the next 9 months, the two companies worked at light speed by collaborating with academic and biopharma partners, across countries, to develop the Pfizer-BioNTech *COVID*-19 vaccine and scale up manufacturing to meet the unheard goal of manufacturing billions of vaccine doses in a short period of time. In 2007, Bristol-Myers Squibb entered into an agreement with Pfizer to jointly develop *apixaban* (brand name Eliquis), an anticoagulant for preventing blood clots and strokes in people suffering from atrial fibrillation.

Licensing. A licensing agreement gives a company the right to produce and sell another company's goods in its market, sometimes a better approach to acquiring innovation than building it in-house.

Under licensing, a company (the licensor) grants the rights to its intellectual property (such as patents, trademarks, copyrights, designs) and manufacturing rights to another company (the licensee) for a certain period of time in return for royalties. The royalties can be payable as a one-time lump sum, or as a percentage of sales (which is more common), by the licensee during the term of the license. A licensing agreement typically specifies the geographic area where the licensee can sell the products manufactured under license and using the licensor's brand name.

Another type of licensing, which is more common, occurs when a company allows (licenses) another company to use its trademark on its products, such as t-shirts and caps. The idea is that consumers will be more likely to buy a product if it has a well-known trademark (brand). There are many other kinds of licensing, such as a physician receiving a license to practice as a medical practitioner. Such licensing, which is not innovation, is beyond the scope of this book.

In life sciences, major pharmaceutical firms often license other companies' drugs and compounds to market them through their global network, rather than developing them in-house. "Externally sourced, midstage drug candidates can represent as much as 50 percent of the largest pharmaceutical companies' total pipelines."[25] Many pharmaceutical firms, in fact, have lists of compounds and drugs on their websites that they are interested in licensing from others. For example, Takeda Pharmaceutical Company Ltd. of Japan lists many areas on its Israel website in which they are interested: "We are interested to in-license late stage, innovative drugs in Takeda's core therapeutic areas – Oncology, CNS and Gastrointestinal diseases as well as niche products in rare diseases – with relatively short time to market… Takeda Israel is actively seeking to utilize its capabilities and partner up with pharmaceutical companies and biotech startups in order to assist them in distributing their products and allow them access to the Israeli market."[26]

Innovation ecosystems. The concept of ecosystems was introduced in Chapter 6:

> An ecosystem is a group of companies from different industries offering bundles of products and services to meet specific customer needs. This concept is based on the idea that customers are not just looking for a specific product or service, but typically a solution to their needs… Ecosystems create value through relationships and networks—linking one group of users with another group of users.

There can in fact be many kinds of ecosystems, such as industry ecosystems, corporate ecosystems, and innovation ecosystems, each consisting of many organizations and individuals with a common objective. An *innovation ecosystem* typically aims to develop technologies and innovations. It can include corporations, entrepreneurs, universities, governments, accelerators, venture capitalists, labs, and so on. The *Swiss Food & Nutrition Valley* is an *industry innovation ecosystem* for food and nutrition. Launched in January 2020, the ecosystem includes the Swiss Canton of Vaud, the Swiss Federal Institute of Technology in Lausanne (EPFL), the Swiss Hospitality Management School in Lausanne, and Nestlé. It aims to attract talent, startups, and investors to develop innovative, sustainable solutions for quality food and nutrition.[27]

Corporate venture capital. Corporate venture capital (CVC), a subset of the traditional venture capital (VC) industry, involves major companies investing in nascent startups developing new or complementary technologies in which they are interested. This is a way for them to test ideas at a relatively low cost and acquire the innovations if the startups are successful. Many major MNEs have active CVC funds to invest in startups with promising innovations. Google Ventures (now GV) is the world's largest CVC investor. Alphabet's VC arm, GV, provides seed, venture, and growth stage funding to technology companies. Since its founding in 2009 as Google Ventures, GV has funded over 500 portfolio companies with an emphasis on enterprise, life sciences, consumer, and frontier technologies. Currently, GV has 400 active portfolio companies across North America and Europe and has had 65 IPOs and 175+ mergers and acquisitions.

Some of the other prominent CVCs are Intel Capital, Salesforce Ventures, Qualcomm Ventures, Comcast Ventures, Novartis Venture Funds, Samsung Ventures, Siemens Venture Capital, Fidelity Biosciences, and so on. CVC investing is quite prevalent and increasing in the computer and IT, biotechnology, and energy sectors.

Outsourcing innovation. For decades, MNEs from developed countries have been outsourcing corporate functions such as manufacturing to developing and middle-income countries that offer skilled workers at low cost. In the 2000s, they began to offshore even core innovation and R&D functions to their captive centers and third-party vendors abroad. While MNEs have been performing R&D in foreign countries for a long time, what is relatively new is that they also now perform (and outsource) R&D in emerging markets.[28] They do so because of the availability of low-cost talent in many emerging markets, the availability of third-party innovation services providers with the requisite expertise, and proximity to their major markets.

Figure 9.3 showed a basic model (Build|Buy|Ally) for acquiring innovations. When a firm offshores innovation, it can do so by setting up a wholly owned R&D subsidiary abroad, called a *captive center* or a *global in-house center*, or by outsourcing (offshoring) innovation to a third-party vendor in the foreign market. For example, dozens of major MNEs, including Cisco Systems, Computer Sciences Corporation, General Electric, and IBM have captive R&D centers in India; they also outsource innovation projects to local vendors such as Tata Consultancy Services, Infosys, and Wipro Technologies.

Open Innovation

The concept of open innovation, or innovation through crowdsourcing, presented in the opening case to this chapter (InnoCentive), was popularized by Henry Chesbrough in his 2003 bestseller, *Open Innovation: The New Imperative for Creating and Profiting from Technology* (Harvard Business Review Press). He distinguished between closed innovation, where R&D is performed in-house with little external input, and open innovation, where an organization leverages external partners through crowdsourcing or other means to achieve innovation. He highlighted the need for companies to shift from a closed model of innovation to an open model to leverage the knowledge and ingenuity that exists outside the company. Though the idea of open innovation had existed and had been used by companies like IBM much earlier than Chesbrough's publication, his main contribution was to democratize the idea to such an extent that hundreds of business, government, and nonprofit organizations now swear by it. The key ideas of open innovation he proposed are:

- Not all of the world's smartest people work for us, so we must find ways to access the knowledge and creativity of people outside the organization;
- We do not have to originate innovation to benefit from it;
- Sometimes, the best solution to a problem comes from outside the industry that was seeking the solution;
- Making the best use of both internal and external ideas is the winning proposition;
- We should buy others' IP if it advances our business and should profit from others using our IP.

Open innovation thus involves accessing the knowledge and intellectual property of others (outside-in), as well as profiting by allowing others to use our knowledge and IP (inside-out).

Inside-out. As indicated earlier, biopharmaceutical firms routinely license or sell their technologies to large pharmaceutical firms. Licensing one's technology is common in other industries as well. However, companies like IBM, Xerox, and Samsung have thousands of patents that they do not use for various reasons. Chesbrough suggested that firms with intellectual property should profit by letting others use their IP through licensing, for example. Over a decade ago, IBM and some other IT companies allowed free use of hundreds of their patents, creating something like an IP-free zone, pledging not to enforce their IP rights if the patents were used only for open-source applications. This came about with the publication of a 2004 report that showed that the open-source operating system Linux had (*inadvertently*) infringed upon more than 250 patents of other companies. This led to further growth of open-source software, unhindered by legal challenges, and IBM substantially increased its global share of Linux-based software.[29]

Outside-in. The outside-in approach to innovation includes collaborating with individuals and entities outside the organization through crowdsourcing or other means. One of the most powerful open-innovation ideas is prize-based innovation, discussed at the chapter opening. There are several innovation platforms that serve as intermediaries connecting organizations seeking solutions to specific problems and prospective *solvers* from throughout the world, such as InnoCentive, HeroX, Viima, Ennomotive, Kaggle, and many others.

Many large organizations, including P&G, Unilever, IBM, Henkel, and Staples, have their own corporate open-innovation platforms or ecosystems serving their own needs. For instance, Unilever's open-innovation platform, innovate-with-us, is an innovation ecosystem comprising *partners* who work on specific problems of interest to the company. Their partner network includes startups, academics, designers, individual inventors, suppliers, and others with big ideas and disruptive technologies. Some recent successes of the Unilever innovation ecosystem include the Dove Body Wash, Magnum Recycled Plastic Tubs, and Laundry Capsules with Recycled Carbon.[30]

Notes

1 Crowdsourcing is a generic term and has been used for seeking information or ideas from the *crowd* about many different things, for example, innovation, opinions regarding something, or selecting a logo at 99designs.com. Wikipedia is a crowdsourced encyclopedia. Crowdfunding involves attempts to raise money from a large number of people for a project or venture.
2 Innocentive, "What challenges will you solve today?" https://www.innocentive.com/challenge/.
3 Cisco's New Innovation Engine accessed from http://newsroom.cisco.com/feature-content?articleId=1720841.
4 Michael E. Porter, *Clusters of Innovation Initiative: Regional Foundations of U.S. Competitiveness* (Boston, MA: Monitor Group and Council on Competitiveness, 2001).
5 Matt Ridley, *How Innovation Works: And Why It Flourishes in Freedom* (New York: HarperCollins, 2020).
6 Joseph A. Schumpeter, *The Theory of Economic Development* (Cambridge, MA: Harvard University Press, 1934).
7 For more details on R&D, refer to OECD's *Frascati Manual* (7th ed., 2015). https://www.oecd.org/sti/inno/Frascati-Manual.htm.
8 MIT, Spectrum, "The brilliance of basic research," Spring 2014. https://spectrum.mit.edu/spring-2014/the-brilliance-of-basic-research/.
9 Anna Maria Santacreu and Heting Zhu, "R&D: Business spending up, government spending flat," May 14, 2018. https://www.stlouisfed.org/on-the-economy/2018/may/rd-business-spending-up-government-spending-flat.
10 OECD, "Main science and technology indicators," September 2022. https://www.oecd.org/sti/msti.htm.
11 Barry Jaruzelski, Kevin Schwartz, and Volker Staack, "The 2015 Global Innovation 1000: Innovation's New World Order," *Strategy+Business*, Winter 2015, p. 2.

12 Barry Jaruzelski, "Global Innovation 1000: The six characteristics of superior innovators," November 1, 2018. https://www.pwc.com.au/digitalpulse/report-global-innovation-1000-study.html.

13 See, for instance, Simon Hill and Alpheus Bingham, *One Smart Crowd: How Crowdsourcing is Changing the World One Idea at a Time*, 2021; Jeff Howe, *Why the Power of the Crowd is Driving the Future of Business.* (Currency, 2009).

14 Jane McCallion, "10 amazing DARPA inventions: How they were made and what happened to them," June 15, 2020. https://www.itpro.com/technology/34730/10-amazing-darpa-inventions.

15 Wikipedia, "NASA spinoff technologies." https://en.wikipedia.org/wiki/NASA_spinoff_technologies# Health_and_medicine.

16 Marla M. Capozzi, Ari Kellen, and Rebecca Somers, "Making innovation structures work: McKinsey global survey results," McKinsey & Company, September 2012.

17 Accenture, "Innovation architecture: The Dock." https://www.accenture.com/us-en/services/about/innovation-hub-the-dock.

18 Dupont, "Insights and ideas." https://www.dupont.com/locations/wilmington-global-innovation-center/insights.html.

19 Global Legal Hackathon, "#GLH 2022," March 25–27, 2022. https://globallegalhackathon.com/.

20 Microsoft, "The Garage is a program that drives a culture of innovation." https://www.microsoft.com/en-us/garage/.

21 Samsung, "We invest in the boldest and most ambitious founders." https://www.samsungnext.com/.

22 IBM Press Release, "IBM to acquire Cognos to accelerate information on demand initiative," November 12, 2007. http://www-03.ibm.com/press/us/en/pressrelease/22572.wss.

23 CNBC Evolve, "14 years, 4 acquisitions, 1 Bob Iger: How Disney's CEO revitalized an iconic American brand," August 6, 2019. https://www.cnbc.com/2019/08/06/bob-iger-forever-changed-disney-with-4-key-acquisitions.html.

24 Federal Trade Commission, "Antitrust guidelines for collaborations among competitors," April 2000. https://www.ftc.gov/sites/default/files/documents/public_events/joint-venture-hearings-antitrust-guidelines-collaboration-among-competitors/ftcdojguidelines-2.pdf.

25 Laurence Capron and Will Mitchell, *Build, Borrow, or Buy: Solving the Growth Dilemma.* (Boston, MA: *Harvard Business Review Press*, 2012, p. 68).

26 Takeda, "Business development and licensing – Takeda Israel." https://www.takeda.com/he-il/business-development/.

27 EHL, "Swiss food and nutrition valley: a unique innovation and ecosystem," January 23, 2020. https://www.hospitalitynet.org/news/4096666.html.

28 Vinod K. Jain and S. Raghunath, "Strengthening America's international competitiveness through innovation and global value chains." In Ben L. Kedia and Subhash C. Jain (eds.), *Restoring America's Global Competitiveness through Innovation.* (Cheltenham, UK: Edward Elgar, 2013).

29 Oliver Alexy and Markus Reitzig, "Managing the Business Risks of Open Innovation," *McKinsey Quarterly*, January 2012.

30 Unilever, "Innovate with us." https://www.unilever.com/brands/innovation/innovate-with-us/.

Chapter 10

Reimagining Business

Predicting the future is hard. But preparing for its uncertainties, while you lie on the beach, can at least be entertaining. It can also broaden the mind and subtly change your understanding of the present… Speculating about the future, even if it is far-teched, can help people and institutions cope with what comes next.

The Economist, July 6, 2019

When I started working on this book in the spring of 2020, COVID-19 had just been declared a global pandemic, though no one could have then fathomed how it might proceed and the kinds of health, economic, business, and social disruptions it might cause. The pandemic not only killed tens of thousands of people worldwide but also almost completely disrupted how people live, work, play, and do business. More recent developments, such as the war in Ukraine, global energy crisis, rising interest rates, inflation, supply-chain tangles, and impending recession as of mid-2022 multiplied challenges to our lives and businesses manyfold. Now, over two years later, we still can't fathom where all this might lead us. But one thing is certain, the impacts of the pandemic and other disruptions will endure for many years to come, and businesses can't stand still waiting for the elusive silver lining. Although the context and prospects of business are no doubt changing, what will not change is the core objective of business, namely, creating and capturing value for its multiple stakeholders. The other side of the challenge coin is, of course, opportunity—providing an impetus to *reimagine* business. It's a time to reimagine business and the approach to doing business—not an incremental approach, but a near-complete rethinking of strategy and business.

> Organizations that make minor changes to the edges of their business model nearly always fall short of their goals. Tinkering leads to returns on investment below the cost of capital.
>
> McKinsey Digital, "Digital strategy in a time of crisis," April 2020

Company after company is having to rethink its approach to business in this new era of challenges and opportunities. Individual companies are also having to deal with other emerging issues facing them. Starbucks, for instance, has lately had negative press and legal battles, largely due to the decision of employees in some 200 US stores to organize under Workers United, as well as some

DOI: 10.4324/9781003037446-12

silly lawsuits and social media backlash. Inflation had not significantly impacted sales until now, though the COVID-19 pandemic did, especially in China, its second largest market.

On September 13, 2022, Starbucks CEO Howard Schultz and CFO Rachel Ruggeri announced a *reinvention plan* to achieve seven to nine percent annual comparable store sales growth and 10–12% annual revenue growth over the next 3 years. These growth targets are expected to be achieved by growth in global store portfolio, and revenue growth by "priority investments that elevate partner engagement and store efficiency, industry-leading digital programs, an engaged and growing Starbucks® Rewards membership base, game-changing product innovation, and a rapidly expanding global footprint."[1]

Previously, on July 11, 2022, Schultz had defined, with five bold moves, what the company's reinvention would look like[2]:

- 'Re-envision how we bring our mission to life.
- Renew the well-being of retail partners by radically improving their experience.
- Reimagine our store experience for greater connection, ease, and a planet positive impact.
- Reconnect with our customers by delivering memorable and personalized moments.
- Redesign partnership by creating new ways to thrive together.

To begin our journey into the future, it will be helpful to first examine some of the major forces impacting our lives and business in 2022 and beyond.

The Five Megatrends

One can relatively easily identify a dozen or more major trends, I restrict our explorations to five that are especially relevant from the perspective of this book—globalization, digitalization, competition, the fourth industrial revolution, and the new normal.

These are *generic* megatrends that impact most businesses. Individual businesses often specify the megatrends important to them. For instance, Germany's Henkel, a chemicals and consumer products company, has identified four megatrends: platform economy, consumer and customer gravitational shift (personalization, convenience, etc.), outcome-based servitization (outcome-based business models), and lean, fast, and simple.[3] The key megatrends in global power industry identified in the *2022 Megatrends in Power* report[4] are decarbonization, electrification, climate adaptation, and energy transformation. Siemens of Germany based its corporate strategy for more than a decade on the same four global megatrends: demographic change (e.g., a growing and aging population), urbanization, climate change, and globalization. In the mid-2010s, Siemens added a fifth megatrend, digitalization.[5] Individual Siemens divisions sometimes have a somewhat different set of global megatrends. For example, Siemens Mobility added yet another megatrend, sustainability (a sustainable and livable future.)

What is a megatrend? A megatrend is a change that impacts large swaths of the population and fundamentally changes how people live, work, and do business. Megatrends take root slowly and steadily and cannot generally be stopped or reversed. Think of globalization as a megatrend; it has been progressing over thousands of years and continues its forward march, though now with an additional focus—cross-border data flows. Companies typically base their strategy on the megatrends most important to them.

Globalization

Reports of the death of globalization have been greatly exaggerated.[6] Major multinationals like Siemens base their strategy appropriate for a global world. The business world is still highly global, except that the definition of globalization now also includes digital businesses and cross-border data flows, not just trade in physical goods. The pace of growth of goods trade and economic integration did slip in the last decade, but as discussed in Chapter 2, the growth of trade in intangibles, like services and data, is orders of magnitude larger than growth in goods trade ever was. In its June 16, 2022, issue, *The Economist* offered yet another take on *reinventing* globalization—a focus on security rather than efficiency in the wake of supply-chain issues caused by the pandemic and the war in Ukraine. Security in supply chains implies, according to *The Economist*, doing business with countries you can rely on (for instance, if war were to break out between them and you), and your government is friendly with—an antithesis of globalization as we knew it.[7]

Digitalization

We first came across *digitalization* in Chapter 1, where it was defined as the process of moving to digital business; digitalization cannot occur unless the different elements involved in a process have first been digitized. Digitalization thus involves transforming a business process using digital technologies. It makes processes easier to perform and more efficient. It is ubiquitous in our daily lives, so much so it is hard to visualize a world without digitalization. Digitization and digitalization are what used to be known as *computerization* a generation or two ago.

Digitalization continues to define and redefine literally all human activity—aided by progress in digital technologies, such as AI, data analytics, augmented reality/virtual reality (AR/VR), 3D printing, IoT, and robotics. Practically, all innovations and technological developments we see today resulted from digitalization. Digitalization is the name of the game today, and, as a true megatrend, its impact continues to grow. COVID-19 further speeded up its adoption in most spheres of human activity.

Competition

In the global–digital economy, there has been a fundamental change in how firms compete. With new elements emerging onto the global scene, *new technologies* (such as AI and 3D printing), *new players* (digital startups and emerging-market firms), *new products* (IoT devices), *new playing fields* (digital markets), *new challenges* (digital disruption), *new rules of the game* (network effects), and *new market dynamics* (winner-take-all or winner-take-most), competition is now an entirely new ball game!

New technologies. Competition in high-technology industries is very different from competition in old-economy industries. New technologies can provide competitive advantage to a firm, for example, by creating entry barriers against competition; they can also speed up digital disruption of incumbents.

New players. These are companies from emerging markets that have joined the ranks of global competitors, small and medium-sized enterprises (SMEs) new to international competition from both developed and emerging markets, as well as new digital players from everywhere. All these pose negative implications for incumbents in literally every legacy industry.

New products. Digital technologies and innovation are giving rise to new products and services—both purely digital and IoT—whose economics and market behavior are very different from those of physical goods and services.

New playing fields. The fall of the Berlin Wall on November 9, 1989, opened up huge new markets—markets that had been behind the Iron Curtain for over 50 years—for companies from outside the Iron Curtain. The growth of developing economies since the 1990s and 2000s has created a much larger market for companies with international operations or aspirations. These new markets comprise some four billion consumers and millions of businesses—more than the world experienced at any time in the past. And, with the growth of digitalization, the market for digital goods and services is increasingly becoming more important than the market for physical goods and services.

New challenges. Digital disruption is just one of the challenges brought on by digital. Businesses today face many other technology-related challenges such as fast-evolving technologies, budgetary constraints, and security concerns.

New rules of the game. In the global–digital economy, firms have many more competitive tools available to them than in earlier economies. This is partly because it consists of the old economy, the digital economy, and the age of smart machines (the IoTs)—each with its own set of competition rules and competitive tools. Add *disruptive business models* to the rules and tools and you have an unbeatable formula!

New market dynamics. Digital markets exhibit zero or near zero marginal cost of production and distribution and significant economies of scale. Such characteristics, along with network effects, whereby a product becomes more valuable the more users it has, can generate winner-take-all or winner-take-most market dynamics.[8]

Truly, competition in the 2020s is an entirely new ball game!

The Fourth Industrial Revolution

Each of the first three industrial revolutions lasted around a hundred years, give or take a decade or two, each merging into the next industrial revolution. The fourth industrial revolution began in the 2000s, though it is hard to specify an exact year when it began; it's a continuous process of innovation and change in industry and business. As discussed in Chapter 8, it refers to the use of digital technologies to transform industry, business, and life in general. Also called *Industry 4.0*, the fourth industrial revolution has revolutionized and continues to revolutionize manufacturing and supply chains, led by automation, industrial internet of things (IIoT), AI, data analytics, and other digital technologies. Smart autonomous systems use computer-based algorithms to monitor and control physical things like machines, robots, and vehicles without human intervention—impacting life in general. "These innovations bridge the physical and digital worlds and make smart, autonomous systems possible."[9] This trend started only in the last two decades and will likely continue to create even more innovations for at least the next few decades, or until it merges with the next megatrend!

The New Normal

The much talked-about *new normal* is here; it is redefining and will continue to redefine life, work, and business for a long time. According to the Urban Dictionary, it means "the current state of being after some dramatic change has transpired. What replaces the expected, usual, typical state after an event occurs. The new normal encourages one to deal with current situations rather than lamenting what could have been."[10] Though megatrends generally take root slowly and steadily, the new normal arrived very fast after the onset of the COVID-19 pandemic.

What's new in the new normal? Let us explore just two aspects.

Technology. Technology is a defining trait of the new normal. Practically, everything in the new normal is technology-driven. In fact, a February 2021 survey by the Pew Research Center suggested that the new normal in 2025 will be far more technology-driven and present even more big challenges than before the pandemic. "…people's relationship with technology will deepen as larger segments of the population come to rely more on digital connections for work, education, health care, daily commercial transactions, and essential social interactions."[11] Some consulting firms[12] are already talking about the *next normal*, led by frontier technologies like AI, machine learning, blockchain, IoT, and autonomous vehicles. These are technologies already developed, but now being applied in new contexts, or yet to be mass marketed. A June 2022 McKinsey & Company survey found that US consumers expect to spend almost four hours per day in *metaverse* in 5 years.[13] (While there is no accepted definition of metaverse, experts think of it as *the internet of the future*—a virtual world, which users access with VR and AR headsets.)

Lexicon. The new normal has unleashed a new lexicon. It has brought terms, both pre-existing and new, into everyday conversation. Pre-existing terms have sometimes acquired new meanings or at least new connotations. New terms help to convey emerging trends in the new normal. In fact, the phrase *new normal* itself has a new meaning and is now used extensively in conversation, press reports, and scientific papers. Two commonly used terms in the new normal are WFH (working from home) and hybrid working. Related to WFH, hybrid working means working at one's regular workplace and offsite. It might include working at home, self-isolation, quarantine, lockdown, or being gig workers or essential workers. Terms like these help us make sense of changes that are now part of our daily lives.

One aspect of the new normal, appropriately termed, is the *great resignation*. Millions of workers in the US (and elsewhere) have voluntarily left (or have considered leaving) their jobs since 2020, seeking a better work environment, better pay, less stress, or for any number of other reasons. More than 40 million US workers left their jobs in 2021. Surveys by Microsoft in March and by McKinsey in June 2022 found that about 40% of workers were thinking of leaving their jobs for one reason or another.[14] This is the new normal and a megatrend!

Strategizing for the New Normal

In an earlier chapter, strategy was defined as a company's approach to creating and capturing value and establishing and sustaining competitive advantage. However, strategy is an often-misunderstood concept. Ask ten managers what strategy is, and you will likely get ten answers. Ask ten academics the same question, and you will likely get twenty answers, though sometimes with some common elements. According to Professor Michael Porter of the Harvard Business School, "Strategy is making trade-offs in competing. The essence of strategy is choosing what not to do. Without trade-offs, there would be no need for choice and thus no need for strategy."[15] Henry Mintzberg, the Cleghorn Professor of Management Studies at McGill University in Canada, defines strategy as the "pattern in a stream of decisions."[16] He clarifies,

> We are the blind people and strategy formation is our elephant. Since no one has the vision to see the entire beast, everyone has grabbed hold of some part or other and 'railed on in utter ignorance' about the rest.[17]

A.G. Lafley, former Chairman, President, and CEO of P&G, and Roger Martin, former Dean of the Rotman School of Management at the University of Toronto, write in their popular *Playing to Win: How Strategy Really Works* 2013 book, "In short, strategy is choice. More specifically, strategy is an integrated set of choices that uniquely positions the firm in its industry so as to create sustainable advantage and superior value relative to the competition."

From a company perspective, does strategy still matter? If companies abandon strategy, what do they lose? How confident are leaders about their company's strategy? What are they most concerned about? Strategy&, the strategy consulting arm of PricewaterhouseCoopers (PWC), developed the *Strategy Profiler* to answer questions like these. Here are some of their findings, based on a 2019 survey of more than 6,000 corporate leaders and senior managers, of whom one third were from the C-suite[18]:

- 43% of leaders say their companies are "very clear" about how they add value for their customers (57% are probably not clear or are clueless about how they add value to their customers).
- 37% feel their value proposition is "very relevant."
- 21% say their company has no list of strategic priorities.
- 37% of respondents say their company has a well-defined strategy—a clear sense of where it's heading.
- 35% think their strategy will lead the company to success.
- 37% feel they provide a unique advantage to their customers in most of their businesses.

Findings like these do not look at all promising. However, the PWC survey also found that companies with well-defined and well-executed strategy performed better than companies with incoherent strategy.

- 47% of the companies that get strategy right are twice as likely to report above average profits compared to companies with incoherent strategy.
- 48% of the companies that get strategy right grow three times faster than companies with incoherent strategy.

According to Paul Leinwand, Strategy&'s Global Managing Director and co-author of the Strategy Profiler report,

> We call these companies super-competitors. What sets them apart is that they have a coherent strategy. But that's not all — they also make sure to live that strategy every day. They carry it all the way through every aspect of their execution.[19]

Clearly, a well-defined, well-understood, and well-executed strategy is essential for superior performance.

Several arenas have been explored in this book. It's time now to collate and organize our thinking into a set of ideas for strategizing for the new normal.

It's a Global–Digital World

The confluence of global business and digital business, first explored in Chapter 1, continues apace led by technology, innovation, and growing interconnectedness between the physical and digital worlds. Business today is global and digital, almost by definition. Practically, every company today is global—whether it does business abroad or competes with companies from abroad. Most businesses are already digital, have elements of digitization embedded into their systems and operations, or are tending toward a digital future. And with an estimated eight billion individuals in

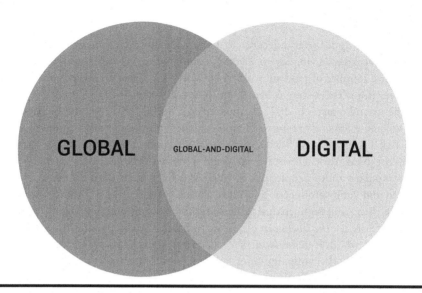

Figure 10.1   It's a global-digital world.

Source: Figure 1.1, Chapter 1 (this book).

the world (as of November 2022), hundreds of millions of businesses, and over 13 billion devices connected to the internet, they are all now part of the global–digital world.

Digital changes everything—products, processes, strategies, and performance—transforming business, industry, and how people live, play, and work.

What does digital offer business? Reach *and* richness and improved performance, in addition to many other benefits discussed in this book.

Reach and Richness

The reach–richness concept, developed by Philip Evans and Thomas Wurster, who in their 2000 book, *Blown to Bits*, presented the economics of information embedded in physical versus digital goods. *Reach* refers to the number of people who share certain information about a good, while *richness* refers to six aspects of information—bandwidth, customization, interactivity, reliability, security, and currency.[20] Global offers reach to a business; digital offers both reach and richness to the business.

Reach or richness had been the traditional tradeoff in business for a very long time; more reach meant little richness and vice versa. A company's strategy can focus on rich information by offering customized products and services to a niche market or reach a larger market without customization—sacrificing richness for greater reach. That was the scenario until the arrival of digital technologies and digital business models. Digital products, as discussed in Chapter 3, are extremely customizable and scalable, permitting a firm to offer differentiated products to different market segments, even personalized products to individual customers, and allowing it to charge different prices to different customers—without compromising cost or reach. A digital product not only has richness but also reach (via the internet), thus weakening, even eliminating, the reach–richness tradeoff of earlier eras.

Digital increases a product's reach. The paid circulation of *New York Times* print-only editions has been declining for over a decade. In December 2021, its average daily paid circulation was 343,000 on weekdays (Monday to Friday), compared to 1.3 million in 2011, and 820,000 on Sundays.[21] The number of paid subscribers of *New York Times* digital edition has been rising consistently over time. There were 6.14 million paid subscribers of the Times' digital-only news product for the second quarter of 2022, compared to 831,000 for the second quarter of 2014.[22]

Digital increases a product's richness. Digital enriches most aspects of peoples' lives and work. It can offer a rich, unique, and flexible experience to large numbers of people simultaneously. For instance, the New York Times Advertising's *T Brand Studio* creates multimedia, branded storytelling campaigns about people, places, and ideas for its clients. With editors, designers, art directors, video and audio producers, and creative technologists, the T Brand Studio works with clients to design their campaigns spanning both digital and traditional media. The Studio worked with Verizon to create its *The Evolution of Speed* campaign to demonstrate what 5G can do and is already doing in the world. It demonstrates to business audiences 5G's transformative potential to move industry forward. The campaign offers audiences rich interactive digital experiences as well as a print campaign in the paper.[23]

Improved Performance

It is easy to see how digital improves organizational performance. The list of the Top 10 most profitable companies in the world includes not only hi-tech companies but also four Chinese banks that make extensive use of digital technologies.

The ten Most Profitable Companies in the World (August 2022)

1. Apple
2. Microsoft
3. Industrial and Commercial Bank of China
4. China Construction Bank
5. Alphabet
6. Agricultural Bank of China
7. JP Morgan Chase
8. Alibaba Group Holdings
9. Bank of China
10. Intel

Source: Matthew Johnston, "10 most profitable companies in the world." Investopedia, August 27, 2022. https://www.investopedia.com/the-world-s-10-most-profitable-companies-4694526.

A 2019 survey of 1,200 senior executives by Deloitte found that companies at higher levels of digital maturity[24] were three times more likely to significantly outperform their industry average on key financial metrics than companies at lower levels of digital maturity. The survey concluded that companies at higher digital maturity levels benefit in dimensions like these: improved efficiency, higher revenue growth, enhanced product/service quality, and better customer satisfaction.[25] (These findings were re-confirmed by Deloitte Digital's 2020 survey.) Similar benefits of digital initiatives were also confirmed by Boston Consulting Group research, which found that digital initiatives enable companies to redesign processes from the ground up, leading to fundamental changes in how work gets done. Such transformations help companies improve their performance along several dimensions, including sales, marketing, pricing, customer service, manufacturing, and supply chains.[26]

Value Creation and Value Capture

This section on value creation and value capture is discussed more fully in Chapter 7; see also Figure 10.2. To create value, find ways to serve customers better than competition, keeping company operations efficient and effective. This may involve approaches such as innovation, lowering cost, offering a differentiated product so that it meets the specific needs of the customers being targeted, offering a full line of products, leveraging network effects, and providing enhanced benefits to increase customers' willingness to pay. For digital and IoT goods, the most important factor in value creation is network effects, whereby the value created by a product or service increases, exponentially, as the number of users of the product or service increases.

When a company creates value, it is also able to capture some of it for itself. So, value-creation approaches also help companies capture some of the value so created. Companies capture value from the prices they charge for their products and by keeping their costs low. In addition, as discussed in Chapter 7, companies capture additional value through approaches such as product servitization, service productization, and pricing innovation.

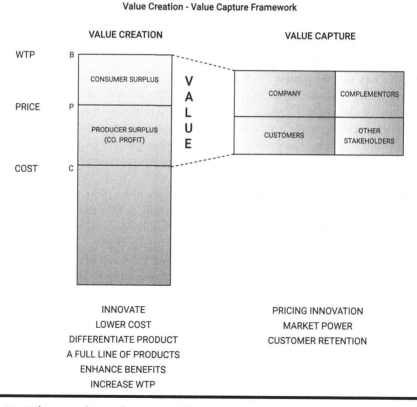

Figure 10.2   Value creation–value capture framework.

Source: Figure 7.2, Chapter 7 (this book).

How can a legacy business benefit from network effects? They can benefit from network effects by first undergoing digital transformation, and second, adding digital and/or IoT products to their product portfolio. If a company's existing physical product can be converted into an IoT product by embedding it with sensors and connecting it to the internet, so much the better. If not, consider developing digital or IoT products organically or acquiring a company that has such products. However, diversification through the addition of new products or product lines to a company's existing portfolio can open up other issues, which need to be carefully considered. Diversification for its own sake rarely works; a company's shareholders can themselves diversify their investments rather than having the company management do it for them.

The seven aspects of value creation and value capture are presented below.

1. Globality

Often confused with globalization, *globality*, according to the Merriam-Webster Dictionary, is the condition of being global. In my view, globalization is a journey, not a destination, and globality is a particular stage at a point in time during globalization's onward march. Globality is a destination at a point in time—recognizing that the end state of globalization is nowhere in sight and may not be reached during our lifetime and beyond. It's the global reality at a specific point in time. As of the autumn of 2022, the global reality (globality) consists of physical and digital goods and services, cross-border data flows, intangibles, developed and emerging markets, and other factors—offering both opportunities and challenges for business.

How to Leverage Globality

Overcome liability of foreignness. Firms new to foreign markets, even firms that have been abroad for some time but entering a new market, often face a variety of managerial, operational, and competitive challenges due to lack of understanding of the market—cultural and business practices, social, geopolitical, and regulatory challenges, and much else—or simply because they are a foreign company. This is known as *liability of foreignness*, which imposes additional costs for MNEs in host markets compared to their domestic counterparts. Some suggestions for overcoming the liability of foreignness are given below.

The real estate industry has the cliché, location–location–location. A similar cliché can be helpful for MNEs in foreign markets, localization–localization–localization. The more localized a foreign MNE is in a market, the less its exposure to liability of foreignness. It can adopt practices such as hiring local staff and executives, using local supply chains, involvement in local civic activities, joining local chambers of commerce, a bilateral chamber of commerce, a local trade association, supporting local causes, and giving greater autonomy to local subsidiaries abroad. Being a partner in the progress of the host nation sends a powerful signal to the market about your good intentions.

Benefit from what the host market has to offer. Most countries offer incentives to foreign companies to attract FDI (foreign direct investment) into the country. In the US, for instance, incentives are typically offered by state and local jurisdictions and, depending on the investment involved, can be worth millions of dollars to the foreign enterprise. Countries often have special economic zones, foreign trade zones, and industry clusters that can be used by foreign companies to their advantage. General Motors, for instance, set up its auto assembly plant in the Katowice Special Economic Zone, Poland, during the 1990s. Another often overlooked resource is the major universities in host markets. Many have incubators that can be used by foreign startups and other companies as a means of entering the market at low cost and low risk. An association with a university provides many other advantages as well, such as access to professors and researchers, their research output, student assistants, and the opportunity to work with professors on joint projects.

Learn from emerging markets. MNEs can learn a great deal from emerging markets, such as frugal innovation, innovative marketing approaches, and the ability to serve the bottom-of-the-pyramid consumers, among other skills. Frugal innovation, born in India, is an approach to innovate and design products and services using minimal (financial, material, institutional) resources and at the lowest possible cost. Individuals and companies improvise, using ingenuity and whatever resources they can find, to do what needs to be done. Necessity is truly the mother of invention.

Deal with and leverage institutional voids in emerging markets. Emerging markets often face *institutional voids*, for example, inadequate legal protections, under-developed capital markets, lack of intermediaries such as certification agencies, and so on. An advantage that emerging-market firms have over firms from developed countries that do not typically have to contend with such issues at home is that they have learned how to deal with institutional voids. (As I write this, an Indian entrepreneur, Gautam Adani, was just declared as the third richest person in the world, after Elon Musk and Jeff Bezos. Among other things, he must have successfully leveraged the institutional voids in the country.[27]) Institutional voids can be a source of advantage for both domestic and foreign companies if they have or can develop local knowledge and capabilities to substitute for the missing institutions. For instance, if a market lacks a certain intermediary, an entrepreneur could create value by creating an intermediary to fill the gap. Obtaining such knowledge and capabilities can help the MNE in not only the country where it obtained the knowledge and capabilities but in other emerging markets as well.[28]

Learn from developed-country markets. Just like developed-country MNEs can learn from emerging markets, MNEs from emerging markets can learn from developed markets. Emerging-market companies starting on their internationalization journey can learn a great deal from their counterparts and institutions in advanced countries—such as business and management practices, brand building, dealing with media, accessing capital, and much more.

Be a good corporate citizen. Much has been written about corporate citizenship and what it means to be a good corporate citizen. Suffice to say that a business must be socially responsible and meet its legal, economic, and ethical responsibilities toward not just its shareholders but toward its broader group of stakeholders. Businesses should aim to create higher standards of living and better quality of life in the communities where they operate. Companies strive to achieve such objectives through initiatives such as corporate social responsibility and increasingly through corporate philanthropy. For obvious reasons, giving back to the society is especially important for firms operating in foreign countries—developing or developed. Corporate philanthropy is based on the idea that successful businesses must recognize their *noblesse oblige* to give back to the societies where they operate. *Noblesse oblige*, a French phrase, implies that people of noble (high) birth have the responsibility to act with generosity toward those less privileged.

2. Competition's New Logic and Logistics

Digitalization is changing business in profound ways—especially how to operate and how to compete. Given that most markets now are effectively *digital markets*, the old logic and logistics of competition no longer work for an increasing number of products and services. Even physical product companies compete in digital markets—they sell online through e-commerce, offer online product information to prospective customers, and compete with companies that also sell online.

Some Features of Digital Markets[29]

Companies selling digital goods and services generally have high fixed cost, low variable cost (recall the *zero marginal cost* characteristic of purely digital goods), and exhibit network effects—the right prescription for them to become dominant players in their markets. As a result, digital markets can be highly concentrated, especially due to network effects, scale economies, and the need for large amounts of data to make them work. (Not all digital markets have such characteristics though; markets for only purely digital goods and services and IoT goods exhibit network effects.) The stronger the network effects in a market, the greater the degree of *concentration*. (See Box 10.1.) A large installed base of users also acts as an entry barrier for new entrants in the market, even if a potential new entrant offered a better product. The addition of more and more customers due to network effects increases a dominant firm's attractiveness, which, in an extreme case, can lead the dominant firm toward monopoly (recall the *winner-take-all* market dynamics).

BOX 10.1 INDUSTRY CONCENTRATION AND COMPETITION

An *industry* is a collection of firms offering goods or services that are close substitutes of each other. Alternatively, an industry consists of firms that compete directly with each other.

The term *industry structure* refers to the number and size distribution of firms in the industry under consideration. The number of firms in an industry may run into hundreds or thousands or more. If all firms in an industry are small in size, relative to the size of the industry, it is a **fragmented** industry. If a few firms control a large share of the industry's output or sales, it is a **concentrated** (consolidated) industry. An oligopoly is a concentrated industry where a very small number of firms accounts for a very large share of the industry's output. The type of competition in fragmented industries is generally very different from that in concentrated industries. By looking at the structure of an industry, one can often learn a great deal about competition, rivalry, entry barriers, and other aspects of competitive dynamics in that industry.

Fragmented industries sometimes have commodity-type products (such as primary metal) and exhibit low entry barriers. The existence of low entry barriers in an industry encourages the entry of new competitors into the industry whenever profits are high. These entries lead to excess capacity in the industry, and industry members begin competing on price to use their capacity and to maintain their market share. As a result, such industries may experience boom-and-bust cycles, even price wars. In such a situation, everyone's profits are hurt and some companies leave, are acquired by larger competitors, or are forced out of the market. From the perspective of incumbents, a concentrated industry has a more attractive industry structure. Such industries may exhibit high entry barriers, differentiated products, established brand names, and high profitability. However, in some concentrated industries, incumbents fight with each other tooth and nail and hurt industry profitability as well as their own, as in the airline industry. In other concentrated industries, incumbents compete on non-price factors and tend not to disrupt industry structure through unilateral competitive actions, as in the cola industry.

Companies in digital markets have the ability to charge different prices to different customers; this is called price discrimination. It is enabled by data analytics and pricing algorithms used by digital companies. They can employ personalized pricing for different customers, depending on their willingness to pay, even charging a zero price (e.g., search engines) or a price below their marginal cost. A newspaper or magazine with substantial advertising revenue often charges a price below its marginal cost of production.

In multi-sided markets, search platforms like Google, Bing, and Baidu (in China) are essentially harvesters of personal information, which they sell to advertisers who pay for accessing the platform; their services are free on the consumer side of the market.

Competition in many digital markets is sometimes competition between ecosystems. Successful digital players may build their business model to incorporate complementary goods and services around their core business. As discussed in Chapter 6, an ecosystem is a group of companies from different industries that offer a bundle of goods and services to meet specific customer needs. This is based on the idea that customers aren't just looking for a specific product or service but a solution to their needs. The solution often involves a joint offering by many companies, including even companies from different industries. Digital processes are extremely scalable, scopable, and can connect with other digital businesses relatively easily to offer integrated products and services. Many of the fastest growing companies (such as Apple, Amazon, and Google) are ecosystems where they themselves act as a hub for networks of customers, suppliers, and providers of complementary goods and services. They derive competitive advantage not just from their scale, scope, and the ability to generate network effects but also from their ability to connect different businesses and aggregate data flows between them through data analytics. Such ecosystems can improve customer experience and may even lead to lower prices.

How to Establish and Sustain Competitive Advantage in Digital Markets

Companies establish and potentially sustain competitive advantage in digital markets through technological innovation, network effects, complementary products and services, scale and scope, and business models. (Refer to Chapter 7 for detailed discussion of these approaches.)

3. Innovation's New Logistics

Innovation is an important feature for most businesses and is especially important for digital businesses that continually give rise to new products and services. Successful digital companies in one area can relatively easily expand into newer, adjacent domains organically, through M&A, or through alliances (recall the *Build|Buy|Ally* framework). Innovation and startup activity have also led to shorter product life cycles as well as shorter R&D cycles, posing competitive threats to incumbents—both legacy and digital incumbents. Sometimes, an established player acquires a startup with promising innovation even before it has a marketable product. Major multinationals also often have corporate venture capital (CVC) units to invest in nascent firms with promising technologies. (See also Chapter 9 for more discussion on innovation.)

4. Disrupt/Cannibalize Yourself

Steve Jobs once said, "if you don't cannibalize yourself, someone else will."[30]

Joseph Schumpeter, writing in 1934, powerfully suggested that capitalism or the free market is an evolutionary process of innovation, entrepreneurial activity, and *creative destruction*. Industries contain the seeds of their own destruction through incursions by both new and established firms using innovative products and strategies to destroy the incumbents' advantage.[31] According to Thomas K. McCaw, who wrote Schumpeter's biography[32]:

> The main takeaway is the absolute relentlessness of creative destruction and entrepreneurship. In a free economy, they never stop – never. Schumpeter wrote that all firms must try, all the time, 'to keep on their feet, on ground that is slipping away from under them.' So, no serious businessperson can ever completely relax. Someone, somewhere, is always trying to think of a way to do the job better, at every point along the value chain. Whatever has been built is going to be destroyed by a better product or a better method or a better organization or a better strategy.

Schumpeter's seminal insight about competition is true more today than ever before. Many industries, especially those with rapidly evolving technologies, are subject to Schumpeterian creative destruction. Companies in such industries should cannibalize their own products and innovations before others do it for them. (In fact, companies in all industries should attempt to do so.) As was observed earlier, Apple's iPod, along with iTunes, had disrupted the music business when it was introduced in 2003. Later, iPod itself was disrupted when Steve Jobs decided to introduce the iPhone in 2007, which incorporated a fully functional MP3 player. The iPod was a $5 billion business for Apple at the time, which Jobs cannibalized despite internal objections to the idea and went on to create even more value for the company.

The business world is replete with examples of companies that suffered because they didn't want to cannibalize their cash cows. Encyclopedia Britannica and Kodak (Eastman Kodak Co.) are classic examples of Schumpeterian creative destruction that killed their successful products, to which they hung on a bit too long. There are also examples of companies, like Schibsted of Norway and Apple, that took the risk to self-cannibalize their successful products and eventually created even more value for their customers and themselves. For Schibsted, a Norwegian media group, advertising in its newspapers had been its major source of revenue. In the mid-2000s, Schibsted decided to offer online classifieds to advertisers free of cost, thus cannibalizing its cash cow. Today, much of Schibsted's earnings come from online classifieds.

5. The Fourth Industrial Revolution

As was observed in Chapter 8, the world is currently in an early phase of the fourth industrial revolution, also known as *Industry 4.0* or *smart manufacturing*—led by automation, IIoT, AI, data analytics, and other digital technologies. This is where the physical truly meets digital. Smart autonomous systems use computer-based algorithms to monitor and control physical devices like machines, robots, and vehicles. Industry 4.0 is (should be) a major part of any company's digital transformation.[33]

The emphasis in Industry 4.0 is on the creation of smart (intelligent) products, smart factories, and smart assets (assets embedded with sensors, software, and technologies).[34] It enables decision making in real time, improves productivity and quality, and replaces manual work with IIoT equipment. For instance, if a machine breaks down, inbuilt sensors alert operators who may not be co-located with the equipment, even triggering a service request—without human intervention. Beyond making manufacturing operations more efficient, IoT-enabled robots can work in dangerous conditions, keeping workers safe. Besides, the IoT has enabled newer business models, such as product servitization, digital add-ons, and outcome-based business models.

While industrial companies can create and capture value without going the IoT route, the IoT (and IIoT) business models can be applied in situations where non-IoT business models cannot. Recall examples like Rolls-Royce and Philips Lighting that use the product-as-a-service (PaaS) model for some customers. Their customers make no capital investment, pass the risk of ownership to the manufacturer, and still receive guaranteed equipment performance. Businesses using the IoT (or IIoT) business model have the opportunity to create and capture value through any and all five layers of the IoT model: physical thing, sensor and actuator, connectivity, data analytics, and digital services (as shown in Figure 7.2).

6. *Disruptive Business Models*

Chapter 6 presented several business models, many of which employ disruptive technologies. The concept of *disruptive technologies* was first explored by Harvard Business School professors, Joseph L. Bower and Clayton M. Christensen, in their 1995 article in *Harvard Business Review*, as technological innovations that completely alter the way businesses and industries operate.[35] Many articles and books later, Christensen's groundbreaking work on disruptive technologies was refined and expanded to include other ideas, such as innovations that create a new market for an existing product which ultimately overtakes the existing market. However, most technologies and innovations are not disruptive by themselves; they need *disruptive business models* to make them work. Here's a brief discussion on several disruptive business models; refer to Chapter 6 for more details on each.

Free offerings. Companies like Google and Baidu offer their search-engine services free of cost to users; they make money through advertising by selling access to users and user data to advertisers. The real innovation here is innovation in pricing—changing the payer from users to service providers. (Refer to "pricing innovation," Chapter 7.) Companies that offer their products or services free of cost disrupt their industry practices, eventually others are *forced* to do the same. Charles Schwab, the discount brokerage firm, is a case in point (Chapter 3).

Freemium. Under this business model, the seller offers a basic version of a product to customers for free but charges a price for enhanced (premium) product features. Hence, *freemium*. Thousands of companies use the freemium business model to build initial demand for their offerings. It makes sense especially for digital-product companies because the marginal cost of production and distribution of a digital product is effectively zero.

Access over ownership. This model is based on customers' increasing preference for *access* over *ownership*, for example, Netflix offering customers access to thousands of movies and Spotify offering access to millions of songs to listeners without expecting them to buy even a single DVD or song. Access to a product or service is offered through *subscription*, paid monthly or annually. Some of the more common applications of the subscription business model are product-as-a-service (PaaS), software-as-a-service (SaaS), and infrastructure-as-a-service (IaaS), though its potential applications are limited only by the ingenuity of the business looking for new ways to monetize its products and services.

Product-as-a-service is also called *product servitization*. Under PaaS, the product is expected to perform without any quality problems since the manufacturer is paid for the service the product provides, not the product *per se*. This is essentially a ***payment-by-results*** (or ***outcome-based***) business model.

Productization of services. The counterpart of servitization of products for services is *productization of services*. Service businesses often bill their clients based on the time and materials (T&M) model, which implies that to double their revenue (for instance), they must nearly double their professional manpower. Not so for product businesses. They don't need to double their manpower and investment in plant and machinery to double output. Products are scalable, services are not.

Productization of services makes a business scalable, repeatable, more efficient, and thus potentially more profitable. Productization at professional services firms can involve developing products that operate on their own or automatically, without necessarily needing services of a human being. H&R Block, for example, not only offers income tax-preparation services to clients, it now also has tax-preparation software products that individuals and businesses can use on their own to prepare their annual tax returns at substantial cost savings. Tax-preparation software has created a second revenue stream for H&R Block, further distinguishing its business model from competitors' business model.

Data monetization. Most companies collect data from their customers, which can be used to potentially cut costs, improve performance, increase revenue, even create new service offerings. Some companies, such as major retail chains, social media platforms, and IoT (IIoT) device users collect massive amounts of data (Big Data) from customers in the normal course of their business operations, which they can monetize in multiple ways. Rolls-Royce, for instance, uses data on engine performance that it gathers continually to plan maintenance and repair activities proactively to minimize disruption, thus adding to its bottom line. Sometimes, companies with massive amounts of data even sell anonymized and aggregated data, called *data-as-a-service* or *data syndication*, to third parties who then mine it for business insights.

Platforms and ecosystems. Platforms are intermediaries that connect and facilitate transactions between two or more sets of users, such as sellers and buyers or producers and consumers. Some prominent examples are Amazon, Facebook, Google, and Uber. They create value by enabling interactions between one set of users with another set of users, capturing value by charging them fees for making the connections and providing them services. An ecosystem, as discussed earlier, refers to a group of companies from different industries offering bundles of products and services to meet specific customer needs. The solution often involves a joint offering by many companies, including companies from different industries, to meet specific customer needs.

Platforms and ecosystems are digital businesses, even though their participants could be buying or selling physical products and services. As such, these business models benefit from all five characteristics of digital products (Chapter 3): network effects, zero marginal cost of production and distribution, non-rivalry, no need for inventories, and customizability.

7. Exponential

The *exponential* characteristic of purely digital and IoT goods derives from Moore's Law and Metcalfe's Law. Besides, purely digital goods have zero or almost zero marginal cost of production and distribution and they are extremely scalable and scopable. In 1965, Gordon Moore, the founder of Intel Corp., suggested that about every 18 months to 2 years, it is possible to double the number of transistors on a computer chip without a corresponding increase in cost; it came to be known as the Moore's Law and has worked well ever since.

Digital and IoT products also exhibit network effects, meaning such products have increasing returns to scale. This is the Metcalfe's Law, whereby the value of a network grows exponentially as the number of the network users increases. Network effects combined with Moore's Law and learning-curve effects (the more units are produced in a factory, the lower the average cost of production due to learning or experience effects) can lead to a *winner-take-all* market. Physical products, by contrast, do not exhibit network effects; they have diminishing returns to scale.[36] Not just the number of transistors on a computer chip, all kinds of phenomena exhibit exponential behavior, such as internet connectivity, sales of smartphones, and spread of epidemics.

According to futurist Ray Kurzweil, Google's Director of Engineering and co-founder of the Singularity University in Silicon Valley, "once a technology becomes digital—that is, once it can be programmed in the ones and zeros of computer code—it hops on the back of Moore's Law and begins accelerating exponentially." For instance, the digital representation of analog objects (digitization) completely transformed the business of photography and activities related to photography, to a scale quite unimaginable just a decade ago. Worldwide, 1.72 trillion photos are taken each year, which equals 4.7 billion per day.[37] These are stored in the cloud managed by Google, Facebook, WeChat, and others.

This is the basic premise of the exponential power of digital, which Kurzweil refers to as "the law of accelerating returns." At the earlier stages of technology growth, the change is so little as not even to be noticed. (One becoming two, two becoming four, four becoming eight, eight becoming sixteen, and so on). Once it crosses a threshold, technology's growth and impact is hard to miss. According to his computations in 2001, there had been "slightly more than 32 doublings of [computer] performance since the first programmable computers were invented during World War II."[38] That was as of 2001. Now, imagine how many doublings have occurred since then—not just of computers but of everything that runs on computers!

Notes

1 Starbucks press release, "Starbucks enters new era of growth driven by unparalleled reinvention plan," September 13, 2022. https://stories.starbucks.com/press/2022/starbucks-enters-new-era-of-growth-driven-by-an-unparalleled-reinvention-plan/.
2 Starbucks press release, "A message from Howard Schultz: The next chapter of Starbucks reinvention," July 11, 2022. https://stories.starbucks.com/stories/2022/a-message-from-howard-schultz-the-next-chapter-of-starbucks-reinvention/.
3 Henkel, "Digital transformation." https://www.henkel.com/digitalization/digital-transformation
4 Black & Veatch, "2022 Megatrends in power." https://www.bv.com/sites/default/files/2022–03/22_Megatrends_Clarion_FINAL__.pdf.
5 Sarwant Singh, "Roland Busch, COO & CTO of Siemens: The fifth mega trend that is changing Siemens' future," *Forbes*, May 29, 2019. https://www.forbes.com/sites/sarwantsingh/2019/05/29/roland-busch-coo-cto-of-the-fifth-mega-trend-that-is-changing-siemens-future/?sh=17e8b06587d8.
6 With apologies to Mark Twain, who is often misquoted as saying, "The reports of my death have been greatly exaggerated." The correct quote is, "The report my death was an exaggeration," which appeared in the *New York Journal* of June 2, 1897. https://oupacademic.tumblr.com/post/48310773463/misquotation-reports-of-my-death-have-been.
7 The Economist, "Reinventing globalisation," June 16, 2022. https://www.economist.com/leaders/2022/06/16/the-tricky-restructuring-of-global-supply-chains.
8 Erik Brynjolfsson, Andrew McAfee, and Michael Spence, "New world order: Labor, capital, and ideas in the power law economy," *Foreign Affairs*, July/August 2014.
9 SAP, "What is industry 4.0?" https://www.sap.com/insights/what-is-industry-4-0.html.
10 Urban Dictionary, "New normal." https://www.urbandictionary.com/define.php?term=New%20normal.
11 Pew Research Center, "Experts say the 'New Normal' in 2025 will be far more tech-driven, presenting more big challenges," February 2021. https://www.pewresearch.org/internet/2021/02/18/experts-say-the-new-normal-in-2025-will-be-far-more-tech-driven-presenting-more-big-challenges/.
12 McKinsey & Company, "The next normal." https://www.mckinsey.com/featured-insights/the-next-normal.
13 Cara Aiello, Jiamei Bai, Jennifer Schmidt, and Yurii Vilchynskyi, "Probing reality and myth in the metaverse," McKinsey & Company, June 13, 2022. https://www.mckinsey.com/industries/retail/our-insights/probing-reality-and-myth-in-the-metaverse.
14 Tristan Bove, "Great resignation shows no signs of slowing down: 40% of U.S. workers are considering quitting their jobs—here's where they are going," July 21, 2022. https://fortune.com/2022/07/21/great-resignation-40-percent-want-to-quit-where-are-they-going/.
15 Michael Porter, "What is strategy?" *Harvard Business Review*, Nov-Dec 1996.
16 Henry Mintzberg, "Patterns in strategy formation," *Management Science*, May 1978.

17 Henry Mintzberg, Bruce Ahlstrand, and Joseph Lampel, *Strategy Safari: A Guided Tour Through the Wilds of Strategic Management.* (New York: The Free Press, 1998). p. 3.

18 Strategy&, "The strategy crisis: Insights from the strategy profiler," 2019. https://www.strategyand.pwc.com/gx/en/unique-solutions/cds/the-strategy-crisis.pdf.

19 Roger Trapp, "Even today, having a strategy is more important than you might think," *Forbes*, February 28, 2019. https://www.forbes.com/sites/rogertrapp/2019/02/28/even-today-having-a-strategy-is-more-important-than-you-might-think/?sh=35af59fd649f.

20 Philip Evans and Thomas S. Wurster, *Blown to Bits: How the New Economics of Information Transforms Strategy.* (Boston: Harvard Business Review Press, 2000). p. 25.

21 Statista, "Average paid and verified weekday circulation of The New York Times from 2000 to 2021." https://www.statista.com/statistics/273503/average-paid-weekday-circulation-of-the-new-york-times/.

22 Statista, "Number of paid subscribers to New York Times' digital only news products from 1st quarter 2014 to 2nd quarter 2022." https://www.statista.com/statistics/315041/new-york-times-company-digital-subscribers/.

23 New York Times, "The evolution of speed." https://www.nytimes.com/paidpost/verizon-5g/the-evolution-of-speed.html.

24 "Digital maturity" refers to an organization's ability to quickly respond to developing trends in technology. For an organization to be able to respond quickly to shifting technology requires investments in technology-enabled initiatives and in leadership capabilities needed for digital transformation.

25 Ragu Gurumurthy, David Schatsky, & Jonathan Camhi, "Uncovering the connection between digital maturity and financial performance." https://www2.deloitte.com/us/en/insights/topics/digital-transformation/digital-transformation-survey.html.

26 Otso Ojanen, Christian Gruß, Mikko Nieminen, Rich Hutchinson, and Lars Fæste, "Ten digital moves for a quick performance boost," March 19, 2020. https://www.bcg.com/publications/2020/ten-digital-moves-for-quick-performance-boost.

27 Nicolas Vega, "Meet billionaire Gautam Adani, a college dropout who just became the third richest person in the world with $137 billion." CNBC, August 30, 2022. https://www.cnbc.com/2022/08/30/billionaire-gautam-adani-college-dropout-to-worlds-third-richest-person.html.

28 Tarun Khanna and Krishna G. Palepu, *Winning in Emerging Markets: A Roadmap for Strategy and Execution* (Boston: Harvard Business School Press, 2010). Chapters 2–3.

29 See also, OECD, "Digital economy, innovation, and competition." https://www.oecd.org/competition/digital-economy-innovation-and-competition.htm.

30 Ross Kimbarovksy, "If you don't cannibalize yourself someone else will." https://www.crowdspring.com/blog/if-you-dont-cannibalize-yourself-someone-else-will/.

31 Joseph A. Schumpeter, *The Theory of Economic Development* (Cambridge, MA: Harvard University Press, 1934).

32 Sean Silverthorne's interview of Thomas K. McCaw, "Rediscovering Schumpeter: The power of capitalism," Harvard Business School Working Knowledge, May 7, 2007.

33 SAP, "What is industry 4.0? https://www.sap.com/insights/what-is-industry-4-0.html.

34 SAP, *op. cit.*

35 Joseph L. Bower and Clayton M. Christensen, "Disruptive technologies: Catching the wave," *Harvard Business Review*, January-February, 1995.

36 Carl Shapiro and Hal R. Varian, *Information Rules: A Strategic Guide to the Network Economy* (Boston: Harvard Business School Press, 1999).

37 Matic Broz, "Number of photos (2022): Statistics, facts, and predictions." Augusts 27, 2022. https://phototutorial.com/photos-statistics/#:~:text=Photo%20Statistics%20(Top%20Picks),or%204.7%20billion%20per%20day.

38 Ray Kurzweil, "The law of accelerating returns." March 7, 2001. https://www.kurzweilai.net/the-law-of-accelerating-returns.

Index

Note: **Bold** page numbers refer to tables; *italic* page numbers refer to figures and page numbers followed by "n" denote endnotes.

Accenture plc 154
access over ownership 99, 177
Advanced Regenerative Manufacturing Institute 6
Age of Discovery 22
Airbnb 16, 47, 52, 59, 76, 88, 109
Alexa 40
Alibaba Group 9, 125, 134
alliances 157–160
Alphabet 42, 106, 109, 158, 159
Amazon 37, 39, 40, 42, 49, 50, 52, 76, 77, 81, 83, 84, 106, 108, 109, 125, 178
Amazon Web Services (AWS) 44, 100, 103, 109
Apple 46–47, 50, 52, 70, 77, 78, 81, 83, 84, 87–89, 98, 106, 110, 125, 126, 155, 176
ArcelorMittal SA 29
artificial intelligence (AI) 38–41
Asimov, Isaac 42, 43
The Atlantic (magazine) 7
autonomous vehicle (AV) industry 72
Axon Group 29

B2B (business-to-business) businesses 131–133
    eCommerce Platforms 108, **108**
B2C (business-to-consumer) category 126–127
    eCommerce Platforms 108, **108**
Bethlehem Steel 7
Bharti Telecom 30, 31, 103
big data 40, 42, 79, 81, 104, 107, 178
blockchain 45
BMW 71
Bosch 139–140
    digital strategy 141–143
    digital transformation 140–141
Bosch Rexroth 98, 143
Brazil, Russia, India, and China (BRIC) 9, 10, **11,** 18n15
Brooks Brothers 49
Build|Buy|Ally framework 153–160, *153*
Business and International Education (BIE) grant 6
business in the 2020s 7, 8

business platforms 49–50
Business Roundtable (BRT) 119

Category Offense 121
CEMEX 29, 59
Charles Schwab Corporation 35–36
Chinese corporates 29
cloud 44–45
cloud computing 13, 28, 38, 40, 44–45, 100–102, 126, 132
Coca-Cola's Minute Maid Pulpy 28
co-development alliances 158
cognition 39
command economy 62
competition 15–17
    new logic and logistics 173–175
competition as a new ball game
    new challenges 16, 166
    new market dynamics 16, 166
    new markets 16, 50
    new players 16
    new playing fields 16, 165–166
    new products 16, 165
    new rules of the game 16, 166
complementors 120
computerization 15
concentrated (consolidated) industry 174
Consumer Direct Offense (CDO) 121
consumer surplus 119
convergence 9, 25
Copycat Building 6
corporate venture capital (CVC) 158–160, 175
Corus 29
Costco Internet Business Solutions Group (IBSG) 60
Costco Wholesale Corporation 60
COVID-19 28, 43, 163
crossing the chasm 35, 53n1
creative destruction 48, 149, 175
critical mass 107
cross-border licensing agreement 70

crowdsourcing 145, 150, 152, 153, 160, 161n1
Crown Cork and Seal Company 6
culture
    high context 64–65
    low context 64–65
CytroBox 143

Daimler AG 29, 72, 93
data-as-a-service 105, 178
data centers 44–45, *45*
data monetization 104–105, 178
data syndication *see* data-as-a-service
Debenhams 49
Department of Defense 6
digital add-on 99
digital business 3
    artificial intelligence 38–41
    blockchain 45
    business model 92
    characteristics 75–76
    cloud 44–45
    cost reduction 51
    creating new markets 51–52
    definition 75
    economics 36–38
    first movers, fast seconds, and imitators 89–90, **91**
    5G 46
    global strategy for 88–94
    increasing customers' willingness to pay 52
    innovation 52
    IP protection 93–94
    licensing and partnering 92–93, **93**
    marketing strategy 91–92
    network effects 88
    robotics 41–43, *42*
    software localization 90–91
    technology and innovation 88–89
    3D Printing 43–44
    value capture with technology 50–52
    value creation 50–52
digital business models 97
    data monetization 104–105
    digital add-on 98, 99, 103, 133, 176
    direct selling 98–99
    disruptive 177–178
    ecosystems 108–110, **110**
    freemium 101–102
    infrastructure-as-a-service (IAAS) 45, 100, 101, 177
    vs. operating model 97
    outcome based 102–103
    platforms 105–108, **108**
    product-as-a-service (PaaS) 45, 100, 119, 126, 134, 135, 138, 142, 143, 177
    for professional services firms 111–113
    Razor and Blade 103–104
    rent (or lease) instead of buy 98
    software-as-a-service (SaaS) 45, 100–101, 177
    subscription 99–101, **101**
digital disruption 46–50, **48**, **49**
digital economy 5, 8, 15, 16, 18n24, 38, 166
digitalization 15, 77, 165
digital markets
    advantage 175
    business model 126
    competition and competitive advantage in 123–126
    complementary products and services 124–125
    economics of 117–118, **118**, **119**
    features of 174–175
    network effects 124
    scale and scope 125
    technological innovation 124
digital products 36–37, **38**
digital services 136, 138
digital strategy 117
    Bosch 126, 133, **139**, 139–140, 141–143
    definition *116*, 117, **118**
    for global B2B businesses 131–143
    for global B2C businesses 115–129
    implementation in legacy businesses 116, 126, 130n15, 142
    Nestlé 127, 128–129
    Peloton 82–88, *84*
    Spotify 76, 77–82, 85, 87, 88, 91, 123, 124
digital technologies 13, *14*
digital transformation
    Bosch 126, 140–141
    definition 77, 126
    Nestlé 127–128
    Peloton 76, 82
    Spotify 76
    XCMG 134
digitization 15, 77
direct network effects 124
direct selling 98–99
direct-to-consumer (D2C) model 121
disruptive business models 177–178
Dongfeng Motor 29
DreamWorks Animation 58
Dropbox 52, 102
DuPont de Nemours, Inc. (DuPont) 154

East India Companies 21, 33n6
Eastman Kodak Company 48–49, **49**
economic competition 15
economic globalization 19, 20
economics concepts
    diminishing returns to scale 36, 37, 118, 178
    increasing returns to scale 17, 36, 37, 52, 118, 178
    resource scarcity 36, 117, 118
economics of digital products 36–38, **38**
economic systems 61
    command economy 62
    market economy 62
    mixed economy 62

ecosystems 108–110, **110**
  innovation 159
electrocardiogram (ECG) machine 27
Eli Lilly 145
Embraer 30, *31*
Embraer's risk-sharing partnerships 30, *31*
exponential characteristics of information
      technologies 46

Facebook 28, 37, 47, 49, 52, 81, 85, 88, 104–106, 124,
      127, 178, 179
fifth-generation cellular communication network (5G)
      46, 170
Ford 4–5, 29, 72, 93
foreign direct investment (FDI) 26, **26, 27,** 72
  reverse 28–30, **29**
foreign-market
  entry modes 69–73
  exporting/importing 69–70
  foreign direct investment 72
  franchising 70–72
  learning about 69
  licensing 70
  Netflix 57–59, *58*
  PRISM framework of foreign market selection
        59–67, **61,** *61*
  selection 59
  strategic alliances 73
Fortune Global 500 (FG500) companies 9, **11**
Four-firm Concentration Ratio (CR4) 67
Foxconn 42
fragmented industry 174
franchise agreement 70–72
freemium 78, 101–102, 177
free offering 101, 177

G7 (Group of 7) 18n14
General Electric (GE) 27, 30, 43, 132, 133, 136,
      158, 160
General Motors 41, 172
general purpose technologies (GPT) 13, 18n18, 46, 89
global business 3, 115
global–digital economy 4–5
global–digital world 3, *4*
global flows 32
Global Innovation 1000 study 28
globality 172–173
globalization 8–9, 164–165
  economic 19, 20
  growth of, recent periods 23
  information and communication technologies 25
  multilateral institutions 24
  multinational enterprises 25
  paradox *20,* 20–23, **22, 23, 24,** 32
  reversal of attitudes 25–27, **26, 27**
  reverse innovation 27–28
  reverse outsourcing/offshoring 30–31, *31*

today *vs.* earlier eras 31–32
  types 19
globalization–localization dilemma 87
global middle-class consumption **12**
global strategy
  for digital business 88–94
  Peloton 86–87
  Spotify 81–82
Google 25, 37, 47, 49, 50, 72, 88, 101, 103, 105,
      109–110, **110,** 122, 123, 125, 127, 147, 149,
      155, 158, 159, 175, 177–179
Google Cloud 44
greenfield investment 26–27
gross domestic product (GDP) 9, **10**

Harvard Business Review (HBR) 50
Hazed & Confused 78
HCL Technologies 29
Herfindahl-Hirschman Index (HHI) 67, **68**
high-context cultures 65
Honda 41, 72, 73
how innovation happens
  invisible hand of the market 149, 153
  serendipity 148, 149, 153
  visible hand of management 149–153, *150,* **151–152**
how to innovate
  Build|Buy|Ally framework 153–160, *154*
  open innovation 160–161

IBM 29–31, 103, 142, 155, 156, 160, 161
IBM Cloud Services 44, 101
Ignition Park 5–6
Imagination Technologies 70, 92
Indian companies 29, 40
indirect network effects 124
Industrial Internet of Things (IIoT) 98, 132–133
  advantages 133–134
  asset tracking 134
  automatic fulfillment 134
  Bosch 139–143
  CAPEX to OPEX 134
  changes manufacturing 133
  compliance monitoring 134
  preventive maintenance 133
  remote monitoring and diagnostics 133
  remote software updates 133–134
  value creation-value-capture 135–138
  Xuzhou Construction Machinery Group Co. Ltd.
        134–135, **135**
Industrial Revolution, First 4, 7, 13, 20, 38
Industrial Revolution, Fourth 131–133, **132,** 166, 176–177
Industrial Revolutions 4–5, 8, 176–177
Industry 4.0 131–133, 176
industry structure
  consolidated (concentrated) 67, 142, 174
  fragmented 67, 142, 174
  perfectly competitive 67

information and communication technologies (ICTs) 25
information rules 16
information technologies (IT) 46
    artificial intelligence (AI) 4, 13, 36, 38–41, 97, 128,
        141, 142
    blockchain 45, 79
    cloud 44–45, 47, 78, 101, 102, 134, 142
    5G 46, 170
    robotics 4, 41–43, 42
    3D printing 13, 14, 43–44, 87
infrastructure 64
    cloud 44
    e-commerce 60
    5G 46
infrastructure-as-a-service (IaaS) 45, 100, 101, 177
ING 39
InnoCentive reinvents innovation 145–146
innovation 13, 52, 147, 175
    digital 13, 89, 128
    technological 4, 5, 48–49, 124, 142
    technology and 88–89
    pricing 122–123
    reinvent (*see* reinvent innovation)
    reverse innovation 27–28
institutional voids 173
institutions 63–64
Intel Corporation 37, 51, 142, 160, 178
intellectual property 64, 70, 88, 89, 92–94, 145,
        158–161
intelligent machines 37–38, **38**
interdependence 8, 9
International Monetary Fund (IMF) 8, 17n14, 24
Internet of Things (IoT) 98
    key characteristic 116
iPhone 39, 40, 46–50, 52, 54n27, 83, 88–90, 98,
        116, 176
iPod 47, 155, 176
ITT Corporation 28
iTunes 47, 107, 155, 176

John Deere 4
joint ventures (JVs) 30, 72, 158
J. Walter Thompson 39

knowledge-intensive portion, global flows 32

Laws of Robotics 43
learning curve 37, 89, 178
lexicon 167
liability of foreignness 172
licensing agreements 70, 92–93, 158–159
low-context cultures 65

machine learning (ML) 40, 51, 59, 76, 79, 112, 121, 128,
        154, 167
Made in Space, Inc. 44
Mahindra & Mahindra 30

Marco Polo 21, 33n3, 33n4
market dynamics 15, 16, 65, 123–125, 165, 166, 174
market economy 62
marketing mix 91–92
market potential 60, 65–66, 68
Mary Kay Cosmetics Inc. (MKC) 66
Mary Kay Inc. (MKI) 66
McKinsey Global AI Survey 40–41
McKinsey Global Institute 32, 33n23
megatrends 164, 166
Mercedes-Benz 41
Merrill 35
Metcalfe's Law 118
Microsoft 17, 28, 36, 39, 44, 52, 53n19, 90, 98, 100–101,
        108, 110, 118, 120, 123, 155, 158, 167
Microsoft Azure 44, 101
Mittal Steel Company 29
mixed economy 62
Moore's law 37
Moore's Technology Adoption Life Cycle 53n1
Morgan Stanley 41
Movile iFood 30
multi-homing 107
multilateral institutions 5, 8, 9, 23, 24
multinational enterprises (MNE) 25
multi-sided markets 175

Navistar 30
Nestlé 127
    digital strategy 128–129
    digital transformation 127–128
Netflix 25, 57–59, *58*
Networking Autonomous Vehicle (NAV) 142
new normal 164, 166–169, *169*
Newsweek magazine 7
new technologies 16, 165
Next Rembrandt *39*, 43
Nike 121
non-rivalry 118
North American Free Trade Agreement (NAFTA) 24
Nuance Communications 92

Oil Recovery Institute 146
oligopoly 67, 174
One Medical 4
open innovation 146, 160–161
Oracle 6
outcome-based business models 102–103
outsourcing innovation 160

paradox of globalization *see* globalization
pay-per-click 103
pay-per-use models 103
Peloton 82
    bike 83, *84*
    connected fitness 83
    creates and captures value 86

declining performance 84
first-mover advantages 85
first-mover strategy 86
global strategy 86–87
innovation 86
localization 87
mobile app 84
network effects 85
partnering 87
technology 85–86
Pew Research Center 27, 33n13
physical incumbent businesses 4
platforms 105–108, **108**, 178
political economy 61
political systems 61–62
democratic 62
totalitarian 62
price carrier 122
price comparison websites (PCWs) 49–50
price-setting mechanism 122
pricing innovation 122
PRISM framework 59–67, **61**, *61*
Procter & Gamble (P&G) 28
producer surplus 119
product-as-a-service (PaaS) 100, 177
productization of services 112–113, 177–178
product servitization 100, 122
PSA Peugeot Citröen 29

Razor and Blade model 103–104
referral-service businesses 122
reimagining business
five megatrends 164–167
global–digital world 168–169, *169*
growth targets 164
improves organizational performance 170
new normal 167–168
reach–richness concept 169–170
value creation and value capture 171–179
reinvent innovation
ally 157–160
build 153–155, *154*
buy 155–157, **156, 157**
InnoCentive 147
invisible hand of market 149
multiple potential sources 147
open innovation 160–161
serendipity 148
visible hand of management 149–153, *150*, **151, 152**
Renaissance District 5
Rent the Runway 50, 99
representative democracy 62
Research and Development (R&D) *150*, 150–152, **151**
resources 63
reverse FDI 28–30, **29**
reverse innovation 27–28
reverse outsourcing/offshoring 30–31, *31*

risk 8, *31,* 36, 41, 59, 60, 62, 64, 68–70, 72, 73, 89, 92–94, 98, 100, 102–104, 134–136, 155, 157, 158, 173, 176, 177
rival 21, 36, 37
rivalry 118
robotics 41–43, *42*
Roche 41
Rolls-Royce 71, *71*, 136
rust belt 5, 6

Salesforce 76, 77, 101, 108, 160
Samsung 47, 82, 89, 90, 110, 155, 160, 161
SAP 29, 99, 103, 104, 106, 108, 109, 134, 137
Science, Technology, Engineering, and Mathematics (STEM) 6
serendipity 148, 149
Sheffield, City of 7
SIGMA AIR UTILITY 102, 103
Silk Road 3, 20, *20*
Siri 39–40, 47, 116
size of middle class 10, **11**
Skype 25
smart machines 3, 5, 16, 17, 36, 37, 38, **38,** 52, 76, 82, 87, 88, 92, 166
smart manufacturing *see* Industry 4.0
smartphone 47, **48**
social democracy 62
social, mobile, analytics, and cloud (SMAC) 13
society 64–65
software-as-a-service (SaaS) 100–101
software internationalization 90
software localization 90–91
Spice Routes 3, 20, *20*
spice trade 32n2
Spotify 77–78
creates and captures value 80–81
fast-second strategy 81
global strategy 81–82
innovation 80
localization 81
network effects 78–79, *79*
partnering 82
technology 79–80
Starbucks 163, 164
state-owned enterprises (SOEs) 9, 28, 29, 62
strategic alliances 73
strategizing for the new normal 167–169, *169*
Strategy& 151, 168
Studebaker 5–6
subscription business model 50, 99–101, **101**, 123
subsidiaries
wholly owned 29, 69, 72, 160
substantive 39
SunNight Solar 146
Suzlon Energy 29

Tata Consultancy Services (TCS) 29, 112, 160
Tata Motors 29
Tata Steel 29
technological innovation 4, 5, 48, 124,
    142–143
technology 13–14, 166–167
telehealth products 14
Tencent Holdings 9, 49
TESCO 30, 57
Texas Instruments 6
3D printing technology 13, *14*, 43–44
time and materials (T&M) billing rate 111
totalitarian 62
Turner Broadcasting 58

Uber 16, 47, 49, 52, 73, 76, 81, 88, 105, 107, 123, 125,
    125, 178
Uber's Super App opportunities 125, *125*
University of New Hampshire 6
University of Notre Dame 6
UPS 42, 43, 124
US Commercial Service 69
US, Mexico, Canada Agreement (USMCA) 24

value creation - value capture approaches
    118–120, *120*
    analytics 138
    competition's new logic and logistics 173–175
    connectivity 138
    cost reduction 51
    creating new markets 51–52
    digital service 138
    disrupt/cannibalize yourself 175–176
    disruptive business models 177–178
    exponential 178–179
    framework 120, *120*
    framework for IoT businesses 135–137, *137*

Fourth Industrial Revolution 176–177
globality 172–173
increasing customers' willingness to pay 51, 52, 81,
    86, 120–122, 128, 171
Industrial Internet of Things (IIoT) 135–138
innovation 51, 52, 80, 86, 175
Innovation's new logistics 175
physical thing 137
reimagining business 171–179
sensors and actuators 137–138
Vanguard 35
Visa Inc. 155
Volkswagen (VW) 71, 93
Volvo 29, 100

Walmart 59, 104, 109
Walt Disney Company 157
Warner Brothers Television Group 58
Wazoku 146
WeChat 47, 179
WhatsApp 47, 49, 52
Whole Foods 4
willingness to pay (WTP) 37, 52, 81, 86, 91, 119, 120,
    121, 122, 171, 175
Wing drones 42
winner-take-all 16, 17, 37, 52, 88, 123–125, 129n10,
    166, 178
Wipro 102, 160
Wolters Kluwer 155
World Bank 24, 47
World Trade Organization (WTO) 8, 24

Xuzhou Construction Machinery Group Co. Ltd.
    (XCMG) 134–135, **135**

zero marginal+101:127 cost 16, 17, 36, 48, 88, 104, 107,
    118, 126, 149, 166, 178

Printed in the United States
by Baker & Taylor Publisher Services